THERE'S NO BONES IN ICE CREAM

Sylvain Sylvain's Story of the

NEW YORK DOLLS

THERE'S NO BONES IN ICE CREAM

Sylvain Sylvain's Story of the

NEW YORK DOLLS

by Sylvain Sylvain

with Dave Thompson

Cover designer Raissa Pardini
Picture research by the authors.

ISBN: 9.781.78558.513.5
Order No: OP57233

Exclusive Distributors
Music Sales Limited
14/15 Berners Street
London, W1T 3LJ

Music Sales Pty Ltd
Australia and New Zealand
Level 4, 30–32 Carrington Street
Sydney
NSW 2000
Australia

Printed in Malta.

A catalogue record for this book is available from the British Library.

Visit Omnibus Press on the web at www.omnibuspress.com

Contents

Introduction

WE WEREN'T WRONG. WE JUST FOUND A THOUSAND WAYS NOT TO BE RIGHT

Whenever anybody asks me about the New York Dolls, what we did and why we did it, the first thing that comes to mind is a Bugs Bunny cartoon I saw when I was small.

Bugs and Daffy Duck are vaudeville performers, but they are clearly at very opposite ends of stardom. All Bugs needs to do is walk onto the stage and raise his arms in the air, and the audience will go nuts. Daffy, on the other hand, can juggle, ride a unicycle, juggle *while* he's riding the unicycle, and he barely gets a single clap.

Bugs comes out again, whistles two notes, and the place goes crazy. Daffy returns and nobody makes a sound. This time, however, he knows what to do.

First he drinks "a generous portion" of gasoline. Then he downs a bottle of nitroglycerin. He swallows a box of dynamite, washes that down with "a goodly amount of gunpowder", adds some uranium-238, and then jumps up and down while instructing, "shake well".

Finally, he lights a match.

He holds it in his hand for a moment, and the audience is paying attention at last – a long, drawn-out "oooooh" of anticipation. "Girls, you'd better hold onto your boyfriends," he warns, and then he swallows the match.

There is a massive explosion, and feathers fly everywhere. The audience, too, erupts in a shattering standing ovation, the biggest ever heard. Even Bugs is impressed. "They want more!" he shouts, but Daffy, ethereal and ghost-like, floating up towards the sky, can only sigh, "I know, I know. It's a great show, but I can only do it once."

That, for me, was the story of the New York Dolls. Not that we could only do it once, because reincarnations of the band have had several lifetimes since then. But we knew from the outset what Daffy only realised at the end. When you take the stage, no matter who you're sharing it with, you've got to promise to die. To detonate. To fly as high as you can and then, like the Fourth of July, explode like a sky full of fireworks. And that is all you need to know about showbiz. The audience wants blood, and you have to provide it.

Caligula would have been proud.

Hell. Caligula would have wanted to join in.

Many people have told their stories of the New York Dolls; their recollections of the first time they saw us, the first time they heard us. You can go online and study virtual encyclopaedias of every concert we played, every song we recorded, every review we received. Even today, there are people out there who weren't even born when the group broke up, but who know more about us than we Dolls ever could.

Keep searching. You can find testimonies from musicians who say we changed their lives, and damnation from rivals who thought we were terrible. You will find sneers and cheers, fact and fiction, rumours and lies, and pie in the sky.

And why? Because, while we may not have sold many records nor racked up any hits, in terms of the stain that we left on the sheets, the New York Dolls were bigger than a lot of the people who did.

That is not what this book is about, because those things are only visible from the outside. Inside the storm, in the heart of the beast, you aren't even aware that there is a storm, or even a beast. You're just a rock 'n'roll band, doing and playing and dressing in all the things you ever dreamed of, and if we were famous for being infamous, as some people like to insist, both the fame and the infamy were mere by-products of everything else.

We never sat down and mapped out a game plan; there was no round table in some bunker-like headquarters where we spent hours with strategists, consultants and their ilk, and brainstormed the outrage that would win the next headline. Nobody told us to behave like we did. We did it because that was who we were and that was what we wanted to do. And when it was done, we did something else. Other people turned the New York Dolls into legends. We just went along for the ride.

And yet ... when I look back on that three-year span in which we held the world in the palm of our hands, and then had it snatched away again; and the years since then, when we were reborn as an historical precedent, year zero of punk, the Roanoke colonists of the new wave's new world (check your history books ... you'll see what I mean); when I compare our fate and fame with those of so many of the groups who once outsold us, one famous saying keeps coming back to mind, a phrase that you used to see a lot on the streets of Paris, daubed on walls, or spray-painted on placards.

À vaincre sans péril, on triomphe sans gloire – "To vanquish without peril is to triumph without glory."*

Like Daffy Duck in that cartoon, we vanquished, we triumphed. And we wanted to give them a killer show every night. Lead, follow, or get out-of-the-way; it's a rich man's war, but a poor boy's fight.

* Pierre Corneille, 1606-1684.

Chapter 1

COCA-COLA WHISKEY

One of my earliest memories is of my homeland being bombed by the British.

First the sirens, shattering the evening with their banshee howl, and the panic on the streets as people ran for whatever shelter they could find. Then the blackout, plunging a city of three million people into darkness. And then the bombs.

They were not falling directly on us, which was why, after a while, I would be allowed to stand on the balcony overlooking the darkened city, staring out past the towering tops of the mosques as they were silhouetted against the moonlight, towards the horizon.

Even from eighty miles away, though, I could see our searchlights struggling to pick out the enemy aircraft. I could see the glow of the flares that lit the bombers' path, and I could hear the rhythmic crumpf crumpf crumpf of each successive bomb blast.

Behind me, my father would be crouching beside an illegal radio, a big, brown Bakelite contraption, listening into the news as it broke across the shortwave networks, telling us to hush if we so much as gasped or spoke. He was taking no chances – he'd even broken the little light that once lit up the radio dial, to make sure no-one knew what he was doing. And we would hush because who knew what technology was raging against us? If the bombers could see the tiniest light, then perhaps they could hear the softest murmur. At any moment, the bombers, British

Valiants and Canberras, might turn their attention away from the airfields that were their supposed target and seek out the child who had just spoken too loudly.

In fact, the next day you would hear that they had, that Cairo Radio was reporting that the outskirts of Cairo had been hit with incendiaries, and charred bodies still lay where they had fallen amid the ruins. The British and the French, who fought alongside them, denied the rumours, of course, insisting that their only targets were our airfields.

But when you're five, you don't know who to believe.

You just know you're being bombed.

Egypt in October 1956 was a land in turmoil. Almost precisely four years earlier, in 1952, Gamal Abdel Nasser Hussein, a lieutenant-colonel in the Egyptian army, had masterminded the overthrow of the monarch, King Farouk. He installed a new government and proclaimed Egypt a republic, shattering the centuries of foreign power and influence that had ruled the nation until then. First the Ottomans, then (briefly) the French, back to the Ottomans, and then the Brits. Five hundred years of outside occupation were ended, to be superseded ... by what?

The revolution was bloody. There was rioting in the cities; foreigners were attacked and even murdered by gangs of nationalist supporters. Buildings were damaged or even destroyed – Barclay's Bank and the Shepheard's Hotel, the Turf Club with its famous collection of rare paintings. But slowly, order was restored and, in 1953, a one-party political system was introduced. Three years later, in early 1956, Nasser was proclaimed president – the role he had been working towards since the revolution.

Nasser was not necessarily a bad man, despite the manner in which he was portrayed elsewhere. He simply wanted the land to be free. But freedom, he learned, comes at a cost. Foreign investment was withdrawn; multinational companies fled. The Aswan Dam, the centrepiece of his vision for a new Egypt, was dealt a body blow when the British and Americans withdrew their support.

So Nasser took the only option that was left to him. For almost a century, the Suez Canal had provided the world's seafarers with a shortcut between India (and, more recently, the oil fields of Arabia) and Europe. It was controlled by the British, who reaped the profits as well. Nasser announced he was nationalising it.

In the Arab world, it was an incredibly popular move. Elsewhere, however, it was viewed as tantamount to a declaration of war, and was treated as such. With Israel already conducting operations in the Sinai, in the east of Egypt, Britain and France piled in, all expecting the so-called Suez Crisis to be over in a matter of weeks. Instead, it became one of the pivotal events in post-World War Two history.

In Britain, the bombers' failure to crush Egyptian resistance brought down the government. In France, it precipitated the surge of nationalism that brought war to Algeria. And in Egypt, which emerged so triumphant from the fray, it brought about the expulsion of some 25,000 people, as Nasser purged the country not only of British and French citizens and sympathisers, but also of Jews of every nationality. The Mizrahi family, my family, was just one of the thousands caught up in the nightmare.

I was born in Cairo on February 14, 1951 – St Valentine's Day, of course. My mother, Marcelle, was of Syrian descent – her mother, my grandmother, hailed from Aleppo but came to Egypt as an orphan child. There she met my grandfather, a rabbi, and started their family; mom was born on September 19, 1923.

They weren't well off. As a child, I remember visiting them in another part of Cairo. My brother Leon and I always addressed them as Nonno and Nanna, which is Italian for grandma and granddad, but I'm not sure why. Like Jews all over the Middle East, our first language was French; that was the language I grew up with and, in many ways, it remains the language in which I am most comfortable. True, I failed French One at school in America, but nevertheless, that was my native tongue.

My father David's side of the family, the Mizrahis, were originally from Izmir in Turkey, although the name Mizrahi is Sephardic Jewish and traces back even further to Spain and Portugal. I never met my paternal grandmother, who passed away before I was born, and I barely recall my grandfather – he died when I was two years old.

But they raised dad well. By the time he left school, he spoke five languages and quickly found a career in banking, handling foreign exchange. I remember being taken to see him at work at the Cairo branch of the National Bank of Egypt; my mother would lift me in her arms and hold me up to the bars that screened the tellers from the public. It was left to me to wonder why dad left the house every day, if all he did was sit inside a cage.

He obviously enjoyed it, though; he worked there for twenty-five years.

Mom was an incredibly beautiful, incredibly sexy lady. I remember dad hung a framed copy of Marilyn Monroe's *Playboy* centrefold over their bed – he was wild about her. Mom just shrugged. She didn't care, and she didn't need to. Years later, she told me she had so many boyfriends when she was young, she could have chosen any of them – and that dad certainly wasn't the best-looking among them, either. When they married, one of her former suitors actually sent him a threatening letter!

Most of what I know about life before Suez comes either from stories that my brother or my parents told me, or from tiny threads of my own memory, few of which are coherent enough to weave together.

I do know that the king was everything when I was born and that he was a very big man. Apparently, he passed a law that said he was the only person allowed to own a red car, so if you ever saw a red car, you knew it was the king, a huge Cadillac convertible with Farouk taking up the entire back seat. Behind him would be all the other limousines, all black, all covered, and they were for his wives.

That all ended with the revolution, and there were stories about that as well – how Nasser's tanks rolled down the street on which we lived, the Qasr el Nile, firing into the cinemas and the foreign businesses. The street itself was Cairo's answer to Fifth Avenue or Oxford Street, packed with western stores and offices. That's why he targeted it.

The damage must have been quickly repaired, however, because I vividly recall us meeting up with dad's younger brother, my Uncle Ralph, and going to the movies.

We saw everything. Mom and dad were both huge movie fans – American, British, French, Arabic, it didn't matter. Plus, Egypt at that time was the Hollywood of the Middle East, with its own movie industry and stars like Omar Sharif and his wife, Faten Hamama.

We saw some incredible movies. Dean Martin and Jerry Lewis were absolute superstars to us, though I also remember some incredibly boring ones; one, starring Spencer Tracy, was basically three hours of a man in the sea. I sat there thinking, "Oh no, what *is* this?" I'd fall asleep, wake up after ten minutes, he was still in the sea. I'd go to the restroom, return and, yep, still in the sea. On and on and on. I blame the movie's title; I thought we were going to see *The Old Man* and *the Sea*. Not *The Middle-aged Man* in *the Sea*. But I didn't mind. I devoured everything. Movies were my life, too.

I was especially enamoured of cowboy movies. In fact, I couldn't get enough of them, and my sole goal in life was to be a cowboy. Preferably one of the singing ones, like Roy Rogers or Gene Autry.

So, and not for the last time, I started to work on my father. "I want a guitar, I want a guitar, I want a guitar." And finally, he cracked. After a fashion. Instead of a guitar, he got me a child-sized oud, an Arabic stringed instrument, handmade by one of the merchants down the road.

I didn't care too much – I had no intention of playing the thing. I just wanted to look like I did. For the same reason as I wore a fez instead of a cowboy hat and, instead of drinking whiskey, I had a bottle of Coca Cola. Painstaking accuracy was not my concern; my imagination could fill in all of the gaps. And so I'd take one of dad's hammers, bang a nail into the bottle top, and then pour myself measures into one of his shot glasses, all the while studying the hand of poker I'd dealt myself. I may have been an Egyptian Jew, but in my heart I was Billy the Kid.

Aside from the movies, a lot of my inspiration came from the American cowboy comics my father used to bring home for me. That was why I started drawing, trying to copy the cowboys, the clothes, the cacti, the lot. And I loved the browns. There was a special shade of brown that those old pulpy comics seemed to reserve for horses and corduroy pants, and I must have spent hours mixing the colours together until I could duplicate it to my satisfaction.

I say American comics. But not exclusively. My favourite – far and away, more than any other comic book hero – was Lucky Luke, who came from France. He was so cool, a bit like Lee Marvin in *Cat Ballou*, but even cooler than that. He smoked, he drank ... even his horse behaved as though he was drunk. Lucky Luke was probably my first true idol.

I talk a lot here about foreign influences, but nothing was more powerful in my mind than the land in which I was growing up.

Egypt is a beautiful land, and not only the pyramids and the Cairo museum, and all the relics of the ancient past. All those years of foreign occupation had left their own magnificent marks on the landscape: the colonial buildings that could have stepped out of Whitehall; mosques that belonged in the *Arabian Nights*; the babble of languages and accents that filled the streets from dawn to dusk; and over it all, the blazing Egyptian sun. The Coptic monastery out in the desert, where the cowled monks blew the most intricate glass.

It was a land of marvels: elephant rides at the Cairo Zoo, the slow, lazy flight of the ibises, the snakes and lizards that were a part of daily life.

The dolphins dancing in the waters off Ras-el-Bar, the coastal resort on the mouth of the Damietta River where we occasionally spent our summers.

Egyptian wildlife seemed fearless to me. One day, I was sitting on a stool in the kitchen with my mother while she was cooking. She was an amazing cook, and she'd just finished preparing a chicken. She took it from the oven and placed it on top of the stove, next to the gas tank, and left the room for a moment.

Suddenly, exactly as she walked out, a huge black bird swooped in through the open window, picked up the chicken in its talons and flew out again. I was still speechless when mom came back in.

But, of course, there was also the other side of life. Political rallies were commonplace and often overflowed into violence. One time I was out with Zahora, my nanny – a beautiful big woman who wore immense golden earrings, and who paraded around, the happiest person in the world. She sang all the time – she'd pick me up from school and she'd be singing. We'd go shopping and she'd be singing. In fact, the only time she didn't sing was as we passed Tahrir Square while Nasser was holding another of his rallies, and the tanks rolled slowly around the streets, chewing up the tarmac with their massive, clanking tracks. Without a word, she grabbed me and thrust me beneath her skirts. She was so protective, she wouldn't let anybody touch me.

There was also poverty. There were beggars, there were vagabonds, there were cripples and amputees, bundles of rags that you might not even notice until a hand reached out from the filthy folds in the hopes of a few *milliemes*. There were street urchins collecting cigarette ends off the street, so that they could be recycled into "new" cigarettes to sell; and a man who walked the streets with a great tank strapped to his back, holding a tube. He was selling a home-made liquorice drink and once I persuaded mom to let me try it. It tasted disgusting.

All of that, however, was a world in which we had no part. Our home was as spectacular as any, a large apartment in a lovely old building, a little like the ones you see on the Upper West Side in Manhattan. Great arched windows looked out across the city; vast columns surrounded the entranceway; intricate carvings adorned the walls.

We even had a balcony overlooking the courtyard, and I remember one day when I was playing out there with Leon, holding stools like they were guitars, with rubber bands stretched out as strings, and strumming them like we'd seen in the cowboy movies, or heard on our father's radio.

Suddenly, we heard my mother yelling for us, almost screaming our names, so we ran inside and found her sitting on the toilet, with everything shaking all around. We were in the midst of what is now remembered as the Alexandria quake of September 1955, one that was felt as far away as Greece and Syria, and we musicians hadn't even noticed. But still she grabbed us both, pulled us to her, and the picture is still etched in my mind – the three of us cowering in her arms in the bathroom until the rattling finally subsided.

Or ... another memory. One time, our carpets, which were these great, elaborate old things, needed re-dying – the fabric lasted forever, but the colours faded through use and sunlight. Today, probably, you'd just send them out to be "professionally" restored. Back then, a couple of workmen would call at the house, carry the carpets down to the street below, and lay them out on the reservation in the middle of the road. They did the dying there.

Another time ... more than one time, in fact ... if we needed to purchase a new mattress, the vendor would come to the house with all the materials and make the thing right there in the room, fitting it to the bed, letting you test it to see if it should be softer or firmer, and not leaving until you declared it just right. And every week, somebody would come with a huge copper burner of incense and swing it around the apartment. It killed the stench from the streets, and a lot of the bugs as well, particularly in the summer, when the temperature soared into the mid-90s without any expectation of rain, and it was too hot to even complain about the heat.

Anybody who could afford it got out of the city during the worst of those weeks, and we were no exception. One of our hideaways was Ras-el-Bar, where we'd join my Aunt Susan and her family and feast on fresh seafood that mom purchased from the brightly coloured fishing boats. But more frequently, we'd take a bus to Alexandria, on the Mediterranean coast, and rent an apartment, one block from the beach. My father would commute back to Cairo for work, but the rest of us would stay for the entire season.

We would spend the day on the water's edge, either watching mom as she swam or staring in amazement at the Arab youths who would stand on the cliffs close by and dive into the sea from there. Then, at night, we'd go out to the outdoor cinemas – imagine a drive-in without the cars – to see what was showing there.

Hula-hoops had just been introduced and I was a hula-hoop expert. One day they had a contest at the cinema and, while I can't remember if I won, I do know I had a phenomenal routine, bringing the hoop up to my neck, then down to my knees, and back up to my neck again. I could also flip it backwards, catch it and throw it, knowing it would come right back to me.

It wasn't all an idyll, however. One year, I awoke to find a very painful boil beginning to erupt on the side of my nose, right by my right eye. Mom immediately blamed it on these three siblings who lived nearby, whose faces were blighted by the worst acne you can imagine. I don't think it was that, but mom was both adamant and furious. "Why did you go talk to them?" she shouted at me when the boil first started developing. "You touched them! This is why this happened."

The boil continued to grow, and now I was getting sick. Finally, she took me to the nearby Jewish clinic for treatment, but, ill as I was, if I'd known what was about to happen, I'd have refused to leave our apartment.

Of course, I was terrified from the outset, flinching every time the doctor even came close to me. Clearly, he decided, this was not going to be a straightforward procedure. Suddenly, five people grabbed me and held me down, impervious to my screaming and struggling. Mom was escorted into another room, and with me still kicking up as much fuss as I was able, one of the doctors jabbed a long needle into the heart of the boil and started to drain it. I still have the scar.

For the most part, of course, those summers in Alexandria were precious to us all, and so was another family tradition that I have never forgotten. Dad was a member of a country club located in the shadow of the pyramids and, every few weeks, we would take a hansom cab through the streets of Cairo and out to Giza, to explore the area, laze by the swimming pool, or visit the other clubs – there were many of them in the neighbourhood, including the Auberge des Pyramids, where Uncle Ralph played accordion in a band.

That was really swanky. While the adults were off doing whatever, I'd sit with Ralph's daughter, my cousin Mereille, and we'd watch the procession of stars as they passed through on their way to the casinos, people like Omar Sharif and Akim Tamiroff, who would later star in *Touch of Evil* and the original version of *Ocean's 11*. Years later, after the

Dolls got together, we used to stay up all night watching movies on late-night television. First there'd be *The Late Show*, then *The Late Late Show,* and after that, *The Late Late Late Show*. So many of these old movies became touchstones for us – *Touch Of Evil* was one of them.

The other star we used to see a lot of was Omah Kaseen, the biggest singer in Egypt. She was gorgeous-looking, always dressed in black, and the moment she started singing, all the Arab men would stand up and go "whoooooo" – instant orgasm. In fact, she was just like that Bugs Bunny cartoon. She could scratch her head and sing a line, and the whole place went crazy.

Music was everywhere – not just at the clubs, but in the city as well. Everywhere you went, you'd hear people playing some instrument or other, street musicians in every other doorway, or groups and singers in the cafes and coffee houses.

It was no different at home. Dad was really into Benny Goodman and swing, the kind of music that Uncle Ralph played. But mom went the other way, and I followed her. She was always singing, always finding the pop songs on the radio, and every so often we'd go to the movies together to see the musicals that my father wouldn't be interested in.

More than anybody, mom filled me with a love of music and, when the time came, she encouraged me to make it myself. I'm not saying she was the New York Dolls' biggest fan, but when we played the Paris Olympia, that was one of the proudest moments of her life. She called up all our relatives, people she'd never even mentioned the band to in the past, and told them all about it.

Not only because we'd achieved something that she could relate to, but because she knew they would appreciate it too. Telling them we'd headlined Max's Kansas City would have meant nothing to them – "What's he doing in Kansas City?" they'd have asked – but the Paris Olympia, that was the big time.

Chapter 2

I'LL MAKE A MUMMY OUT OF YOU

I started school the same year as Suez. My brother attended the Collège-des-Frères, a French Catholic school in a downtown neighbourhood known as Bab el-Louk, an imposing cream-coloured edifice whose staff were renowned for their strictness. I would probably end up there myself one day.

For now, however, I attended Lycée Français du Cairo, one of the French international schools that are scattered around major cities across the world. That's where I discovered how brave I was. I was the only kid who didn't pee his pants on the first day.

Aside from that, I didn't do too well at school, although it would be several decades before I was diagnosed with dyslexia and understood why. But I do not fault my teachers. When I was at school, it would be years before dyslexia became a part of the language, and while the condition had been identified back in the 1800s, it remained barely known outside the scientific community, and completely unheard of in schools. As far as some of the teachers were concerned, I was just a kid who had a hard time reading, a harder time writing, and was destined to spend my academic career lodged firmly at the back of the class.

I hadn't wanted to go to school anyway, and the way I was treated just made me even more determined. But mom would not hear of it. Every day, off I would go in my freshly pressed uniform (how I hated it), then sit staring helplessly into space while the teachers tried to drill French and Arabic into my head, not even imagining that there might actually be a reason why I was having so much trouble grasping either. Because – and let me tell you – even the smartest pupils were having problems at first, with two different languages not only written in two different alphabets, but which read in totally opposite directions, too.

There was one saving grace, a young French teacher who took a liking to me, and maybe even had an inkling of what was going on. Because one of the first things she did was hand me a diploma, written in French, the only kid in the class to receive one. It didn't make the learning any easier, but it gave me the confidence to at least try harder, if only to justify her faith in me. And it worked. I was still dyslexic, and still had problems. But I had stopped giving up at the first sign of trouble.

My parents tried to help, of course; my father even hired a tutor, one of his colleagues from the bank, to help me with my Arabic. But he was the worst tutor you could imagine; if I even started to stumble or struggle, his response was to pull terrifying faces at me, as though fear would help me learn faster. Instead, I didn't learn anything.

What Arabic I did pick up, then, I learned on the street. Everywhere I went, for instance, I'd hear the word "hashish" – I didn't know what it was; I didn't know what you'd do with it. But I'd hear my parents say "Ah, they're doing the hashish" as we walked past people ... it was everywhere. So I knew that word.

Other words I picked up: "Khara" which means "shit"; "Gaatak dahya" ("go to hell"); "yaatak Darba fi 'albak" ("drop dead"). But Arabic also has the best curses in the world – "Ah, I shit on your face." "You deserve to be hit with a hundred shoes." "May the house fall on your head." Mom was great; when she got mad with us, she would slip out of her native French and let fly with the most brightly coloured Arabic curses she could muster.

The funny thing is, it was no different when I got to New York. Ninety per cent of the English I heard spoken had the word "fuck" in it. Ninety per cent of the Arabic I heard was the same.

My poor father, though. I mentioned before that my father could read, write and speak five languages, and here was I having problems with just two. There was, however, one he wasn't so good at, and that was Hebrew. That's why my grandfather, the rabbi, gave him a book in which all the prayers and the things he had to read at holidays were spelled out phonetically. But he would still lapse into English on occasion, especially at Passover. This was after we left Egypt, and we would gather together to hear him read the passage about the Jews being thrown out of Egypt in Biblical times. Then he'd pause before adding, "And we were schmucks enough to get thrown out again."

The 1956 Suez Crisis changed everything. Not at first, though. I remember the bombing clearly, and how we would all huddle together at my grandfather's house – the entire family, uncles, aunts and cousins alike, gathered together in this vast apartment until the all-clear sirens sounded.

But once that was over, life looked like carrying on as before, at least from my five-year-old perspective. It is only with hindsight that I can piece together the first skeins of all that was to transpire.

We'd moved by now, away from the house with the balcony and into a gorgeous penthouse atop a brand-new six-storey building, not far from the Egyptian Museum. Here, the balcony was as big as the apartment, and there was a vast winding staircase that went up the centre of the building. There was also an elevator with a huge, heavy metal grille, which I once caught my finger in, so I remember that elevator very well. I can also still visualise the moment when my fingernail went flying across the floor. I screamed my lungs out, bringing all of the other residents pouring out of their apartments before the doorman, a really sweet guy, sent someone to bring my mother downstairs and take me to the clinic.

And not long after that, although I'm sure the events were in no way connected, Nasser decided to nationalise the Suez Canal. It was July 1956, and our lives were about to come crumbling down.

Dad's subterfuge with the radio notwithstanding, my family tried to let the events pass us by. There were demonstrations in the street, attacking the most obvious signs of Britain's former colonial influence; and once Israel became involved, invading the Sinai, a certain amount of anti-Jewish sentiment, too, began to manifest.

But it was not only the mobs who raised their voices. The government, too, began to take a harder look at the so-called outsiders who now called Egypt home.

One of the first things Nasser did when the bombing started was ban people from listening to the BBC, whose World Service was popular throughout the country. Of course they still did, dad included, but now people were actually being arrested for doing so.

And still we were surprised when they came for him.

It wasn't because of the radio. Anyone suspected of any British or French sympathies was being rounded up, and the very fact that dad worked at the bank while the British pound was the main currency was deemed sufficient grounds for suspicion.

Dad was not considered especially high profile, I don't think – they only sent one uniformed officer to collect him, although I remember my mother screaming and crying as he left. I don't recall how long he was gone, or much about what happened while he was away. He was sent to a camp, presumably where everybody was processed and their backgrounds checked and checked again. Then they were either released or ... I don't know what.

Dad came home, but he remained under house arrest, and he wasn't the only one. I had other family members, distant relatives and friends as well, whose fathers were taken away too. And then other things began happening.

Suddenly you couldn't go shopping or walk down the streets without Arabs jostling you or calling you names. Nationalism was taking over, with all the awful connotations that that entails.

Egypt had always been so open: Jews, Coptic Christians and Muslims living side by side without problem. Even after the formation of Israel in 1948, there was no real animosity. But after Suez, and after Israel was pulled into that, now the abuse was uncaged. Years later, in my late teens, I had this really strange dream. I was in the womb, about to come into the world, and God was talking to me, saying, "Guess what, man, you're going to be born. You're going to be born, and you're going to speak French," and I was saying, "That's great, terrific, thank you." And then he says, "The only thing is, you're going to be born a Jew. In 1951. In Egypt."

And I replied, "Why am I the chosen one? Next time choose someone else."

Life turned completely upside down. We went from being well off, happy, enjoying life to the full, to – the complete opposite. Jews had been teachers, bankers, merchants – and now, no longer. Life changed completely, not only for the Mizrahis, but for every Jew in Egypt. You couldn't go out after dark; you couldn't walk around the streets any more.

One evening sticks in my mind. It was before dad was arrested, and the air raids were still underway. But the adults were already aware that things were changing. This one night, we were getting ready to drive over to my grandfather's house to sit out the raid. Various uncles and their families would be there as well, and we were just getting ready to go down to the taxi when dad looked down and saw what I was holding in my hand – my beloved cowboy gun.

"No Sylvain, you don't want to be taking the pistol."

I threw it out of the window.

Dad's bank was nationalised and he was thrown out of his job. He was a Jew and therefore he couldn't be employed there. Only Egyptians could work in government-controlled professions. It didn't matter that he'd given twenty-five years of his life to the bank. He was out. Suddenly, we were living off whatever we had left, whatever he had saved. My Uncle Ralph owned his own business, something to do with pharmaceuticals, so he wasn't affected too badly. But dad knew nothing other than banking.

He needed a new trade – something that would not be prohibited, something that would bring in some money. He seized upon tailoring.

Overnight, the penthouse changed beyond recognition. All the pictures came off the walls, disturbing the little lizard that lived behind one of them. Out went the furniture, and in came a massive dining-room table, and that's where dad and Uncle Victor taught themselves how to cut shirts ... I still have some of the shirts they made. They had a pile of books filled with patterns to be traced, and that's how I learned as well. I looked, I copied, I helped wherever I could.

Mum had an old Singer sewing machine in an oval wooden box. It operated with a hand crank, and it was gorgeous. She started sewing the shirts, and she would make me do the cranking; she'd do the first spin with her right hand and then, once it got going, I'd keep it spinning. Dad and Uncle Victor would be cutting and tracing, mom would be sewing, and I'd be doing whatever I could.

Thanks to the tailoring, money was flowing in again, and continued to do so for the remainder of our time in Cairo. Of course there wasn't as much as before, but it was enough to live on. Food was getting scarcer, though – and not just for us, for everybody. Since Suez, hardly anything was being imported. Every so often, down in the square outside the Egyptian Museum, the authorities would bring in a truck full of frozen American chickens, and everybody would converge on it, pushing and shoving until they got their hands on one of those precious birds.

One day, though, we knew that Jews would be banned from receiving even a chicken. It was time to get out.

But where? Dad began writing to different embassies, asking if there was any possibility of their nation accepting us. Dad, and every other Jewish family in Egypt. Most of his letters went unanswered.

A few friends had better luck, or perhaps they were less fussy than mom and dad. Many people went to Israel, including my Uncle Max and his wife. Others went to different parts of Europe. Some of our distant cousins wound up in Belgium, others in the UK.

Some even went to Brazil, including my dad's sister, Aunt Loretta, her husband and their two children, Lucien and Lillian, and I didn't see them again until 2009, when the New York Dolls had a gig in São Paulo. But we arranged to meet, and it was just in time. A year later, Lillian passed away. I was devastated, but I was so thrilled that we had met up again, and to discover that she was exactly like my father; she was a translator, and she also spoke five languages. In fact it was Lillian, shortly before she left for Brazil, who taught me my first ever English phrase. It was "shut up".

Years later, I asked my father why we didn't go to Israel, and he said "Sylvain? This – meaning the wars and the conflict – is going to go on for a hundred years." And, of course, he was right. In fact, getting ahead of myself, when we did finally escape, my mother turned to Leon and me and said, "Don't tell anyone you're Jewish." Because she knew. There is prejudice everywhere.

It was either late 1958 or very early 1959 that dad's efforts finally paid off. We had been accepted by France: mom and dad, myself and Leon, Uncle Victor, Uncle Ralph and their families too. I don't know how much paperwork was involved; I do recall us going to a little photographer's studio to have our picture taken for the family passport; and, after that, the last of the packing and the seemingly endless round of goodbyes to friends and families.

Our luggage was as tightly regulated as our lives had become. Nasser had not only nationalised industry and commerce. He had also nationalised all the country's assets, regardless of whether or not they were public property: money, jewellery, antiquities, anything of value that you might think you owned. I used to hear my parents talk, worrying about what they were going to do, how we were even going to survive once we left the country.

There were rumours that some people were buying diamonds and jewels and then swallowing them before they left the country. It was that bad. Dad, thankfully, chose a less drastic route. He decided to take us on shopping sprees, buying clothes not just for the immediate future, but for years after as well. We'd walk into a place that sold nothing but leather, and he bought us all leather jackets.

Then we'd go next door and he'd buy us shoes, dozens of pairs in every size, so we'd never need to buy any more, ever. I had sufficient pairs of these little brown English shoes to fit me until I was twenty-one! I'd ask, "Why? These don't fit me," and he'd say, "Not now. But they will." That's what we did for what felt like weeks; we bought clothes.

Then he had someone make us a set of big wooden chests, five or six of them; we painted them brown, we stencilled our names all over them, numbered them, and everything we could carry went into them, including the sewing machine. Other things were given to friends, to the Arabs who had never turned against us, neighbours, friendly shopkeepers. Most of what we gave away I have forgotten, but one particular item remains with me today.

A guy came over and my mother handed him a big green duffel bag, stuffed with who knows what. It was only as he turned to leave, that I saw something hanging out of it.

It looked like one of my old toys. I was such a freak with my little guns and cars; I used to take them apart to find out how they worked, and this bag was absolutely full of them. I was in tears, I was screaming, "Give them back, give them back." But to no avail. Off they went, together with everything else that my poor mom and dad deemed expendable.

Looking back, I cannot imagine the hell that my parents were going through, giving up everything they had known and worked for, just to start again in a new land. But for me, watching that duffel bag full of toys bump out of the penthouse on a stranger's back was trauma enough.

At last, the big day arrived.

I'd just celebrated my eighth birthday a few days earlier, and maybe I thought of this latest adventure as a part of that. Catching the bus to Alexandria – the same journey we had made so many times before during the summer, but with a very different destination. Like seaside towns the world over, Alexandria was dead in the winter. The beach was bare, the hotels were empty. I'd never seen the city so deserted. In the summer it's a really beautiful place, there's so much to see and do. But in winter, it's desolate.

My father had booked passage on a merchant ship sailing out of the western harbour. I don't know why, because everybody else flew. But no; we were to go on this funky-ass Greek merchant ship called the *Medea*, a journey that would take five days. Our destination was Marseille, the final port of call. Mom was already contemplating that with growing alarm when we were ushered into the customs office.

First, they went through each of the crates we had so painstakingly packed, checking for anything that might be considered contraband and, of course, helping themselves to anything that they personally took a fancy to. Then a couple of customs officers came and took my parents into separate rooms, where they would be searched.

And I mean searched. They had heard the rumours of how and where people were hiding their valuables, and they had no compunction about searching every possible place. I could hear my mother crying in the room, and, all the while, I was watching other people – non-Jews – just walking straight through the customs building, without so much as a glance.

Finally we were out on the dock, watching the crane loading our belongings onto the ship. The first pallet, with half of our crates aboard, made it safely onto the deck. The second, however, was not so lucky. Maybe the pallet slipped, or perhaps the ropes broke. Either way, half of our crates, half of our belongings, crashed into the water and sank straight down.

I remember my mother screaming, while dad held her and tried to calm her. "It's okay, it's okay, don't look at it." But of course you couldn't help but look.

Once aboard the *Medea*, we discovered we were among the fortunate passengers; we had a cabin with wooden bunk beds. Other people didn't even have that; they'd be sleeping outside, with just canvas and the ship's superstructure to protect them from the elements. And there were a lot of elements to beware of: wind and rain and towering waves, bitter cold, and then, shortly before we were due to arrive at the ship's first halt, in Greece, a massive storm blew up.

That baby started rocking. The Greeks started praying, the Muslims started praying, we started praying, all of us convinced that we were going to die aboard this dinky little boat in this heavy, heavy storm. But we got through it, and now all we could think of was how great it would be to feel dry land beneath our feet once we got to Greece. Dad had vacationed there once when he was a kid, and he was bubbling over with excitement.

Except it didn't work out that way. The Greek authorities would not allow us off the ship. We had to stay aboard while the seamen did whatever business they had to conduct. Thank you, Greece.

Soon enough, though, we were on the move again, heading now for Italy, and this time dad did manage to get ashore. I don't remember the port we docked at; what I do know is it was snowing, it was freezing, and it was so windy that the beautiful hat he was wearing was literally snatched off his head and deposited into the sea. I remember thinking, "Please, dad, why don't you just stay away from water?"

Finally, after five days that might have been five weeks, we reached Marseilles and, for the first time in a long time, people were nice to us. They welcomed us with smiles, they helped us with our baggage, they were ready for us. We handed over our papers and, all the while, I'm sure mom and dad were waiting for another kick in the teeth from officialdom.

It didn't arrive. Instead, we were assured that we could move any place we wanted to, and stay for as long as we liked. We were permanent residents of *la belle France.*

Chapter 3

LES CHAUSSETTES NOIRES

We took the overnight train to Paris. It was a long journey, and of course it was too dark to see anything more than the stations we passed through. But still we were too excited to sleep, and when we stumbled out at the end of the journey, our first Parisian dawn greeted us with damp and cold.

We made the most of it, though. One of the first things I remember from Paris was dad going out and buying cold milk. We didn't know what it was! In Cairo, milk came straight from the cow. It wasn't pasteurised; it had to be boiled before you could drink it. Now he was handing us cold milk in little bottles, and chocolate as well. The first day, that was our first treat. I loved it.

But the weather was a terrible shock – cold and rainy all the time, with grey skies that seemed to go on forever, and everybody hurrying here and there, hopping around the puddles and sheltering in doorways. It would almost have been funny, a scene from a slapstick movie, if we hadn't been doing the same things ourselves.

I also remember seeing couples kissing in the street, which is another thing I'd never seen before. In Cairo, my father got into trouble for kissing my mother on a bus; the Arab passengers were furious, they got really mad. And Uncle Victor once got thrown out of a casino, again for trying to kiss a girl. But in France, what a different way of life. Teenagers were making out on the corner. My eyes were opening up – this, at least, was like the movies coming true.

Home was to be a single room in the Hotel Hollande, on the Rue Cadet. It's a market street in the ninth arrondissement, right off the Rue du Fabourg Montmartre, in an area where many Middle Eastern Jews had settled. And when I think back, the room was tiny. There were four of us crammed in there … five after my sister Brigitte was born … and mom wasn't even allowed to cook in there. Of course she did, and every so often, you'd hear a knock on the door and the landlord shouting, "Mrs Mizrahi, it's not permitted to cook in the room," because he could smell it. And she'd be yelling, "No, it's the fish market downstairs, it's not us." Because that place did stink, especially during the summer months.

The toilet was down the hallway, and the only amenity we had to ourselves was a basin that we took turns to wash in. There were rats and bugs, if not in the hotel, then certainly on the street outside.

We couldn't even surround ourselves with possessions – those that had survived our exile were still crated up, locked away in a storage place dad had rented. And we came to this from the penthouse. My poor parents – they tried to look on the bright side, and they disguised their feelings well. They stood strong. But it was an enormous culture shock.

Yes, things were bad in Egypt. Yes, they denied my father work; yes, they took everything away from us. But we loved Egypt, we absolutely loved it. And now we were in this cold, damp, cramped single room in a cheap hotel. It seems unbelievable today, looking back on how everything unfurled. Particularly as France was having its own problems as the Algerian war began to pick up pace, and again you could see that suspicion building, people eyeing you on the street, knowing you were "not one of them".

Children are tough, though, they adapt, and I quickly discovered Paris was as alive with adventure as Cairo. The Rue Cadet itself was amazing; it was a busy street market, every shop window stuffed with some other fabulous foodstuff. We were right above the fish market, but across the street was the *boucherie chevaline*, selling horsemeat. Then, down the road, there was the wine merchant, whose stock comprised two big barrels, one full of red wine, and one full of white. I used to love it when dad would send me down there to get him a few bottles of red. I was eight, and the guy would just fill up the bottles for me.

It was loud, it was crowded, it was smelly, it was messy. Fourteen years later, back in France with the New York Dolls, I took David Johansen with me when I went back to revisit the area, pointing out the hotel where we lived, the shops that I remembered, and trying to recreate for him the sights and sounds of my childhood.

It didn't work. The street was clean, the people were smart, the shops were tidy, the rats had gone. Even the smells seemed less pervasive and, later on, I overheard him telling someone the story and he was saying, "It looked really nice, it was like Greenwich Village."

One thing hadn't changed, though. We bought bread and cheese and a bottle of wine, and returned to our own hotel, L'Ambassador, for lunch. And it was just like when I was a kid, no eating in the rooms! I don't know how they knew, maybe they smelled the cheese, but we had just tucked in when there was a banging on the door. I opened it to the bellboy, gesticulating wildly in his little jacket, his bowtie, his hat, going, "*Non, non, ce n'est pas autorisé*" – "This is not permitted." So, pretending I only spoke English, I replied, "We're fucking Americans, man, we can do whatever we want," and slammed the door in his face.

My brother and I were sent to school, at l'École Victoire on the Boulevard de la Villette. It was an all-boys school with a reputation for toughness, particularly where the teachers were concerned. They could spank you for any reason at all, and they did. In the lunchroom, for example, you were not permitted to place your elbows on the table, just your forearm. Have you ever tried to eat soup like that? Believe me, you'll learn fast because the moment your elbow touched the table, even if it was only for a moment, you'd get a mighty slap around the head.

Or in class; imagine you are a little behind your classmates in reading, and imagine you cannot catch up, no matter how hard you try. You're at your desk, head down, doing your best to shape the letters into something you could pronounce, and whack. The teacher would come up behind you and smack the hell out of you. Then they'd send you into *le coin*, the corner, to stand there with your hands raised above your head. After half an hour, you'd be in agony.

There was just one escape route. The school was so crowded they opened up an annex a few streets away. Every morning, we would have to follow the teacher to this other building, and it was astonishing. Every corner we turned, another couple of classmates would have absented themselves from the back of the line, and by the time we got to the school, half the pupils were gone, all cutting out and heading off to play pinball and smoke cigarettes in the cafes.

Me included.

I was becoming a little bit of a street kid. Hanging out on corners, wandering the streets ... one of my favourite haunts was Galeries Lafayette, a very upmarket department store on the Boulevard Haussmann. They had a fabulous toy department, with shelf after shelf of little British Dinky toy cars – which would disappear, one by one, into my pockets. Then, when I got home and mom saw me playing with a new one, I'd tell her I won it in the playground, at marbles or something. If you've ever seen French film-maker François Truffaut's *The 400 Blows*, that's exactly my life in Paris. Check it out. The whole school thing, the children filing into the annex – there we are.

The school had a dark history. During the Nazi occupation – still less than twenty years in the past – Jewish children were taken from that school and transported to the camps. There was a plaque on the wall remembering them, but there were also some very strange undercurrents at play.

That Christmas, all of the Jewish youths in the area were invited to a little hall further down the Rue Cadet, where we were told we'd be given gifts – toys and pencils and things like that.

We duly arrived there, to be greeted by a menorah on the stage and a couple of very straight-looking men who talked for a while, and then brought out some singers. They started out chanting, but it was also a little like gospel, and the audience was beginning to fidget a little, wondering what was going on.

Suddenly, one of the leaders kicked the menorah and it fell to the floor.

There was a horrified, puzzled silence – and then the audience rose as one, grabbing chairs and anything else that came to hand, and started hurling them at the stage. Because we'd realised what was going on. They were trying to convert us to Christianity. Can you even imagine?

Once again, music was everywhere, the latest pop hits from America and Britain as well as France, and a whole new wave of local superstars, people like Johnny Hallyday, Sacha Distel, Charles Aznavour, Bob Azzam and, mom's personal favourite, Dalida. (Azzam's maddeningly poppy 'C'Est Écrit Dans La Ciel', on the other hand, drove her to distraction.)

Like us, she was Egyptian. But she also had a fantastic voice, a gorgeous body, and her music was everywhere: 'T'Aimer Follement', 'Romantica', 'Itsy Bitsy Petit Bikini' and the song that soundtracked that entire summer, 'Les Enfants Du Pirée'.

She was so beautiful, and so talented, but the poor thing suffered from depression, and later on she committed suicide. You don't hear her name so much these days: she was a part of that generation of performers who were completely swept away by rock'n'roll. At the time, however, she was a goddess. Another fascination, at least for me, was the Folies Bergère, the cabaret hall that brought us everyone from Josephine Baker to Maurice Chevalier, from the art of Manet to la Belle Époque. Even today, it's probably the most glamorous place in all of Paris, and, luckily for me, it was just around the corner from our hotel.

Not that I ever went in there! In fact, the only reason I even went close was because there was an electronics shop nearby, with a television in the window, and a little speaker hooked up so you could hear it from the street.

Just as we left Egypt, they were beginning to introduce television, and one evening our entire family went to visit a friend of my father's in his nice fancy apartment, where he had just installed one of the first TVs in Egypt. We got to France, and they *all* had television sets! Everyone!

Well, everyone except us. So every day after school, a couple of buddies and I would go and hang out in front of that electronics shop. It didn't matter what the weather was like – which was just as well, because it seemed to be raining, grey and cold most days – there we'd watch the television. Except on *really* rainy days, when it would be just me, standing there watching *The Adventures of Rin Tin Tin* through the downpour.

The Folies' stage entrance was right next door to the electronics shop, and every other day or so, a truck would pull up and disgorge a tsunami of costumes, feathers, sequins and the most beautiful satins.

Well, fuck this *Rin Tin Tin* stuff; I'm looking at this now. I'd watch the costumes, and later, when the dancers came in, I'd be watching them, standing there until it got dark, just revelling in this world of glitz and glitter that was so far beyond anything I had ever experienced in the past.

Not even the clubs around the pyramids could touch the Folies Bergère for sheer glamour and, years later, when the New York Dolls were first starting, that was exactly what I was thinking of – the feathers and the Folies. I was eight years old, nine years old, and I was just absorbing everything.

The movies continued to dominate, too. Every Saturday afternoon, Leon would take me to the Palace, a neon-lit cinema just down the road, where every movie they showed seemed destined to open my eyes a little wider. The British Hammer films – the Draculas and Frankensteins and all those films – were extremely popular, and so were these continental movies in which everybody seemed to be having sex with everybody else. We devoured them.

One Saturday, however, Leon announced, "Okay, we're going to see this American movie," and long before we reached the Palace, we could see an army of teenagers lined up outside.

They looked spectacular – the boys in their pointed shoes and tight blue jeans, chain-smoking Gitanes through thickly nicotined fingers, and all of them seemed to be combing their hair, coaxing it into the perfect quiff; the girls with their scarves flipped over their shoulders, ever-shorter skirts, nylon stockings and ballet slippers, soft fitted sweaters and acres of mascara. And everybody seemed to have an acoustic guitar or a set of bongoes.

Then I saw the first posters. We were going to see Elvis Presley in *Jailhouse Rock*.

Slowly the line snaked its way into the auditorium, and everybody found a seat. But the moment the movie started, they were all in the aisles again, singing and dancing and playing along with the music. It was like *The Rocky Horror Show* is today, except there was no planning, no organisation, no "right" or "wrong" way to respond to what was taking place on the screen.

It was sheer animal exuberance, everybody throwing themselves in whichever direction the mood and the music took them. I say this a lot about the time I spent in Paris, but this time I felt as though I was shouting it from the rooftops. I had *never* seen anything like it, and never felt anything like it either. Because that's when I fell in love with rock'n'roll

I made up my mind to seek out more, but instead it sought me out first. Suddenly, I was hearing the music everywhere. In the cafes, on the jukeboxes, floating out of car radios, drifting from boutiques and record shops. Rock'n'roll was exploding in France – not only the imported British and American stars, but also local talents, people like Les Chaussettes Noires, few of whom could sing or play especially well, but that didn't matter. For the French, it's not the artistry that matters, or how well you can play your instrument. It's the performance that counts. It's the style, it's the energy, it's the show that matters.

That's why people like Gene Vincent and Vince Taylor were so big over there, and, later, Iggy Pop and the Dolls ... the French want to see you sweat, they want to see you work, they want to see Daffy Duck explode.

We were in France for only a couple of years, from March 1959 to March 1961. In fact, we'd barely been there a year before my parents decided they really didn't want to stay. Dad was not getting the kind of employment he wanted, or that he was qualified for – in fact, he was working in much the same kind of shop as the one where I was watching the TV, a little further away.

We were short of money, so we were still trapped in that little hotel room. Even worse, my brother got held back a year in school, and then, without a word to my parents, the authorities decreed that he was to go to a mechanics' school to learn a trade.

Dad was livid. "My son is going to become a *professeur*," he roared, and that's exactly what he became; Leon worked for the New York City Board of Education for twenty-five years. But it wouldn't happen in France.

One day, dad heard about an agency that was helping Jews move to the United States; it not only sponsored their application to the US government, but also vouched to house and find jobs for the families they brought over.

He contacted them and, over a period of several months, the agency filed all the necessary paperwork with the American Embassy and made the financial and moral guarantees that were demanded. Finally, one day, we received a letter instructing us to report to the embassy for physicals and interviews.

It took a long time, what with the photographs, fingerprinting and lots of sitting around, although as far as I was concerned, it was a done deal. The doctor who gave me my physical had told me so. "Ah, you're going to go to America," he said to me, and I nodded. "That's right, I am."

Most of the everyday communication about our case was handled through the agency, so we heard very little. At last, however, a letter arrived, offering us a list of American cities in which we could settle.

Cleveland was one of them, I believe, and so were Baltimore and Philadelphia. But we had some friends from Egypt who'd moved to Brooklyn, so there was only one place on the list that we were interested in – Buffalo, New York. I still remember dad putting down the letter and asking, "How far can it be from there?"

About 400 miles, dad. And it is always snowing.

Chapter 4

JUNK SCIENCE

It took us four days to cross the Atlantic Ocean, less time than we spent crossing the Mediterranean! There again, the SS *United States* was the fastest boat in the world at that time, and probably the most beautiful as well.

We took the train from Paris to the harbour at Le Havre, and my God, I'd never seen anything so vast as that ship. She had elevators, swimming pools and theatres. Of course, we were travelling third class, so we couldn't really walk around the nicest parts, but even where we were, it was hard to find things to complain about. I didn't even mind the sea sickness, although it really only struck me once, as I was riding the elevator one day. My stomach lurched, I turned and *bleaugh*. All down the operator's pants. Every time he saw me after that, he'd tell me to stand on the other side of the carriage.

It was raining as we entered New York harbour, but that didn't stop Leon and me from standing on deck to glimpse the Statue of Liberty through the fog, just like the old Ellis Island immigrants used to. "At last," she seemed to be saying, "you've made it."

We docked at the American-Holland Line pier and were met by somebody from the Jewish society, who took us to check into an old hotel on 46th Street. It was a big place with musty, cold rooms, but of course we were too excited to notice.

I don't think anybody slept that night – how can you sleep your first night in Manhattan? There is so much noise coming up from the street, so many strange smells to breathe in, so much activity on the sidewalk down below. You want to listen, inhale and watch it all. Even the air felt different. I couldn't wait to get out and explore, but there was no time for that. The following morning, we were taken to Grand Central Station, and they shuffled us off to Buffalo.

We got there and it was snowing.

Buffalo is the second largest city, after New York City, in New York State, perched on the easternmost shore of Lake Erie, with Canada on the other side of the river. At least back then, it was very industrial, very working class, pocked with neighbourhoods that you shied away from walking through without even knowing who lived there. Again, a culture shock for our parents, and a surprise for Leon and me. We'd been expecting ... well, I don't know exactly what we were expecting. But cowboys, Cadillacs, and what our Parisian sojourn had taught us to call "American champagne" – Coca Cola – were a large part of it. Where were the movie stars, where were the mobsters, where were Dean Martin and Jerry Lewis?

They weren't in Buffalo. Very little was.

We had a home to go to: the ground floor of a two-family house at 987 Lafayette Avenue, right off Main Street, in the centre of town. The place was furnished, probably back in the forties from the look of things, but everything was solid, and it would suffice. The society had even bought us food and stocked the refrigerator; and my father had a job to go to the next day, at a nearby pharmacy. Even us boys had been catered for; we'd be starting school the next day at PS 56.

Those first days were a blur. We bought our first television, second-hand, from a shop on Main Street for $50; we went to Sears and picked up a record player for Leon, and we unpacked all the discs we'd had in France. Then Leon came home with 'Peppermint Twist' by Joey Dee & The Starliters, and I played that song a hundred million times, until I had completely scratched the shit out of it. Mom used to beg me, in French, "Please don't play that thing again," and then the sudden shift to Arabic: "May the house fall on your head if you play it again." But of course I did.

The greatest thing, though, was the upright piano that also came as part of the furniture. It was situated in the warmest part of the house, beside one of the heat vents, and I probably gravitated to it in the first place because I was always freezing. But I used to monkey around with it too, and I quickly realised that I could figure out tunes. Soon I was playing along with the records we were playing, not always in time – occasionally, I'd have to pause while I hunted down the correct note. But once I found it, I would remember it, and my mother was not slow to notice.

Of course the piano wasn't my first musical instrument. There were the stools back in Egypt, and my oud, too. I didn't "play" either, but I always consider that was my musical awakening. Then there was Uncle Ralph with his accordion, showing me how things worked and encouraging me to sing along with him.

But again, my mother was the one who had the great love of music – not just Arabic stuff, but Jewish songs, western songs and things from the movies, too. So I had a musical background. It just wasn't formal, and I don't think I ever considered becoming a musician; it was completely subconscious, absorbing everything, learning without knowing I was learning. And once we came to America, I was falling in love with new songs every day – Carole King writing the most beautiful ballads ever written: 'It Might As Well Rain Until September', 'Halfway To Paradise', 'Take Good Care Of My Baby'. Phil Spector, The Chiffons, The Shirelles, that whole girl group explosion that would eventually peak with what I consider the greatest musical partnership of them all, Shadow Morton and The Shangri-Las.

Those sounds, those voices, those looks. From 'Leader Of The Pack' to 'Past, Present, Future' and all songs in between, there has never been a more perfect combination. And maybe that, a decade later, is why my own brush with Shadow left me feeling so downhearted.

Rock'n'roll was built upon the premise that "you're a punk and you shouldn't worry about it". Disobedience and delinquency were hard-wired into the best songs from the beginning, but so was the sense of being an outsider: being "weird" or "freakish", somehow different to all of their friends. Which, when you remember how old many of the writers were, makes perfect sense.

People like Carole King, Neil Sedaka, the cream of the Brill Building crop, were all in their teens or early twenties, and that's why their music spoke so loudly to their audience. They knew what we were thinking. To a kid like me, someone who was always getting bullied for being too small, too foreign, too puny, too *whatever*, those songs were lifesavers.

What they couldn't help me come to terms with was Buffalo. We stayed there for a whole year and it felt like ten. It felt like twenty to my poor mother. She cried every damned day we were there; she just couldn't believe that *this* was America. None of us could.

I've already told you that when we were on the boat, I thought everything in America was Marilyn Monroe, and cowboys and Indians driving Cadillacs. The first shock came when I got off the boat, because it wasn't like that at all. And once we got to Buffalo, it wasn't like anything.

The deal was we had to stay in Buffalo if we wanted the organisation to continue to support us. We had to stay in the house they gave us, and my father had to stay in the job they'd given him; and, for as long as we did so, they would make sure we were okay.

But mom couldn't stand it. She didn't want to leave the house; she wouldn't even go out to the supermarket, so I used to earn a quarter every day if I went to the stores to pick up whatever she needed. That's how much she hated it. For her, it was the worst curse ever. Life was nothing like the way we once had it, and while going from good to bad is awful enough, going from good to bad to even worse was totally unbearable. They might as well have sent us to Siberia. In mom's mind, they already had.

In truth, it wasn't so bad for me. I was earning a quarter every day, plus a dollar fifty allowance every week. I was buying new toys all the time, the little metal ones like the scuba diver you wound up and then placed in the water, to watch him kick his way across the bowl.

Leon and I got our first bicycles, and I even had a girlfriend, much to my brother's teasing delight. Our sister Brigitte was growing up and wobbling around in her walker, and that was always fun to see, and I was watching all the television shows in my own front room, rather than standing in front of an electronics shop in the cold. I was devoted to *American Bandstand*, but I would watch anything. My mom would be going, "Come on, it's getting late, it's 10 o'clock," and I'd be "Don't worry, don't worry, I'm just watching this." I was devouring it all.

Even school wasn't so bad. They put me in the fourth grade, which was lower than I should have been, but in a way it helped. I arrived in America with just the one English phrase that my cousin Lillian taught me – "shut up" (and how useful that proved). But learning a foreign language by exposing yourself to it, rather than sitting down and "learning" is the only way to go – within six months I was fluent in English, purely from going to school, watching TV and hanging out with other kids.

Of course that method does have its drawbacks. The slang comes first, and the curse words, because naturally you gravitate fastest to the words you hear the most. My ten-year-old vocabulary was still more *Leave It To Beaver* than anything else, at least at first, but I was doing all right.

I was also lucky to have a terrific teacher, Mrs Salt, who not only paired me with her best student, she would also tutor me privately, outside of class. The only thing I was slow with, of course, was reading and writing, because, again, dyslexia really wasn't known at that time.

At first they gave me the benefit of the doubt, a foreigner learning a new language. But one day, when I clearly hadn't improved, I was called out of class and sat down in the lunchroom, all on my own, and told to take an IQ test. Of course I didn't realise that at the time, but they had plainly decided that I was too busy talking to my friends, or daydreaming or whatever, and they wanted to see what I could do when there were no other distractions. I must have done okay, too, because I was back in class soon enough, and I never heard about it again.

Bullying, however, was a problem.

Remembering what mom had warned us, I never told anybody that I was Jewish, or Egyptian. Everybody thought I was French, so all the teasing I got was about that – things like "Do you eat snails?" or singing little songs: "All the girls in France don't wear their underpants."

But there were darker moments too, like the time Leon and me were out and a bunch of boys started to chase us, wanting to steal our bikes. Then there were the wannabe hoods and bullies, wearing their omnipresent black leather jackets and swaggering up to say, "You don't speak English – fuck you."

There was one boy in particular, a sixth grader who lived a little further down Lafayette Avenue. I had to walk past his house all the time to go to school or the supermarket, and he bullied the shit out of me, making fun of my brown shoes, the way I combed my hair, the way I wore my scarf flipped over my shoulder in the French style, instead of knotted at the neck like Americans. He'd pick on me for anything, and every other word out of his mouth was "fuck" – "You're a fucking this, you're a fucking that" – and while I was terrified at first, after a time I decided I'd had enough.

One day I was with my friend Charlie and I told him I was going to get this kid. But how? As Charlie put it, "He's ten feet tall, and you're the shortest kid in my class."

Easy. "I'm going to get his little brother." Because everybody has a little brother, or a little cousin, or a little close friend, and that's how to get at them.

Sure enough, I was on my way home from school one afternoon and I saw this kid, the bully's little brother, walking home. Okay, I didn't really kick his ass, but I did put him down on the ground, then got up really close to his face and said, "You tell your brother, if he fucking touches me again, you're going to die." And guess what? I never got bothered again. The sixth grader would walk past me, growling and sighing and whatever, but he never touched me again. Which is when I realised, in America, this is how I've got to be.

So I was getting along. I still didn't like Buffalo, but I was surviving. Mom, however, was becoming more and more miserable. We'd barely unpacked before we had our first ice storm, which was followed immediately by our first blizzard. Then our second and then our third, one on top of the other. She started getting out a little once it warmed up, but, of course, the bad weather returned soon enough.

Finally, she'd had enough. I don't know exactly what she said, but somehow she convinced my father to go to New York, find himself a job, get an apartment, and then come back and collect the family.

Immediately, he started writing to all of the banks in New York, detailing his experience, his skills, his five languages, his background – and every single one of them passed on him, except one, the Merchant Bank of New York on 47th Street, in the heart of the diamond and gold district. They had a vacancy in their foreign exchange department and, with all of his experience, he was the perfect match.

He had a job; and soon, he found an apartment, out in Brooklyn. Then he came back to Buffalo, we packed up the house, and then we boarded the Greyhound back to the city – a twelve hour journey that was so mundane, I could have shot myself out of boredom. But finally we arrived in New York City. It was spring 1962 and, at last, things could start rocking'n'rolling.

Chapter 5

RIGHT HERE, RIGHT NOW, AND NOT LATER, BABY

We only stayed at that first apartment for a short time, just until dad found his feet at the bank, and found a second job as well. Money was still tight; rent and food were both much more expensive in Brooklyn than they were in Buffalo, while he also had to start repaying the Jewish society because that was part of the deal.

They would support a family for as long as it needed to be supported, but the moment the family flew the nest, all that money had to be repaid. I don't know how much we owed them, but it was more than dad could handle on one income. So, every day after he finished at the bank, he would walk the few blocks to Macy's department store and spend his evenings and weekends working there.

That brought in enough to allow us to move to a bigger apartment, still in Brooklyn, on West 6th and Avenue O, although it wasn't necessarily a step up in the world. There were bugs the size of my thumb that used to scare the hell out of me, and the landlord wouldn't give us any heat. I remember my mother stomping on the floor in her heels, shouting for him to turn the heat on – the original punk rocker!

Sometimes he would, mostly he wouldn't. I remember waking up some mornings, chilled to the bone, with my feet jammed against the radiator at the foot of the bed – at some point in the night, the landlord would have turned it on, and even in the deepest sleep, my body sought out the warmth.

Again, I settled in quickly. My English was more or less perfect by now; people still knew I was foreign, still thought I was French, but the only hardship, if you can call it that, was that none of them could say my name because they thought it was weird. Very early on, I remember someone coming up to me and saying, "From now on, you're Steve, motherfucker." So that's what they called me, at least for a while. But then it became Syl, and that's how it stayed.

All the children from my neighbourhood attended the same school, PS 177 on Avenue P. It was called the Marlborough School – to match the Marlborough Theater, and the Marlborough Pizzeria down the road – and it was packed with some of the coolest guys I'd ever seen. Ricky, for instance. He used to comb his hair straight back on both sides, and then the top was straight down. It looked fantastic. The lame kids were still dolloping on their fathers' hair cream. The cool dudes, like Ricky, were using Yardley gel, as thick as they could put it on.

I also had a Jewish friend named Isaac, who lived in a brand-new building at 7000 Bay Parkway, the kind of place everybody wished they lived in, and he had a great haircut, too. In fact, almost everyone was dressing up – all the cool ones, anyway. And the girls were sexy as hell, too, all trying to outdo each other with those beehive hair-dos that were built like skyscrapers. If skyscrapers were made of pure sex.

We, the boys, did our best to get noticed by them, and occasionally it worked. One day, heading into class, I was walking past two of the girls at the front, on my way to my appointed roost at the very back of the room. Out of nowhere, I heard one of them say, "He's cute." But before I could even start to feel good, the other one retorted, "Yeah, but he's *so* dumb." I got a lot of that.

I continued to struggle at lessons. I got kissed like crazy; there was no shortage of that, but they don't hand out certificates for kissing. I was also a good dancer – they quickly figured that out – and every time there was a music class, I did well there too. But in other subjects, I was slowly fading into my own world, sitting at the back with all the others who weren't doing so well, drawing or daydreaming or whatever. The teachers never asked me anything, they never gave me any encouragement. I was just there to make up the numbers. Mostly they left me alone.

Which, I have to admit, suited me. I'd sit and look at the girls, all of them wearing their tight pink mohair sweaters, all of them looking like

Mary Tyler Moore, Ann-Margret and Mary Weiss. If you were really sweet to them, they'd let you walk them home after school and you could even carry their books for them. And I did it! English class, I was hopeless. But book carrying? Fuck, I was number one. A-plus.

I loved New York City. For the first time since Cairo, I felt that I belonged somewhere. I loved the street, the feel of it, the sound and smell of it, the gunpowder volatility of it. The sounds of Brooklyn being Brooklyn, rough and raw, but it had so much character.

The slang! There was a lot of "snag you", meaning "I tricked you"; and "I got woofed", meaning you'd been taken, caught out. And, if somebody of the opposite sex ever told you to "fuck off", the response was immediate. "I don't fuck off, I fuck *on*." Even today, I know that kind of language a billion times better than I know vocabulary.

I made friends quickly. The Italians really took to me, partly because they thought I was French, but also because I wore my clothes properly; I understood style. Whenever they threw a party in the park, which was a lot, I was always invited along to play squash or tennis or whatever. I got to know these guys, got to know their girlfriends, and everything I saw, fashion-wise, I absorbed. I took it all in and then recreated it in my own look.

I bought a pair of pants. They were a real dark plaid, three greens together. I put them on inside out and then I pinned them up the side, to make them as tight as I possibly could. I'd either sew them by hand or with mom's old Singer, then I'd turn them right side out and they were skin, skin tight.

Thin blue ski jackets. Black mohair sweaters. And if you wore a suit jacket, you had better only fasten one button. If you buttoned two, you were lame shit, and nobody would talk to you. It meant you still liked Bobby Darin and that was the worst. Or The Four Seasons. Even though they were a new group, they were also lame and old-fashioned, so far as we were concerned.

There was a bowling alley across from the school, and that's where we hung out a lot of the time. It had the best jukebox in town, crammed with the music we liked – Gary US Bonds, Sam Cooke, all the girl groups, all the great Phil Spector productions. The Ronettes, 'Be My Baby', David Rose playing 'The Stripper', so much great music.

One girl named Mary always had money and 'Be My Baby' was her favourite song. So she'd call it up on the jukebox, and then the next song would invariably be 'Will You Still Love Me Tomorrow'. And it was so sexy. We didn't know what sex was at that age, but we knew it when we heard it. Especially after we discovered where the jukebox's volume button was.

And guess who was dancing? The other boys didn't dance too well, but little Sylvain was out there with Mary and her girlfriends, dancing together and twirling one another around. Plus it was always dark in there, which meant it was also kind of romantic.

That said, I can't even tell you when I lost my virginity, because every encounter brought on something new and exciting, and you know what high school gossip is like. Girls can be as bad as boys when it comes to telling their friends they've "done it", and as my school days continued, I heard that I'd "done it" a lot. Whether I was aware of the fact or not.

Anyway, those were the cool kids. But there were also the gangs – the Irish over here, the Latinos over there, the Italians some place else. It was all very *West Side Story*, and it was also very violent. Particularly towards girls.

I've already mentioned the songs that brought solace to the weirdos. Well, there was another strain, and it was a big one, which started out from the premise that the guy was a punk, a rough kid and, although it didn't always say it, you inferred that he was knocking his girl around.

The most blatant was The Crystals' 'He Hit Me And It Felt Like A Kiss', and people still look askance when they hear it play. The rest tended to be the bad boy epics that were summed up by The Shangri-Las singing, "He's good-bad, but he's not evil", but still there was a constant undercurrent of violence, not only among the gangs, but just among "regular" kids. Fighting, bullying, violence were all considered "okay", just a normal part of teenage life. A lot of us didn't even think twice, for example, when a gang known as the Park Boys began levying a fifteen-cent entrance fee to the park alongside Sethlow Junior School.

But the guys weren't the only ones who acted tough. The girls did as well. One day, the story went around that two girls were going to be fighting one another in that same park. They were from rival gangs, and the fight was going to be at three, because *everything* is at three. "You're gonna die at three." "I'll meet you in the park at three." Everything. Because that was when school was let out.

There was already a crowd of expectant spectators as the two girls arrived, and they were both so cool-looking, so stylish in their tight sweaters and beehive hair. Suddenly, before they had even started to fight, one of the girls walked up behind the other and bang! She hit her on the head as hard as she could with the looseleaf binder she kept her schoolwork in, then turned and walked away again.

Was that it? No. Because the other girl was on the ground screaming in pain, and there was blood everywhere. While their audience, everybody who'd gathered to watch the fight, stood there in total amazement, wondering what on earth had happened.

Well, what had happened was that when girls fought, they always went for one another's hair first, pulling out great handfuls of it. So this one girl thought she would be really clever and hide a bunch of razor blades in her beehive, to cut up her opponent's hands. The problem was, her opponent got wind of what she'd done.

The other big thing back then was summer camp, sponsored by the local community for children who never managed to get outside of New York City. That first summer in Brooklyn, my parents signed me up, and off I went to Camp Sussex, out in Sussex County, New Jersey.

It was good. They had a lake, they had a little theatre, and there was all kinds of people there: the tough ones, the nice ones, everyone. Including one especially handsome guy, who had all the girls swooning after him because he used to walk around singing Brian Hyland's summertime smash 'Sealed With A Kiss'.

But, of course, there were also bullies and schmucks there, the same as everywhere else.

The very first day, we were all called together to be introduced to one another, shown where the bathrooms and the dining area were, and be given baseball jackets and clothes to wear while we were there, so we didn't spoil our own clothes when we were romping in the woods.

I was taking all this in when a couple of boys called me over to where they were standing. "Hey kid, look at this, look at this!" I looked, and I couldn't see anything.

"No, get closer, look carefully," they said. So, like an idiot, I got closer, bent right over and wham. This one fucker pushed my face straight down into a mass of poison ivy, and then started rubbing me into it.

The next day I awoke and I looked like a fucking monster. My entire face felt as though it were on fire, burning and itching, and I went outside. Every morning, we had to pledge allegiance to the flag. I was crying my eyes out.

Every face turned to look at me, and now the girls were crying as well. At last, a couple of the counsellors came and led me away for treatment. The camp trip was supposed to last for three weeks. I was in the hospital wing for two and a half of them.

I never went back to Camp Sussex. Besides, the beach was far more to my liking.

Brighton Beach was just a bike ride away, so every day that we could, friends and I would ride down there and just hang. Leon even got a job there doing the umbrellas and deckchairs. Or we'd head for Coney Island, which is right next door, because that's where the rides were.

And a lot more besides. In Britain around that same time, they had the Mods and Rockers who would meet on Brighton Beach and beat the shit out of one another, and people often think that was a uniquely English thing.

No. American gangs, as I've already said, would divide down ethnic lines rather than musical or cultural ones. But they still enjoyed a good rumble on the beach, battling their way around, across and through the regular holidaymakers, all waving beer bottles and chains at one another, until the cops poured down from the boardwalk to try to break it up. Which must have been terrifying for all the couples making out under the boardwalk, like The Drifters song said they should.

But have you ever seen a cop trying to run on the beach, in the sand, in his big boots? That alone would pull in an audience, just to watch them flounder.

The other great attraction, naturally, was girls, and they, too, tended to favour the wrong kind of footwear, because they wouldn't take their spiked heels off for anything. Not even the sand. Unless, of course, they wanted to be with Sylvain, in which case they'd have to take them off – and they were still too tall!

The only time they'd remove them was if they wanted to go on the Parachute Jump. Originally designed in the thirties for the military, it was a 250-foot-tall metal tower with eleven steel arms, and a canvas seat and parachute suspended from each one. You would be strapped into the seat, hoisted to the top and then released, with only the parachute to slow your descent. (The so-called Eiffel Tower of Brooklyn still stands today, although it is no longer in use.)

There were dozens of legends about people either falling from the Parachute Jump, or being killed when the shock absorbers at the bottom failed, which of course added to the thrill of riding it. But the biggest killer, or at least the biggest cause of injury, was said to be the spiked heels that the girls were wearing, slipping off a dainty foot and plunging spike first into a luckless passer-by.

Again, this was the stuff of legend and may or may not have been true. But the ride's operators were taking no chances. No spiked heels on the Parachute Jump.

Another regular stop for us was the freak show – a *real* freak show, a relic of the days when they still had proper bearded ladies and tattooed dwarves, and bizarre mummified things in bottles.

But the biggest attraction for me was the music. Those first two summers in Brooklyn, I don't care how much great music came afterwards, or how much I would later love The Beatles and the Stones. For me, 1962 and 1963 were, are, and always will be pop's most glorious, halcyon era.

'Up On The Roof', 'Chapel Of Love', 'It's My Party', 'Palisades Park', 'The Locomotion', 'Let's Dance', 'Breaking Up Is Hard To Do', all of those songs. Gary US Bonds was the most exciting sound you'd ever hear; one of the first things that David Johansen and I ever bonded over was our love of Gary US Bonds.

And all these sounds were best experienced on the sand, at the height of summer, and everyone around you has a transistor radio playing. It was like an army encampment, and they were all tuned to the exact same station, WMCA Good Guys.

What a station. They had all the best DJs – Joe O'Brien, Harry Harrison, Jack Spector, Don Davis, Jim Harriott, Dan Daniel, Ed Baer – and they played the best songs. They even produced the best T-shirts, bright yellow with the smiley face on them, and if you had one of those, you were the coolest of the cool. And that was the soundtrack we grew up with.

Later on, in the New York Dolls, all the little "ooohs"' and "aaaahs"' that were so much of our signature sound, and songs like 'Give Her A Great Big Kiss' and 'Pipeline', I took them all straight from the beach when I was eleven or twelve, years old. I played them all the time when I was a kid, and we played them even more later, when the Dolls were starting.

Yet it was not an easy time to be alive. The Cold War was in full swing, and we were constantly going through drills – what to do if the bomb drops. Even then, I think we knew that "duck and cover" probably wasn't the guaranteed lifesaver that we were brought up to believe, and neither was hiding under our school desks.

But we went along with the charade because what alternative did we have? Particularly as 1962 wore on and the world was convulsed by the Cuban Missile Crisis, and every day felt as though it was going to be our last. When that moment finally passed, there wasn't merely a genuine, palpable feeling of relief. There was also a sense that, if we'd survived that, we could survive anything.

Winter came and with it snow. Not the blinding, deadening walls of white that we'd suffered in Buffalo, but still a hefty dumping, a foot or two that the snow ploughs would then heap into huge hills on every corner, and which we would then set out to conquer, racing to be first to reach the summit, before hurtling down the other side, with a piece of cardboard for a sled.

Deep down, I know my parents still missed Egypt. But America was our home now, and New York City – even out here in the boroughs, in a barely heated apartment – was beginning to *feel* like home to them as well.

But the past still had ways of reaching out to us.

Chapter 6

THE UGLIEST BAND FROM ENGLAND

One day in October 1963, I arrived home from school to find my mother in tears. Edith Piaf was dead.

When we lived in Paris, Piaf was huge. Huger than huge. As far as I was concerned, and many other people as well, Piaf was the *real* France, the truth and soul of France. People loved her, they loved her music, they loved her background, they even loved her scandals, of which there were a lot.

Most of them were to do with sex and drugs, none of which I really understood, but I was aware of them regardless, because my mother used to sit and tell me all the gossip. "Don't repeat this to your father," she'd begin, "but she slept with this one, she slept with that one … ." You think today's stars are scandalous? The tales you heard about Piaf could put them all to shame. And France adored her for it.

She transcended everything; there was something almost messianic about her, a sense that she suffered so that France could live free. Her music could break hearts with a single breath, and then arouse the passions with another. But she was hurting, and it's the kind of hurt that I'd see again with Johnny Thunders. And then she passed away.

Oh my God, it was incredible. Even though we no longer lived in France, we heard the news and we saw the pictures. The whole city came to a standstill; there were crowds on every street. It was all over the newspapers, and the television too. Mom was in tears; everyone was.

Again, no matter that so many miles separated us from the heart of the events, it was the first time I had ever experienced communal grief on that scale, although, of course, it would not be the last.

Just six weeks later, sitting in class one Friday afternoon, we were astonished when a teacher walked in to tell us that school had been dismissed and that we should all go straight home.

At first we thought we'd been granted an extended weekend. But then we discovered the truth. President Kennedy had been assassinated.

We walked home, not quite taking the news in, but still it was the weirdest sensation, passing people on the street and seeing the shock and grief in their eyes. Walking into the apartment, and seeing my mother in tears, staring at the television in mute disbelief.

We were still in France when Kennedy was elected, but he was one of the reasons why we wanted to move to America. It was a time of hope and optimism, everybody was looking to the future, and of course his wife Jackie's family were French – her great-great-grandfather came to America from France. So we loved Kennedy, and we loved Jackie as well.

The weekend started strangely and it only became even more surreal. Throughout the Cuban Missile Crisis, although there would be a lot of interruptions and news updates, there was still shows to watch.

When Kennedy was killed, there was nothing. Just non-stop news, non-stop Walter Cronkite. For three days, that was all we got, and there was no escaping it because, if you stepped outside, all the radios were tuned to the news broadcasts too, and there would be crowds outside stores, or even gathered around parked cars, listening in to the latest bulletins.

Kennedy was assassinated on November 22, the day after Thanksgiving, and that only added to the sense of unreality. Twenty-four hours before, the entire country had been gathered to celebrate the birth of the nation. Now, we were together again, mourning what felt like its death.

It was also just around the time that the stores would have been thinking about putting up their Christmas decorations. Of course they didn't, not that weekend or any weekend after. The holidays were effectively cancelled. New Year's Eve was cancelled and New Year's Day, too. I was even beginning to eye my birthday nervously, wondering whether that would fall prey to the vast cloud of gloom that overhung everything. And then, a whisper out of nowhere: "The Beatles are coming."

History tells us that it was their appearance on *The Ed Sullivan Show* that broke The Beatles in America, and in many ways it was. But the only reason so many people were watching that night's show in the first place was because they knew who was going to be starring on it; and the only reason they knew that was because the radio had been talking about little else for weeks.

I don't remember where I first heard The Beatles, but it was probably in the candy store, coming out of the radio. 'I Want To Hold Your Hand' first, then 'She Loves You', then 'Please Please Me'. We didn't know it at the time, but the group had a solid year's worth of hits behind them in the UK; we thought they were just writing and recording them as fast as we were hearing them, and that made them even more impressive.

The promotion that surrounded them was equally outrageous. The books, the buttons, the board games, the boots, the everything. And, for the first time in the six weeks since Kennedy was shot, you started to see people smile again.

First, it was the kids who'd heard The Beatles first. Then the ones who watched them on the television. Then the newspapers, who finally had something different to write about, even if it was merely the length of the invaders' hair.

Not everybody loved them, after all. Even among my own peers, there were the leering thugs who would jostle Beatles fans and put them down at every opportunity: "How can you like those fags? They want to hold your hand, I wanna grab your tits." They were not going to change for anything.

But I loved The Beatles, and so did millions of others. We were so desperate for something new and exciting to pull us out of the post-Kennedy depression, and The Beatles did it. They dragged us out of the mire and they changed everybody's lives. Even hanging out at the candy store, they were inescapable – you'd go in for the five-cent soda fountain and find yourself staring at a rack of big Beatles buttons ... "I love John", "I love Paul". I had one that said "I love Ringo" because it was a little cheaper than the others, and I didn't care that, if a guy wore that – "Hey kid, you're a faggot." In terms of offering up an easy target for insults, I guess I was just rehearsing for later in life.

Across the country, everyone was glued to their TV set. We sat down and they came on, and the girls in the studio were screaming their lungs out. The Beatles played whatever they played, and you could barely even hear them above the noise. It was incredible. And everybody who liked

The Beatles, they went for the rest of the British Invasion as well, and that's how it divided up. Either you were hip or you weren't.

That's when I started on again at my father, demanding a guitar. Not an oud, not an upside-down stool with the rubber-band strings. A proper guitar. I wasn't doing well at school, but this was something I knew I could do. And I swear I cried and I cried, please, please, please, and I cried even more after my cousin Isaac got a Kent Japanese guitar and a little amplifier. Please, please ... .

Finally (and it felt like six months later, but I'm sure it wasn't), one weekend my father told me to meet him at Macy's where he was working, and there he bought me a sunburst Spanish guitar. It came complete with a canvas zip-up case, and I carried it everywhere.

It wasn't the best instrument around. The neck was warped and every time you hit the bridge, it shifted a little. But I learned a lot on that guitar, and I banged the shit out of it. It got me going. I bought a book that had diagrams of where you put your fingers on the fretboard, and I was learning tunes, things like 'Twist And Shout' and 'Shake It Baby'. I'd go over to Isaac's house and we'd put on records and sing along with them, and try to play along with them as well. That's how I found out I had a voice; I could hear the tone in my ear, and I'd work out harmonies. It all started making sense.

The Dave Clark Five arrived – great music, great songs – and I loved them as well. Hit after hit, and just like we had with The Beatles, we thought these guys were geniuses because we didn't know these records had been hits in England over a period of months; we were getting them one two three, bang bang bang, as though they were turning them out every week. And it was the most amazing schooling; it taught us how a pop group should be, how to write a song, how to behave.

The invasion was upon us; so many different performers, so many great records, and everything changed. How we looked at music, what we wanted from it. We were hearing the blues – Howling Wolf, Muddy Waters, people we'd never heard of. The Rolling Stones arrived. All my friends, the girls, immediately fell in love with Brian Jones and Mick Jagger. Me, I loved them all ... in fact, I loved them so much that suddenly I hated The Beatles. Overnight. The Beatles, they're wimps. I want 'Time Is On My Side', and when 'Satisfaction' came out, it was the greatest thing ever.

They were singing about real life, real people, and all those blues songs that they recorded at the start ... we thought they'd written them, we didn't know. The guy on the radio wasn't going to say, "Oh, this is a cover of an old Howling Wolf song," because he didn't even know. He was just a white guy who had never heard of these people either. But what a change, and I loved it.

The British Invasion hit everybody. Even the old, established artists, Bobby Darin and people like that, were trying to make better records, a little bit folky, a little bit meaningful. And it's incredible to remember not so much how fast things were moving, but how they continued moving.

Movements that take years nowadays were shifting overnight, from one thing to another. If you were playing music from two months ago, you were yesterday's news. It's incredible to think, but between The Beatles playing *Ed Sullivan* in early 1964 and the start of the psychedelic movement on the west coast, it was barely two years.

On February 14, 1964, I turned thirteen, and that meant there were some major changes in store for me. A new school career as I graduated to Junior High; and, as a Jew on the brink of manhood, my bar mitzvah.

That was an experience. Hebrew school, where I was expected to learn all that I needed to know, was an afternoon thing, and immediately my guard was up. I knew I would be tutored by a rabbi, but I was expecting a traditional one, somebody like my grandfather. Instead, this young guy in a sharkskin suit walked in, and *he* was my teacher? I couldn't believe it.

Of course I got over that shock, but it didn't help. His job was to teach me Hebrew – the fourth language, and the third alphabet that somebody tried to cram inside my head. And, like so many teachers before him, when he found conventional teaching methods didn't work, he slapped me. Hard.

Languages themselves, I had already discovered, were not a problem. Immerse me in the culture and I quickly picked up all I needed to learn – French and Arabic in Cairo; more French in Paris; English in Buffalo and New York. I was hanging out with the Italians, and learned some of their tongue; I was going to parties with the Latinos, and I could get along with their language, too. But sit me in a classroom, with a book I couldn't read, and expect me to follow along with anything, and I was a blank page.

That slap was where I gave up on religion. If that's the only way to teach somebody about God, then I didn't want to know. I got through the classes, and I got through my bar mitzvah too, although my only real memories of the occasion are my Uncle Victor, who had recently arrived in New York, turning up riding a brand-new baby blue 1964 Pontiac Bonneville, and, afterwards, when dad took me outside and offered me my first cigarette. At least, he thought it was my first, and I played along, coughing and pulling faces, just like any dutiful son.

That summer of 1964, my Uncle Ralph arrived in America and moved into a beautiful, brand-new building on Hillside Avenue in Jamaica, Queens. Mom fell head over heels in love with the place. Particularly when compared to the Brooklyn apartment, where we still had to fight with the landlord to get heat in the winter, and fight with the bugs, and everything else. "Please," she implored my father, "come on. Even if we take the smallest place we can afford in that building, we'll still be living better than this."

In the end, I'm not sure that we did take the smallest place, but we weren't far away from it. Our $183 rent afforded us a one-bedroom apartment on the seventh floor, which dad quickly converted to two bedrooms with an accordion divider curtain. I shared with Leon, and Brigitte was in with our parents. It was still a long way from the life we had lived in Egypt, but there was definitely a sense that things were improving.

Jamaica was a very divided area back then. On one side, it was essentially a black neighbourhood, with little enclaves of other cultures specked here and there; but on the other, it was what was known as Jamaica Estates, a very wealthy and well-to-do area. It was also where us locals would gravitate towards when the snow started falling and the rich folk needed their driveways shovelled. Or the leaves fell and we'd rake their lawns. If we'd had a lawnmower, we'd have done that too. You could make good money there, and maybe even be invited in for a mug of hot cocoa when the job was done. Usually when the parents were out, and the daughter took pity on you.

It didn't strike me at the time, but that was my first ever experience of class distinction – which, in its own way, is just as broad, and as just bad, as racism. It's what allows women in fur coats to swan past homeless beggars; it's what enables rich politicians to keep taxing the poor while giving breaks to their buddies.

It's just the way things are, and I think the reason I wasn't aware of it was because I had already encountered more overt forms of prejudice everywhere else – visiting a friend, for example, and the whole time listening to the adults swearing about this minority or that one. Walking down the street and hearing a white motorist shouting insults towards a Latino pedestrian.

Johnny Thunders came from that background. One night at Max's Kansas City, I met this beautiful black chick and took her back to Johnny's, where we spent the night together. The following morning, I was making her a cup of tea or whatever, when Johnny walked into the kitchen and said, in absolute disgust, "You fucked a *black* chick?"

I couldn't believe it; I couldn't believe that came out of his mouth, after being the grooviest guy I'd ever met. I know I told him, "My God, she's gorgeous, Johnny," but I really didn't know what else to say. And that went on through our entire lives together. It was his background. It's how he was brought up.

Another time, I was on Christopher Street in Greenwich Village as this gorgeous Asian girl walked by. Suddenly, from across the street, this cry of "Chinese pussy! Chinese pussy!" rang out. I looked, and there was a kid, maybe fourteen or fifteen, obviously on his way home with his mom's grocery bags, smirking and yelling at this poor girl.

I couldn't help myself; I ran to him, pushed him against the wall and asked, "Is this how your mother taught you to behave?" And maybe a warning or two as well. He ran, and I doubt whether my intervention made any difference to his future behaviour. But it might have made him think, or at least look around, before he did that again.

One down, several million to go. One of the very worst things about New York City was the amount of verbal abuse that was going on. It was like Cairo in the years after Suez, only this was on an industrial scale. People genuinely believed they could come out and say what they wanted about anyone, and that caused the kind of divisions which eventually led to gang warfare.

The Italians wouldn't go into the Irish neighbourhood, the Irish wouldn't go into the black, the blacks wouldn't go into the Italian, and so on. And it passed from generation to generation, until it became a way of life. Every day, the wisdom of what mom told us when we got off the boat, about never telling anyone that we were Jewish, was brought home to me – because, of course, I'd heard what people called the Jews they *did* know about.

Moving to Queens was a massive upheaval, and I was horribly lonely at first. All my friends, everyone with whom I'd spent the last two years, were back in Brooklyn, and for the last few weeks of the summer vacation, I was spending upwards of four hours a day riding the subway there and back, just to see my old buddies. I didn't care that the subway took so long; I couldn't wait to be back aboard the train, returning to the friends I'd left behind.

After a while, though, I started to settle, meeting new people and making new friends. First, the other children my age in my building; there were a few girls who intrigued me. I started to walk around the neighbourhood to see what was going on. And in September, I started school, at Robert A Van Wyck Junior High, PS 217. Where I discovered, as is so often the case at school (and, I later discovered, in the music business), it's the bullies and freaks who seek you out first.

They laid traps everywhere. Every day, as I walked to school, I passed a drugstore, just by the subway entrance. There was always a bunch of people there, in their late teens or early twenties, shuffling around on the sidewalk, and looking considerably less than savoury.

Later, I realised why – they were heroin addicts, and when they got into trouble and couldn't get a fix, they'd turn to the next best thing, which was cough mixture, because it contained codeine.

The problem was, drugstore owners caught on fast, and eventually refused to serve them. That's when these people began hanging around outside, looking for somebody who would go in and buy it for them. Someone like little Sylvain, bouncing along the street on his way to class, all curly hair and angelic smile, the kind of kid nobody would suspect.

A couple called me over. "Hey kid, come here."

I didn't know any better. I walked over. "Here's the money. Go into the drugstore, buy us – whatever it was – and if the guy asks, tell him it's for your mother."

So that's what I did. The pharmacist sold me the cough mixture, I handed it over to my new friends, and they were so happy. "Hey man, you're a good dude." They patted me on the back and sent me on my way, and I was floating on air because, hey, I wasn't having a good time at school; I didn't know anyone, I was constantly getting picked on, and here was this pair treating me like their best friend in the world.

This went on for a while. Every time my new pals needed a quick fix, there they'd be as I was walking to school, with a fistful of change and a beaming smile. But the pharmacist was growing suspicious. "How many times is your mother sick?" he asked once, so I changed my story. "No, this time, it's my father … my uncle … my brother … whoever."

Finally, however, he'd had enough. I was kicked out of the store and when I went to tell my "friends" what had happened, they grabbed me and started throwing me around.

It was probably only for a few minutes, if that, but it felt like an age before I broke their grip, and then I ran like hell. Even worse, from that day on, I had to walk the long way to get to school. Where I'd get thrown around some more.

I was forever on my guard; there simply was no way of knowing when your enemies would strike. A few surly-looking youths would block your path and draw a line on the ground with chalk, or their toe of their shoe, right where you had been heading. Then they would dare you to cross it.

Why? Because, if you did, you'd have to fight them. And, if you didn't, you were a punk, in an age when the word had a very different meaning to today. If you were a punk, it meant you were a chicken, that you "punked out" of something.

So yes, I was a punk, and just in case anybody doubted that, I proved it again when I was confronted by the punk test.

This was huge when I was at school, the ultimate way of proving your courage and manliness. Taking your door key, a standard Yale lock key, you placed the teeth against the top of your wrist, and you rubbed them back and forth as hard as you could until it got red enough to scab over. If you did it, you were cool. If you didn't, you were a punk.

I never did take the punk test, which meant I was a punk years before *that* became cool. But it also meant I never had a scabby wrist.

Another day, another encounter. There was a girl in my class, a really tough-looking Afro-American chick, very tall, very skinny, with her hair in braids and brightly coloured beads. She always looked as though she wasn't wearing any clothes – every day, she'd be wearing a thin T-shirt that doubled for a skirt and a pair of the flimsiest Mary Jane shoes you've ever seen, a single layer of gray suede and no sole to speak of.

Her routine never varied. She'd come into class and walk towards me; I would be sitting at my desk and there she'd be, towering over me. Well, she would have towered over me even if I was standing on tiptoe, but now I was positively dwarfed.

She would look down at me, and make a face … she reminded me of that private tutor I had in Egypt, when I couldn't get my Arabic together. Then she would whisper, very softly, "I'm going to see you outside, Littlebit (that's what she nicknamed me … Littlebit). I'm going to kill you."

She never did touch me; in fact, I rarely saw her any place outside of the classroom. But she might well have been the most intimidating person I have ever met, at school or any place else.

The biggest test of all, however, came just a few weeks into my first semester at Van Wyck, the day an older Latino boy came up to me and announced, "Man, you're going to fight my brother. At three o'clock."

What? I'd never seen this guy before, but of course that wasn't the point. I either had to make a stand, or accept that everybody would be kicking my ass for the rest of my school days. And, of course, three o'clock meant it was serious.

So there I was, standing outside while a crowd of other kids gathered around me, and the big guy was standing in front of me, looking really, really mean.

Suddenly, he pushed this boy towards me, and growled, "This is my brother and you're going to fight him." Everyone around us was on edge now, beginning the "fight fight fight" chant, and there was a handful of girls going "Oh no, oh no" and another handful shouting "Go on, hit him."

But I looked at this boy, who seemed no keener on the prospect than I did, and suddenly I recognised him. I'd seen him in gym class, one of the handful of students, like me, who didn't have the requisite gym uniform and were therefore condemned to stand at the back in their underwear. And one time, we'd chatted for a bit.

The tension went out of my body. Instead, I smiled and said, "Hey William," and he replied, "Hey man." But so as not to disappoint our audience, we began scuffing our feet on the ground, exactly like the bulls do in cartoons, right before they charge; we turned in little circles, feinting and jabbing out little punches that we knew the other would dodge. Then we blended together, as though we were pummelling one another, only not quite … and then we walked home with our arms together and we became best friends.

And that is how I met Billy Murcia, the drummer with the original New York Dolls.

Chapter 7

CABARET PAS NORMAL

Yo-yo shops were called that for a very simple reason. If a customer came in, looking as though they didn't have much money, that electric toaster, for example, would cost them $11. But if they looked as though they could afford it, it would be $24. The price went up and down with the customer.

The other name for these places was "the everything store", and that also made sense, because they sold everything. The principal business might be jewellery, but they would sell novelties in there, cosmetics, clothing, all manner of items; in fact, I had a distant relative just down the block on Jamaica Avenue whose store sold exactly that; and another who led off with electronics – radios, televisions, record players and so on.

The name of the store was Douglas Electronics, *not* because anybody connected with the business shared that name but because, since at least the 1920s, it had been the home of the well-respected Douglas Shoes. The new owner kept the old facade, kept the old furniture, and he even kept most of the original signage. He just replaced "shoes" with "electronics" and it was business as usual.

My first ever job was at Douglas Electronics, working through the summer of 1965, and getting my first ever taste of the music industry – with the emphasis on industry.

As the name implied, the shop sold everything electronic, from transistor radios and record players to kettles and kitchen gadgets. Walk past the shop and you could see them all in the window, heaped high in the most enticing piles, a true masterpiece of consumer art.

I'd not been there long when the boss called me over, handed me a copy of *Billboard* magazine and told me to go to such-and-such an address, a record distributors further down Jamaica Avenue, and pick up so many copies of the Top 5 or 10 singles. He would then get to work building a rack to put them all in. "Sylvain," he said proudly, "we're going into the record business."

It worked so well. I got back, we stacked the racks, hooked up a pair of speakers outside the store, and we sold out in one day. So that became a major part of my job, either biking or taking the bus to the distributors, bringing back all the vinyl I could carry, then watching as it sailed out of the store. Sometimes, we'd not even have time to fill the rack before the records started selling, and soon I was picking up LPs as well.

They sold just as quickly, but what was even more important to me was that this was where I really started to learn about music, to hear things that maybe my friends hadn't heard yet, or that I might never have discovered on my own.

Few of us could afford LPs in those days – all we knew of The Rolling Stones, for example, were their hits. Now I had the latest album in my grasp, and if I was lucky, I'd get to hear the whole thing before somebody wanted to buy it.

Even after school restarted, I'd stop by the Douglas Electronics whenever I could; hell, even after the Dolls got going, I was still going to that same distributor, going through the boxes of new and sometimes pre-releases, and picking up everything at cost. "Hey, you paid retail for the new so-and-so album? I got it for a buck."

That wasn't the only yo-yo shop I worked for. Another was geared primarily towards the ladies ... jewellery, stockings, accessories, and that had its advantages too, at least for the cute little French guy behind the counter, flirting with the customers, complimenting them on their purchases.

I didn't care that I was only fourteen. I was meeting girls, going to the movies with them, getting kissed by them, and sometimes I'd even tell them about my band.

Actually, it was more of a duo at that time. At some point, shortly after we met, I mentioned to Billy that I played guitar. "Really?" he asked. "I want to play drums." The very next day, he picked up a snare drum from some used place for a few bucks. Only a snare, but that didn't matter – in those days, if you played drums, that's all you needed: a drum. And if you said you were a drummer, all you needed was a pair of sticks.

From that most unlikely beginning in the schoolyard, our friendship had blossomed into what I can only describe as brotherhood. We went almost everywhere together, and if something prevented us from doing so, we'd make sure to deliver a full report the next time we met. That's how I found out about how great The Beatles were when they played Shea Stadium; Billy's older sister, Elizabeth, took both him and their sister Heidi, but the $5 (plus federal tax, plus city tax) ticket was like $50 to me, so I couldn't go. But Billy not only told me all about it, he made sure I didn't miss a song, or even a solo.

We did go to the 1964 World's Fair in Flushing Meadows, though, and that was amazing, a two-year-long extravaganza of pavilions and exhibitions and concerts and rides, and the great thing was, it was completely free.

At least, it was if you chained your bike up some place outside and then climbed over the fence, like we used to.

We went so many times, and only once did we get busted, coming down from the fence into the arms of these plain-clothes policemen with badges and everything, who rounded us up with a few other intruders, searched us and fined us all the money that we had – and then ran off, because they weren't really cops after all. We'd been woofed, but hey, this is New York. What do you expect to happen?

Once inside, we saw everything we could. The Future City, with a glimpse inside "your house in 1999" (I've since been to 1999 – they weren't even close). A slew of Walt Disney-themed attractions, including an army of singing animatronic dolls, all dressed as children. NASA had a pavilion, promising a moon landing within just a few years. IBM were there with their futuristic electronics; Du Pont, with their Wonderful World of Chemistry; and then there was the Belgian Village, which, for some reason, was the hip spot. And guess who had a job there, although we never met him back then? Arthur Killer Kane, future New York Doll, but, for now, just a kid working at the 7-Up stall.

Maybe the greatest attraction of all, however, were the girls.

"Do you like The Beatles or the Stones?" Introductions were so much simpler back then. Followed by, "Hey, we're going to the Ford Pavilion – you wanna come and ride the Mustangs?"

Ford were debuting their latest model, named for the wartime fighter plane, and destined to become their most popular launch since the Model A. Round and round the pavilion the cars would go, on a sleek moving roadway, and we'd pile into one of the show cars with our new lady friends, two in the front, two in the back … and we'd stay there until the next couple (or, occasionally, a genuine customer) wanted their turn at the wheel.

We told the girls about our group as well. It seemed to make a difference to them.

Billy's home was our first headquarters. The attic was empty, so his mother, Mercedes, let us turn it into our clubhouse, cover the walls in posters and make as much noise as we wanted. Which, when all we had was a Spanish guitar and a snare, wasn't too much.

But then I got my first electric, an Audition guitar, $35 on monthly down payments, and I was so thrilled when I took that baby home for the first time. Only for my mother to kick my ass and call me crazy.

Of course, she also knew how much it meant to me; I think it mattered to her too. She'd seen how well I took to the Spanish guitar, she'd seen me tinkering with the piano back in Buffalo. At school, while I remained at the back of the class for most subjects, I was having no problems at all in art and music. I even did a few junior productions, *HMS Pinafore* and *Fiddler On The Roof;* I sang in the chorus and, for a time, I was even in the school band, although handing me a trombone was not the teacher's smartest ever idea. But mom was proud all the same.

She loved music as much as I did, and it was from her that I got that love to begin with. It was the money that she objected to, as opposed to the guitar itself. Those down payments more or less devoured every cent I earned at the yo-yo shop. But once she accepted that, then she was ready to accept the guitar … on one condition. I had to take lessons.

I think it was that very same day that she walked me to Parson's Boulevard, which was the next subway stop to ours, and hooked me up with the very grandly named New York School of Music, up on the second floor of one of the corner buildings, and left me to take my first lesson.

The school devoured one room, dominated by an upright piano and not much else. The teacher himself looked a little like Nonno, my grandfather, a sweet old guy with a bit of an accent. He sat me down, watched me form a few chords, maybe corrected my fingering a little, and we went into the first song he wanted me to learn, a country oom-pah number called 'Down In The Valley'.

Then home again, I showed mom what I had learned, and for the second time she went crazy.

"That's all he taught you for a dollar fifty?"

It was like the times I came home with a skinny tie, or a dickie shirt, and my dad would tell me to take them back to the store because they didn't sell me the whole thing. "That's all you got?" She never sent me back for more lessons.

To be honest, though, I was stretching the story that I told her a little, not because I didn't learn anything, but because I didn't *want* lessons. Or if I did, I didn't want to learn 'Down In The Valley'. I wanted to learn 'You Really Got Me' and 'Twist And Shout', proper rockers, two-chord masterpieces.

I also wanted an amplifier.

I already had my eye on one. Billy's dad, Alphonso Sr. introduced me to a store called Lafayette Electronics, which was a lot like Radio Shack became, the kind of place you went when you wanted to build your own devices. They sold transistors, metal boxes, loose speakers, lengths of wire, soldering irons, all of that stuff, and they had a catalogue that you could drool over for hours. I know, because I did.

The object of my most rampant desire came already assembled. It was a one-channel, five-watt amp with a twelve-inch speaker. But it had two inputs, which not only meant I could plug in my guitar; I could also plug in a microphone. In my mind, I could do anything with this baby.

Of course, five watts isn't anything, as I discovered once I got it home and hit my first chord. But I also learned that if you turned it up to ten, it distorted like you wouldn't believe and yeah, now we're cooking with gas. 'You Really Got Me' here we come.

It was still just Billy and me, but that amp made all the difference. Now we were loud, too loud even for Mrs Murcia. But not too loud for the parking garage in the basement of my own building, where the superintendent allowed us to plug into one of the outlets in his little office.

We'd have to stop playing every time a car came in but, in between times, we could let rip, Billy bashing his snare, and my five-watt amp cranked up and bleeding, and what are we going to play?

'Wipe Out'! Twenty million times.

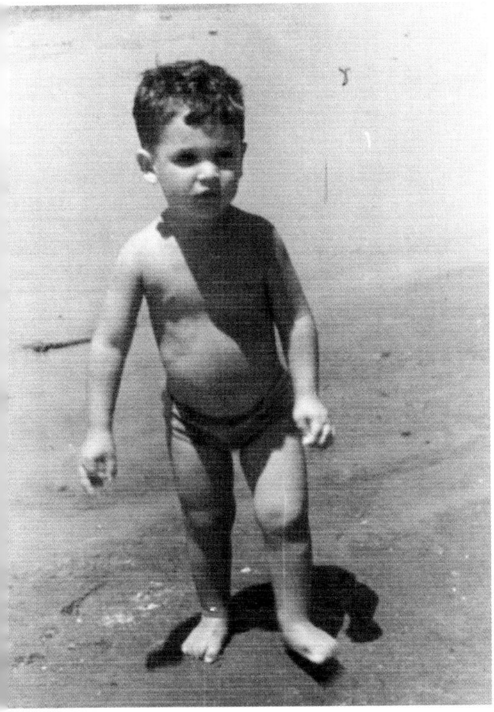

m on the beach at Alexandria, 1954-or-so – the photo was shot y one of those guys who walk around with cameras, offering to ake your picture. Mum said yes.

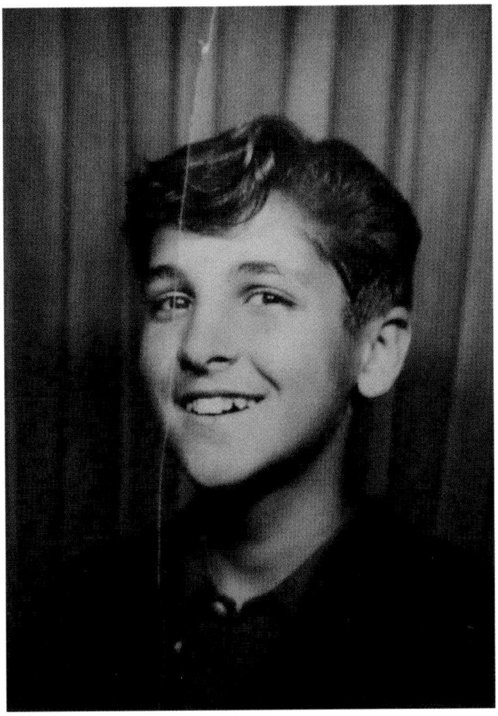

Self-portrait, taken at the Woolworths on Jamaica Avenue, shortly after we moved to Queens. I was 13 and I was already doing my own hair and make-up. Shangri-Las fans note the black mohair sweater.

SYLVAIN SYLVAIN.

My first American bicycle, in Buffalo, New York, 1961!

My sister and I, Buffalo, September 1961.
LEON MIZRAHI.

Uncle Ralph playing at Le Petit Aubergine cabaret, close by the pyramids, early 1950s.

Uncle Victor, wearing one of my hats!
SYLVAIN SYLVAIN

The photo that adorned my permit to re-enter the United States. At the time (early-mid 70s), I was still deemed "stateless".

Central Park, 1965, just before Billy and I formed the Pox. I'm on the left with shades, then it's Billy, George Nayko, Billy's brother Alfonso Jr and Farran, our vocalist.
ALFONSO MURCIA SR.

Billy and I in Central Park, 1965.
ALFONSO MURCIA SR.

We sectioned off one part of the Christie Street loft to hold our clothing, with everything hanging from the overhead pipes. This is the photo that appeared in *Melody Maker* and made us huge stars in England overnight.
LEEE BLACK CHILDERS.

From early 1972, Oz Garcia's original photo of the Dolls – the first ever taken!
OZ GARCIA.

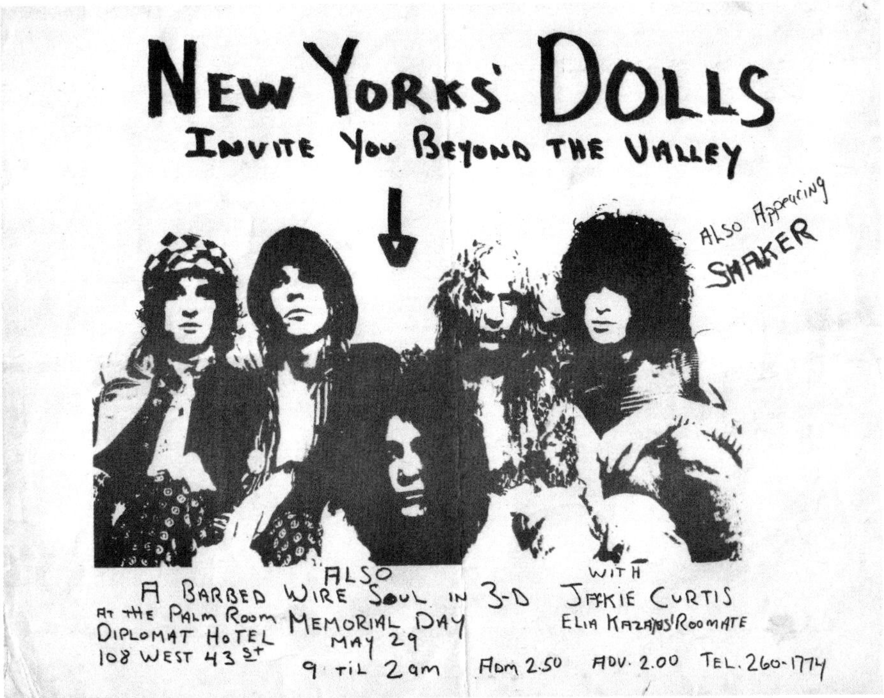

Our first ever flyer, the Dolls at the Diplomat in 1972. Jerry and Buddy Bowser's band Shaker were among the openers. David had to fix a typo in green ink.

JOHNNY THUNDERS

Johnny at the Mercer Arts Center, 1972. He got the top in a trade with David.
LEEE BLACK CHILDERS.

SYLVAIN SYLVAIN

Arthur and I at the Mercer, 1972.
LEEE BLACK CHILDERS.

The Dolls in the Oscar Wilde Room at the Mercer Arts Center, 1972. That's Billy on the far right, I'm playing my Sunburst and Johnn has his see-through plastic Dan Armstrong.

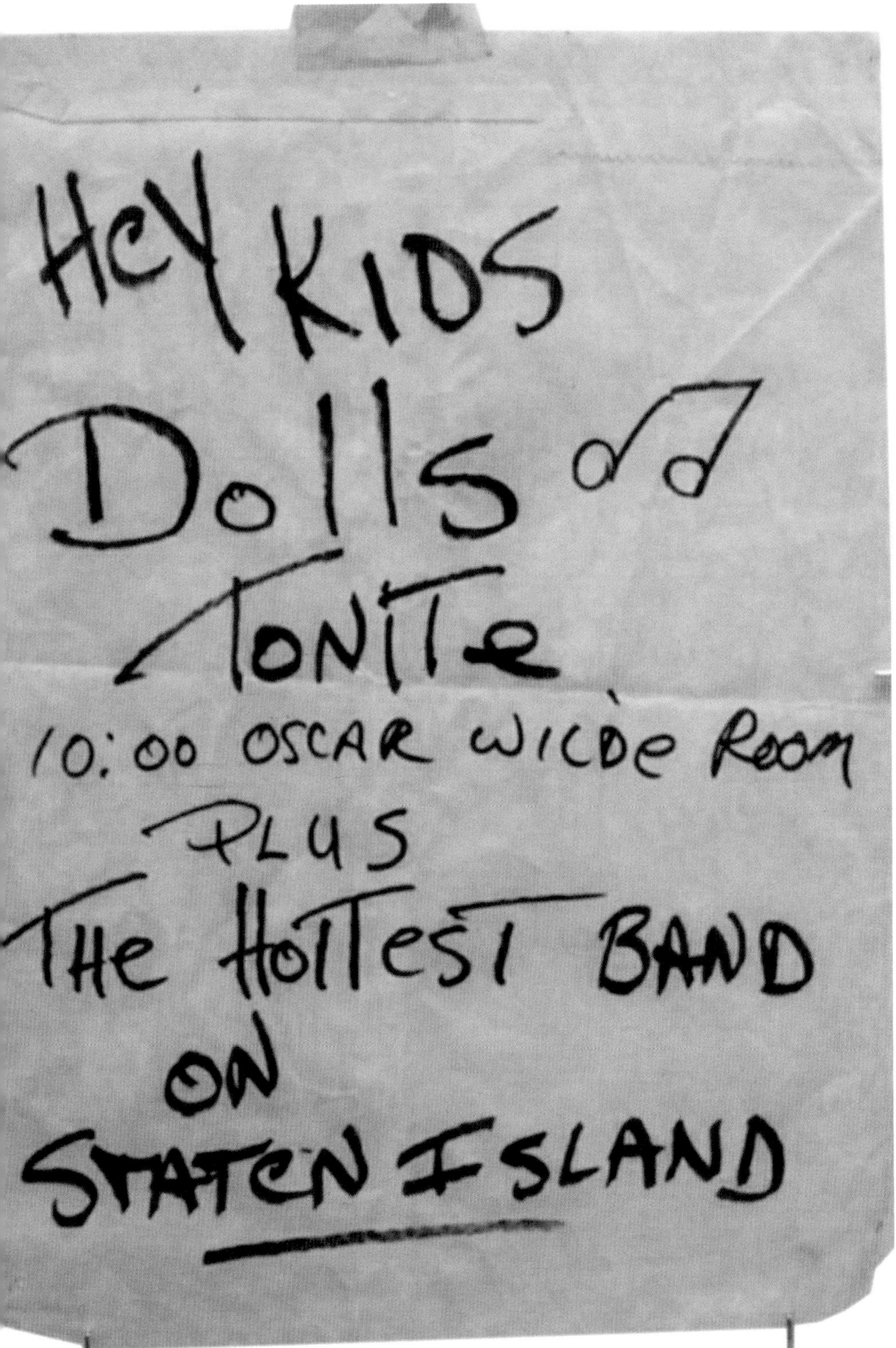

An early flyer for our Mercer Arts Center shows.

The New York Doll Hospital frontage that haunted me every time I stepped out of the Different Drummer.
MIKE SCHNAPP.

Inside the Doll Hospital. I still have the lady on the left, in the orange dress.
MIKE SCHNAPP.

At the Gem Spa candy store on the corner of St Marks and 2nd Ave, an outtake from the sessions for the back cover of the first album. I got my outfit, via Cyrinde, from Rick Derringer.
TOSHI MATSUO.

The Ventures were my guitar gods. Other groups made better records or had a better sound, and I still hankered for the sounds of The Shadows, the British instrumental wizards I discovered when I was living in Paris. Their records were not so easy to find in the States, though, so if you wanted to marvel at great guitar, without the distractions of voice or image or anything, The Ventures were the only place to go.

Plus, 'Wipe Out' has everything: a killer progression, sexy drums, a bit of flash, a bit of aggression, it's really rock'n'roll.

It's impossible for me to overestimate the importance of The Ventures. In fact, I even bought their *Play Guitar With The Ventures* LP, and that taught you everything – the rhythm, lead and bass lines to a bunch of their biggest hits – and when you'd mastered them, you could play along as well as The Ventures themselves. Years later, I taught Johnny Thunders another of their tunes, 'Pipeline' (he recorded a fantastic version on his *So Alone* album) and that's where it came from.

Meanwhile, people were walking around, glancing over at us, and occasionally stopping to watch; and a couple of girls from the building asked if they could come and check us out. Suddenly, we had an audience.

And that's how we started.

I don't believe we stayed in the garage for long; just until Billy's family moved to an even nicer house, and his mom gave us the room in the basement. We dressed it up, painted the walls, rehung our posters and installed black lights and all that kind of thing, and that's where we started to learn all the things that we wanted to. The serious stuff: the things that actually taught you to play, as opposed to learning enough to pick up chicks. Although that part still worked.

Again, word got around. Friends would drop by to listen to us, even though it was still just the two of us, and Billy's parents were as tolerant as they were supportive. There would never have been a New York Dolls without Mr and Mrs Murcia, because they went out of their way to encourage us. Billy's dad even put up with us tearing his MG sports car apart; there was a dead end at the back of their street and Billy and I used to drive it back and forth when nobody was around. Unfortunately, not only could neither of us drive, we didn't know how to, so that poor car never left first gear. You can imagine.

The Murcias had come to the United States from Colombia in 1963; back home in Bogotá, Billy's dad was an engineer – he was responsible for the first ever ice rink in Bogotá! There were three children – Billy and his sisters Elizabeth and Heidi – and I have never met a family like them. They were so sweet, so supportive, and Billy himself was incredible, really smart and really creative. I picked up so much from that guy, and I loved him for it.

One of my favourite stories about him goes back to when he first came to the USA. As I'd discovered, when you start a new school, they ask you what grade you were in and then, if you don't speak English too well, they drop you back a couple of grades to allow you to catch up. Billy's first school was the grammar school right across from where he lived, and sure enough, although he was old enough for seventh grade, they put him in the fifth or sixth, where he wasn't simply the biggest kid in the class, he was probably the biggest in the school.

So when he left that school, and went to register at a new one, he knew exactly what to do. He explained that he'd just arrived in the country, and had been in the ninth grade back home. "Okay," they said, "we'll put you in the seventh", which is where he should have been.

He wasn't at that school for long; I don't know exactly what happened, but he got thrown out. So off he went to another one, and he told the same story again, only this time he said he'd been in an even higher grade. Because the schools never checked with one another, they just believed what you told them, and that was a very important lesson for Billy and for me. You have to take advantage of what you can, because if you don't, you're screwed and you end up with nothing.

Billy and I made our very first recordings in that basement. Billy's dad was as addicted to Lafayettes as we were, and was forever bringing things home to tinker with. Now he had picked up a really nice reel-to-reel machine, and he started to tape us.

We were instantly enamoured. For the first time, we could actually listen back to the music we were making, and not only could we identify the parts that we needed to work on, but we could also celebrate the elements that we got right. It was time to broaden our scope.

George Nayko was a really good-looking guy, a bit like Brian Jones, who could both play guitar and sing – in fact, the first time we heard him was in a school production. We invited him along to try out as rhythm guitarist. We also found a singer, Farran, and it worked; between the two of them, they introduced a whole new dimension to our sound, and a new world of dynamics opened up too – how to play in a way that accentuated the singer's voice, rather than simply bang along as loud as we could and make him scream to be heard above it.

Not that we didn't do that as well, especially at first. But then we'd listen back to a tape and see where we had gone wrong: compare our version of, say, a Mitch Ryder song with his, and work out why his was so much better than ours.

I was also delving deep into the blues – not so much the traditional stuff, but the electric blues that were coming out of places like Chicago and New York, people like the Butterfield Blues Band, as well as all the English groups like the Stones and John Mayall. And I'd recently rediscovered Bob Dylan.

Back in Brooklyn, I spent a lot of time visiting my cousin Dove at his apartment off the King's Highway. We'd take our bikes and go to the beach, or sneak off some place and smoke cigarettes, but we also seemed to spend a lot of time on the street outside his house, listening to the music pouring out of a store across the road.

It was a hand-made leather goods store, owned by this bohemian kind of guy whose door was always wide open, and he would be blaring Dylan from dawn to dusk, the early folk stuff. I liked it well enough, and Dylan remained on my radar. He rewarded me with some of the most dramatic music I have ever heard – 'Positively Fourth Street', 'Maggie's Farm', 'Like A Rolling Stone'; real rebel music, with those Al Kooper organ lines, and the Butterfield Blues Band blasting behind him.

The power of that combination, and the sheer vehemence of Dylan's delivery, overwhelmed me. I never did catch every lyric to every song, but the ones I did get – "You've got a lot of nerve", "How does it feel?" – were so dismissive, so snotty, so angry and questioning, that you almost flinched when you heard them.

It was music made for the moment.

America was going through hard times in 1965. Society was still divided over civil rights, and now a new conflict was making itself felt, as Vietnam commenced its slow creep into the headlines. It was not a war yet, at least so far as media reports were concerned, but it certainly felt as though it was becoming one; and, even in my age group, with four years to go before it could touch us, for the first time you heard people talking about the draft.

Vast cracks were appearing in society. On the one hand, there were the people who were smoking dope and getting high; and, on the other, the ones who were smoking cigarettes and *not* getting high. With The Rolling Stones and Dylan bellowing defiance into our ears, Billy and I naturally fell into the first category.

I smoked my very first joint at the Jewish Centre in Jamaica, Queens. It was not the most obvious hotbed of sedition, but one day a friend of mine named David sidled up to me, and uncupped his hand to reveal the skinniest little reefer you can imagine. "Hey man, want to smoke a joint?"

Yeah, sure! To be honest, I didn't really know what he was talking about. It certainly didn't look like much, this skinny little thing that reeked of oil and tasted like shit. But it made me laugh and it made me feel good, and that was it. Throughout the years that followed, no matter what other drugs and chemicals were on offer, pot remained my first love, and when the mainstream first started to report on its health benefits, I readily added my voice to the chorus of other potheads who asked, "You've only just figured that out?"

David also had a group, although they were considerably better than mine and Billy's. Nevertheless, when the Jewish Centre announced it was going to stage a dance and was auditioning groups to perform that night, we decided to give it a go.

We're into 1966 by now, and Billy's brother Alphonso was playing with us too. Window shopping in Macy's one day, I'd spotted a Hammond B2 organ, a beast of a machine but an essential part of the sound I was envisioning in my head (again, thank you Al Kooper). I told Alphonso about it and, soon enough, it was sitting in the basement, being put through all the torments that an aspiring blues-rock band could devise. We worked so hard to blend it into our sound, although we had to work even harder to transport it to the venue, a few streets and a steep flight of stairs away from home.

We settled on a name, The Devils; we decided which songs we were going to perform; and we smiled broadly at the girls who would be judging the event, walking round the room with notebooks and pens.

There were three acts on the bill. I don't recall the first, but David's group blew all of us away. He was armed with a black Les Paul cutaway, and he played it well. Plus, while we relied on our usual repertoire, they chose a song by Cream, who had just recently broken through, and of course the girls picked them.

We little Devils were shattered, and promptly fled the scene of our disgrace – straight round the corner to Tony's Pizza, where we drowned our sorrows in Coke and pizza slices. Then, the next day, we were back on our feet and preparing, once more, to take on the world.

We continued to play whatever we could learn, whatever we heard on the radio or at the beach, but it wasn't only music that I was picking up on. I was also learning – I guess you could almost call it showmanship, although I thought of it more as self-confidence, without realising that the two often march hand in hand together.

Billy and I had started attending the Friday night dances that were held at the church down the block; then, when our school began doing the same thing on a different evening, we'd be there as well.

Of course, it was attended by all the same kids you saw every day in class, but there was something about low lights and loud music that made everybody look and behave very differently. The girls would dress up and bring these bowls of dip for the refreshment tables; there'd be a disc jockey playing things like the Count Five's 'Psychotic Reaction' with that crazy fuzz guitar that made you feel ten feet tall; and, naturally, everyone would be dancing and making out.

Suddenly I noticed something else that was different. Girls who, in class, barely looked at me were now lining up to dance with me. Because, as it transpired, I was probably the best dancer in the place, and it didn't matter how tired I might be, I couldn't take a break until every girl had had her turn.

I couldn't believe it, but that's when I kinda realised, "Okay kid, you got something. You don't have other things, but you've got *something*."

Natural rhythm. A certain style. Or, as David Bowie put it a few years later, "God-given ass".

Chapter 8

THE TOM JONES SHIRT

Clothes were so important, and I didn't care what people thought. Not even my parents.

The Tom Jones shirt, though, was a genuine flashpoint. And a game changer, too.

In truth, it was just a regular shirt, with a dark brown background and blueish polka dots, and at the bottom it was cut straight across. But the sleeves were puffed, the cuffs had three buttons, and they, the cuffs, were puffed as well. I bought it on Jamaica Avenue, and my mother almost killed me. My father, too. In French we have the slang "PD" – short for "pédé" – which means gay, and though dad didn't say that, I knew he was thinking it. That shirt was too much for him and I had no choice but to return it to the store.

I had to change my strategy. No more showing mom and dad what I'd bought, no more letting them even know I'd bought something. Down in the basement, behind the washing machines in the laundry room, I made myself a little hiding place where I'd stash all the clothes that I didn't want my parents to know I owned. New shirts, tighter trousers, vivid jackets. My brown suede pointy Beatle boots with the Cuban heels, a zipper up the back, and a sunburst stripe down the centre. Check out the cover to the first Question Mark & The Mysterions album – they're wearing them there.

Every morning, I'd walk out of the apartment in whatever clothes they approved of, with my hair combed back, looking slick as you like. Then, down to the laundry room to change into that day's outlandish outfit. I'd mess up my hair, I'd check my reflection, and that's how I'd go to school. When I came home, I'd go straight into the laundry room and change back. Which could be embarrassing if there were people in there, but it was worth it.

Not that my parents were wholly against fashion. Billy and I were not only buying clothes, we were also designing our own, things that we wish we could have bought but nobody was manufacturing. With Billy's sister Heidi and some obliging girlfriends to help with the sewing, and mom adding her knitting skills, we were putting together some great-looking outfits, which we would then wear on our increasingly regular trips into Manhattan.

Often we would even dress the same ... I remember the matching pants we had, in bold black and white checks, and I still don't know where we found the balls to do this, but we rode the subway all the way into the city like that, then walked around Washington Square Park.

We must have looked like a complete pair of idiots, but we didn't care. Greenwich Village was the centre of the New York scene back then, with clubs on every corner and kids on every street, all doing the same thing as we were, hanging out and seeing who we could see.

It might be Janis Ian walking down MacDougal Street in her cape, clutching her guitar on her way to the Cafe Bizarre; it might be David Peel, staging impromptu love-ins in the park; and the friends who would later become Teenage Lust, standing on top of the benches singing songs about marijuana and Vietnam with fifty people all around them dancing with tambourines and bells.

There'd be the runaways dodging the cops; the cops looking out for the dealers; the dealers peddling banana skins, to take advantage of that sudden flash of mass gullibility that convinced people you could get a legal high from smoking the things. 'Hold On, I'm Coming' by Sam & Dave was the monster song of the day, and you couldn't turn around without hearing it; every store would be playing it, every band would be blasting it, every busker would be strumming it. It was an incredible feeling.

Things were changing so fast; you'd blink and something new had come along. I saw this process in action, this non-stop kaleidoscope of new ideas, new sounds, new paradigms – and how quickly they affected people, one afternoon in June 1967.

I'd gone to see The Young Rascals at the Schaefer Music Festival in New York, at the Wollman Rink in Central Park. The Rascals were big back then, and they were definitely one of my favourite bands, but first we had to get through the support act.

I was curious. Their set-up alone blew me away – Marshall stacks on either side of the stage – and I was poking Billy, going, "Fuck, check out those amps!" They looked as big as the Empire State; we were accustomed to those little Fender amps that everybody else used, and here were these monsters. And the other thing? Most amps whistle; the Marshall sustains. It sings, it doesn't scream.

Out came the MC with his English accent. "For the first time in America" ... and on trouped the support act, a riot of colour and clothes, flowery jackets, huge heads of curly hair. I loved them already – I had natural curly hair and I used to get poked all the time: "Syl, why don't you buy yourself some Beat the Frizzies?" There were only three of them, but they looked so beautiful and they hadn't even played a note.

When they did, I was in heaven. I'd already seen Cream and been impressed, but Eric Clapton, Ginger Baker and Jack Bruce were still individual musicians, who just happened to play along with one another. This "Jimi Hendrix Experience" was a true band. An entirely different thing. And when they played 'Wild Thing', I was cumming in my pants.

Hendrix pulled out all the stops. Every sonic trick he would ever be renowned for in the future, including most of the ones he would pull out at the Monterey Pop Festival a few days later, he did them that afternoon. When the Experience left the stage at the end of their set, I don't think there was anybody in the audience who didn't instinctively understand that something major had just occurred; that music itself would never be the same again.

And then The Young Rascals, who we'd paid the dollar to see, came on. They had the hit for the summer, 'Groovin'', and such a fantastic line-up: Gene Cornish on guitar, Felix Cavaliere on organ and Dino Danelli, who remains my all-time favourite drummer, even more than Jerry Nolan.

He was so incredible; the entire band was. They came out of the Action House, which was a phenomenal club out on Long Beach. They'd played all the really big venues in New York City, the kind of places where you did three or four sets a night, so you had to have stamina and really know your shit. I used to play their records at full volume on my little record player, so excited that I would literally take my clothes off and run around naked to 'Mustang Sally'. Poor mom, the first time she came home unexpectedly and saw that!

Back to the Wollman Rink. Out came The Young Rascals and the first thing Gene did was go up to his Fender amp and start trying to get feedback, in the same way that Hendrix had.

But the Fender isn't built like that. She's gonna scream, but she's not going to give you that sustain. So he gave up on that and, with his back to the audience, he started hitting the neck of the guitar against the amp and that was it for me, and for everybody else. Across the room, people were standing up and booing, because it was obvious that he was trying to imitate Hendrix, and doing it really badly.

Now I think about it, God bless him for trying. He had just seen the entire future of rock'n'roll shift before his eyes, and he was trying to shift with it. But all we saw was a guy trying to copy the uncopyable, and we gave him hell.

Hendrix was remarkable, but *all* music was remarkable at that time. All the good music, anyway.

I went to the Cafe Owl to see The Lovin' Spoonful, and that's where I caught another of my favourite groups of that time, The Music Machine. The Blues Magoos, too; they were spellbinding. Another time ... I'm not sure where Billy was, but I was there, standing around outside the Cafe Wha? (which is where Chas Chandler discovered Hendrix), and I could hear a band playing in the rooms above, the Player Theater.

It was warm and the windows were open, and this amazing music was just floating down. Suddenly a face appeared at the window, looking down at me. Frank Zappa! He caught my eye and called out, "Hey kid, come on in!" And for the next forty-five minutes, I sat there, absolutely rapt, while The Mothers Of Invention ran through their soundcheck.

The amazing thing is, this wasn't a big deal. There was a vibe to the Village back then, a sense that anything was possible, and everything was for everyone. There would be musicians playing on every street corner, and Washington Square Park was alive with them, everything from one-man shows to full ensembles, all playing for the love of playing.

One night, Billy and I discovered the Cock and Bull, which was effectively just a basement beneath some store or other; we went in and there was a couple of guitarists jamming rock'n'roll, the blues, whatever came into their heads, both playing through the same Fender amp – exactly the same as Billy and I had always done.

Most of our visits to New York took place either in the late afternoon or at weekends; at any other time, you risked being picked up by the truancy officers, who were really hard cases in those days, prowling the streets looking for anyone who looked as though they ought to be in the classroom. Fortunately – or not, depending upon your outlook – those days were fast coming to an end, at least for me.

Billy and I were attending high school now: Newtown High School in Elmshurst. We were still rehearsing and jamming as much as we could, with Alphonso sitting in when he wanted to. George and Farran weren't around so much now, though, and we were spending time with one of Farran's friends, a guitar player named Mike Turby.

What a talent. First of all, he was great looking; and second, he played in an amazing group. Every neighbourhood in New York had its own answer to the British Invasion – there'd be the local Beatles, the local Who, the local Kinks. Mike played in The Orphans, who were unanimously proclaimed Queens's answer to The Rolling Stones. They sounded like them, and they dressed like them as well, trouping down to Playboy, a boutique just down the road from Douglas Electronics, and then dazzling us all with their purchases.

One night, Billy, Heidi and I went to see them play the Jewish Centre, and it was clear that Mike had an eye for Heidi. Finally, he came over and asked us to introduce him, and we said yeah ... but only if you'll teach us how to play. So he did.

He was older than us, a student at Quintano's, a private school for young professionals – models, musicians, all the showbiz types – across the street from Carnegie Hall in Manhattan. But, for some reason, he took a liking to Billy and me, spending hours with us in the Murcias' basement, him smoking his omnipresent Benson & Hedges cigarettes and teaching me B B King riffs, blues progressions, different bars and scales, things I would probably never have worked out on my own.

He introduced us to new songs, new bands, great rock'n'roll numbers with barely any chords, but all the energy and meaning in the world. Songs that stood up for themselves. He showed me how to write songs, too, and later in the year, when we decided to form a group together, he gave me something even more precious than that. He would play the bass, he said. I should be the lead guitarist.

It was around this same time, while we were playing with Mike but before we became a band, that I started to notice a really cool-looking cat in the lunchroom at school or in the hallways between classes.

Immaculately dressed and great looking too, he was always accompanied by the most beautiful chicks, and that may be what I noticed first. If we could get this kid into our group, then maybe we'd have those same chicks in *our* audience. I mentioned him to Billy; he agreed. So the next time I saw him, in the school lunchroom one day, I went up and asked him straight: "Hey man, me and Billy have got a band, do you wanna join?"

He looked at me, deep brown eyes beneath a mass of painstakingly coiffed hair, sculpted cheekbones and chin, resplendent in whatever outfit he had decided to grace us with that day. "Oh yeah, I know that guy." Then a pause. "The problem is, I can't play anything."

So I said, "It's easy, I'll show you," and he told me he'd think about it.

That was it for a couple of weeks, and then one day he came over and asked, "How many strings does a bass guitar have?" I said four. "And how many does a regular guitar have?" Six. And he replies, "Sylvain, I'm your fucking bass player." And that's how Johnny Thunders, or Johnny Genzale Jr as he was back then, got his start; playing the instrument that he thought would be easiest.

Of course it isn't. It's the bass that holds the bottom, and without that foundation, you don't have the sound that will take you into the next zone. Just like a drummer gives you an accent. Johnny started coming down to the basement, and that's how it was for a while.

But Johnny had a tremendous ego. You could put Elvis Presley, Steve Jobs and Phil Spector all together, and their combined ego still wouldn't come close.

A lot of it was insecurity. Growing up was hard for Johnny; his father had effectively abandoned the family, and while he did show up on occasion, one particular event never left his mind.

Johnny wanted to be a baseball hero. As a kid, that was his only ambition; he would grow up and become a big star. He had the talent, too; he was a great player and people talked about him. He even got scouted by one of the New York teams.

Now he had been invited to a trial. All he had to do was show up with a parent, and play as well as he always did. His father agreed to take him – and he didn't turn up. Johnny stood there waiting, delaying the inevitable as long as he could. "Oh, he'll be right along"; "Maybe he got stuck in traffic"; everything he could come up with.

The old man never showed, though, and – yes, maybe there would be other scouts, other opportunities – but I think Johnny just lost heart. It certainly broke his heart. He'd been let down on what should have been the greatest occasion of his life, and he wasn't going to risk it happening again.

From that moment on, he was determined never to ask anybody for anything again. He would do everything he needed by himself, and if he couldn't, that didn't matter. He'd bluff it.

He was lonely, I realised that. He had girlfriends aplenty, but there were very few males in Johnny's life, very few mates. But he would never risk being rebuffed. Rather than ask if you wanted to hang out, he would always offer an incentive. He always kept an eye open to see what his friends enjoyed the most – the very day after he was introduced to pot, for example, he was calling up saying, "Hey, I've got some pot. Wanna get high?"

Or we'd be sitting around looking at a magazine, raving about the clothes that so-and-so was wearing, and the next day he would have an identical outfit. It was as if he didn't believe that he himself was worthy of anyone's attention, so he needed to sweeten the pill.

I taught him bass and, later, guitar. But almost from the outset, he let me know that it was him who was doing *me* the favour and, a few years later, as we were putting the New York Dolls together, he came up to me and announced, "From now on, I'm the lead guitar player and you're the rhythm guitar player." The funny thing was, I knew he'd been thinking that all along, from the moment I started to teach him to play. Not because he necessarily believed it, but because he wanted everybody else to. Because then, he thought, they would respect him.

He didn't need any of that. When I first met him, and all through the birth of the New York Dolls, Johnny really was an angel of a child: the cleanest guy, the coolest guy, with the coolest records and clothes, and the sexiest, most beautiful girlfriends.

When the band started to take off, all the biggest stars came to see us. But their wives and girlfriends came for Johnny. He had the greatest talent, and he wrote the greatest tunes. He wrote 'You Can't Put Your Arms Around A Memory', for heaven's sake, and when Ronnie Spector recorded it with Joey Ramone, it broke my heart. All I could think of was *if only* he could have been around to hear it.

Johnny would never reconcile with his father; in fact, I don't think he even saw him again until the New York Dolls were playing a show in Coventry, in Queens, in 1974. Without any warning, the old man turned up, showing off his son, the star, to the new Mrs Genzale.

I don't know if she was impressed, but Johnny certainly wasn't. A few days after his father died, late in the eighties, I called him up and said I was sorry to hear the news. Johnny didn't even pause. "Ah, I don't give a fuck."

But deep down, he was still hurt. In fact, I am convinced that one of the things that made heroin so appealing to Johnny was that it gave him a break from an issue that had haunted him since childhood.

All of these thoughts, of course, came later. At the time, Johnny was simply a high school friend and a fellow aspiring musician. Our early friendship lasted for as long as it lasted, but as our mid-teens progressed and other interests hove into view, we would lose touch for a short time.

With the summer vacation looming, I decided to look a little further afield than the yo-yo shops, and further than Queens, too, in my search for a part-time job. Inevitably I settled on Manhattan, haunting the area around St Mark's Place in search of any kind of opening.

I found it on Avenue A, in a battered storefront between 8th and 9th, at Peace Eye, the bookstore that was run by Ed Sanders and The Fugs.

The Fugs were the coolest shit at that time: political street theatre at its most anti-establishment extreme – even their name was an obscenity if you'd read the right books; "fug" is what Mailer uses instead of "fuck" in *The Naked And The Dead.*

Their records and their performances were not so restrained – one of my favourite numbers by them was 'Doing Alright', with that wonderful lyric, "I ain't ever going to go to Vietnam, I'd prefer to stay here and screw your mom." And that at a time, The Fugs themselves acknowledged, when a line like that could get you seriously beaten up.

Peace Eye was the centre of that world, a magnet for every runaway, junkie, peacenik and hippy-before-there-were-hippies in the city. I, on the other hand, was none of those things, just a fifteen-year-old kid from the boroughs who needed some cash to spend. But I was willing to learn!

Unfortunately, my employers weren't so willing to let me. I had only been there a couple of days when one of the men who ran the place discovered that I couldn't read too well. So what did the son of a bitch do? He fired me, on the spot. So much for peace and love, man.

Next, I took a job delivering sandwiches, going from office block to office block with the businessmen's orders. It wasn't quite as glamorous as working for The Fugs, and the dress code was a lot more restrictive (probably because Peace Eye didn't have one), but at least I wasn't going to get fired because I couldn't spell "mayonnaise".

I think I quit the next day.

Money was tight then. I could usually rely on finding the cash to buy things that I genuinely wanted – clothes, records, guitar strings, life's bare essentials. But dad was still working two jobs, and it wasn't cheap raising three children.

We cut corners, and one of those corners was my gym uniform. As far back as my days at Van Wyck, I had always forgone this particular school requisite, because it just didn't seem to matter. They'd simply park me at the back with all the others who didn't have one, shivering in our underwear and complaining that gym was such a waste of time anyway.

Newtown High, however, was somewhat less forgiving. Every class, this utter bastard of a gym master, a California beach dude type who looked like Kookie from the *77 Sunset Strip* TV show, would bawl me out for not having a uniform – a pair of shorts with the school's name printed on them, and a certain type of T-shirt. Available only from the school, for a princely $15.

Every class, I'd make an excuse and tell him I'd have one next time. But I never did, so finally he told me that if I didn't turn up with the $15 the very next day, I would be sent to see the principal. Of course I didn't have the $15, and though I did ask, I knew that my dad didn't either.

It was raining the next day, which meant I took my umbrella with me to school; and, because I didn't want it dripping all over my locker, I carried it with me to the first couple of classes, the second of which was gym.

As soon as I walked in, Kookie asked me where my $15 was, and when I told him I didn't have it, he marched me down the hallway to the staircase that would ultimately lead to the principal's office.

The place was deserted; everyone else was in class. Suddenly, halfway down the stairs, he turned around and laid into me: "You fucking little faggot, I know you've got the money."

He grabbed me, started shaking me, shouting in my face. I was screaming, because this guy was enormous, and I was genuinely terrified. And that's when I did it. I hit him with my umbrella, as hard as I could, and I kept on hitting him, still screaming my head off, until people started pouring out of the classes to see what was going on, and the pair of us were pulled apart.

Now I was definitely bound for the principal's office, and, of course, I was not permitted to say a word. The teacher told his side of the story – that I had gone crazy for no reason at all, and just started beating on him with my umbrella. The principal took out a little piece of paper, signed it and put it away. I had been expelled from school. I was to return the following day with my mother – by which time, a bunch of the other pupils had been convinced to agree that yes, they saw me attack the gym teacher.

I was 16 and my education was over. At the time, I was devastated. But it's strange how things work out. It meant I had more time to spend in Manhattan, more time to make money (I started applying for full-time jobs immediately), and more time to hang out with Mike at Quintano's. In fact, I spent so much time there that a couple of the teachers started treating me as an actual student, even though I never was – Billy and Alphonso would eventually enrol, but I was never able to scrape up the $400 a term tuition fee.

Nevertheless, particularly on warm days when a teacher might decide to hold his class in Central Park, which was only three blocks away, there would usually be a friendly "Okay Sylvain, come along" and there I'd be.

I found an apartment in Manhattan. It was a sublet, $57 a month, which I scraped together from a few part-time jobs and various other little gigs. It belonged to a couple of friends I had from Queens, transients who were constantly travelling to San Francisco and back, and who used the apartment to stash their dope.

It wasn't much. Deep within the Lower East Side, between Avenues D and C, up on the third or fourth floor at the rear of an anonymous, rundown brownstone. I could look out of the window and see kids sitting out back with bags over their heads, sniffing glue.

The apartment's saving grace was that it came with an operating refrigerator – you could seldom rely on the appliances actually working in any of those places. The bad news was that it had no door. They kept it running to cool the apartment down during the summer!

In those days the Lower East Side wasn't much of a destination: block after block of increasingly dilapidated tenements, overcrowded with families and overrun by rats, bums and drug dealers. It was also dangerous as hell, particularly if you were white, or you dressed in clothes that the locals might think strange, or if you were carrying a guitar. I had a few close shaves when I was out, but I was also quick on my feet.

Still, if anybody ever suggested they visit me, I'd do my best to put them off, and they would usually agree. Even out in Queens, we knew that the only reason anyone would wind up on the Lower East Side was because they were broke, and you never, ever went past Avenue B unless you were going to buy junk and you were ready to get ripped off, both going and coming back.

Even I didn't stick it out for long before heading back to Hillside Avenue.

Our social circle grew wider. Alphonso was now dating a girl he met at Quintano's, Ellen Croner, whose parents were probably the hippest adults I have ever met. They lived in Greenwich Village, in a gorgeous modern apartment owned by New York University (Ellen's father was a professor there) at the end of Bleecker Street, and they were forever inviting us to join them at one or other of the multitude of clubs that gave the area its aura.

We saw so many bands, particularly at the Cafe au Go Go, when that was one of *the* premier venues in the Village. That's where I caught Blood Sweat & Tears' first ever show, with Al Kooper on organ and Jim Fielder from the Mothers; that's where I discovered Moby Grape, and oh my God, they were so great – they had hollow guitars and they were playing the blues, Albert King, B B King, Blues Project, all manner of people.

The Croners also introduced Billy and me to the town of Woodstock – famed now, of course, for the festival, but, in 1967, still a sleepy little community in upstate New York, with a vague reputation as an artists' colony. Dylan lived there, and so did The Band, but nobody else had followed them, so it was still very quiet, very peaceful, and every summer the Croners would rent a house there and we spent a wonderful few weeks just relaxing and exploring.

Then, back to the basement to rehearse, with Billy, Mike and I in full Hendrix Experience mode. Jimi's first album, *Are You Experienced*, was released in the US in August 1967, and much as we loved the music, it was the clothes the three of them were wearing on the cover that really knocked us out.

That was it. All I wanted was to look, play and smell just like that. I already had the black velvet jacket and the curly hair. We already had all we needed for a three-piece band. The sewing machine would do the rest.

But we still needed a name. Something short, something memorable, something that sounded English.

We called ourselves The Pox.

Chapter 9

TENDER BUTTONS

In hindsight, you could say that things moved quickly for The Pox, although to me, with absolutely nothing to compare it to, our progress felt perfectly normal. We formed a band; we told a friend, whose father happened to own a recording studio; we auditioned; we were signed … easy.

Mike Brown was the friend – lead singer with The Left Banke, whose most massive hit, 'Walk Away Renee', overshadows the wealth of other music for which they were responsible. His father was Harry Lookofsky, a violinist by trade (you can hear him, too, on 'Walk Away Renee'), who also owned a small studio next to the Brill Building on Broadway.

Mike made the introductions and off we went, up to the third-floor studio, where burlap sacks were nailed to the walls to provide a degree of sound proofing, and a handful of Vox Super Beatle cabinets stood in for decor. Harry ushered us in, sat us down, and, for a while, we chatted. Then he asked to hear what we'd got.

We were prepared for the moment. We'd written a handful of songs by now, including one called 'Epitaph', which we really felt strongly about. That would be our opening shot, but just as we were getting ready to start, Harry looked directly at me and asked, "Do you sing?" And when I said yes, he told me to show him.

This was awkward; Mike was our lead singer, but I wasn't going to disappoint Harry Brown. I started out with The Beatles' 'Yesterday', followed through with 'Michelle', and that was it. Harry told me to take lead vocals.

Mike was fine with it; he was as excited about this whole affair as I was. Harry seemed to like it as well, because the next thing we know, he's having contracts drawn up and, a short while later, on April 18, 1968, Billy, Mike and my father (I was still just seventeen, a minor in legal terms) were signing on the dotted line.

What did the contract offer? Well, there was no money, for a start. But Harry would represent us, record us and, hopefully, find a record deal for us; and, in the meantime, we were to go out and make a name for ourselves.

That, too, proved surprisingly easy – at least, compared to the situation a few years later. When the New York Dolls first began looking for gigs around Manhattan in 1972, there were so few functioning venues that we had to invent our own. In 1967, on the other hand, the streets were lousy with them, with one of them sited more or less directly opposite Harry's studio.

The Crawdaddy, like so many other venues, was little more than a converted basement. In an earlier lifetime, it had been Birdland, where Charlie Parker got his start. Now it was owned by old-time rock'n'roller Lloyd Price, the voice behind the hits 'Personality' and 'Stagger Lee'.

Price performed there on a regular basis, but the actual day-to-day business was handled by two fellows named Timothy something, and Mike Quashi, a professional dancer who later became one of the powers behind Max's Kansas City. His big thing was to strip down to a loin cloth, grab a spear and perform the limbo – in fact, he was known as the Limbo King, although right now he was simply a lovely guy who liked our sound (although he did think we were too loud) and gave us a gig the following weekend. The adverts he drew up were headlined "Go Catch The Pox."

We landed another gig at the Cafe Bizarre, which was where you played if you couldn't get a gig at the Wha? or the Owl; and we had a few other shows as well, including one ... the biggest of them all ... in the Grand Ballroom of the Hotel Diplomat, opening to a roomful of hippies for a band called The Group Image.

It was the largest audience we'd ever seen, and of course we were nervous. I was also out of tune, but there I was, riffing on my cherry-coloured SG, trying to get the sound when, all of a sudden, these hippies who'd been drifting around all evening, all fringes and sandals and peace signs, gathered as one and rushed to the stage, all of them going crazy.

Whoah, that felt good!

We went into 'Epitaph'; the crowd was still with us. Our second song went down even better; the third was going gangbusters – and crash. The juice went out. The guitars, the mikes, the amps, the stage lights. Everything.

The headliners had pulled the plugs on us. This was meant to be *their* night and we were blowing them off the stage completely.

It didn't stop us. The guitar and bass were dead, but Billy just kept going, powering into a massive drum solo and not stopping until the headliners physically marched on stage, carried off our gear and started to dismantle the drums around Billy as well.

I cannot recall how many shows The Pox played altogether; not many, for sure. More of our time was spent in our basement, lost within marathon jams that lasted for hours and hours.

We learned so much in those sessions; everything that Billy and I brought to the New York Dolls was born in that basement, trying everything we could think of and figuring out what worked and what didn't.

We'd hear a song on the radio and, if it felt right, we'd learn it and then unlearn it sufficiently to make it into our own. The first time I heard Hendrix's version of 'Hey Joe', I was telling Billy, "We need to learn it" – not because we didn't have enough of our own songs to play, but because there were certain standards that audiences expected to hear, or some that they needed to hear. It was like when Hendrix picked up on The Beatles' 'Sergeant Pepper' and Dylan's 'All Along The Watchtower', when even the original versions of those songs were still brand new. Audiences remembered things like that.

Every so often, we'd take a break and troop on up to the kitchen to hang with Heidi, make coffee and have something to eat. For the most part, though, it was the three of us just taking off, getting high from the music and the solos and improvisation. Or, on occasion, other things.

None of us drank alcohol – maybe a little wine occasionally, but no spirits, no beer, and nothing to excess. But there would be occasionally a little pot floating around, and that's when we would really open up and talk to one another.

It was during one of these sessions that I finally shared my deepest secret with my bandmates. Or, as I thought of it, I finally took off the dark glasses I had been wearing my entire teenaged life.

Up to this point, everybody knew me as the French kid, born and raised in Paris, then coming to the States in time for my teens. I don't know why I'd stuck with the story; partly, I suppose, it was because of my mother's insistence that I should never let on that I was a Jew; but also it was because I'd been "French" for so long, it would be bizarre to change that now. And because being French went down a lot better with the ladies than being Egyptian. But when Mike suggested that we all cleanse ourselves with one massive revelation, I knew what I had to do.

So I spilled the beans ... and they didn't believe me. I was, as they said in those days, "full of shit". But I didn't care. As far as I was concerned, I'd done it, and I resolved there and then I would never again hide away the person I was. Which, of course, would have its own particular consequences once the Dolls got going.

The Pox did not last long. One afternoon, Mike announced that he wouldn't be around the next day. He had to report to the draft board, the first step towards being conscripted and sent to fight in Vietnam.

We were horrified. "What are you going to do?" But he told us not to worry.

If you were sick, they weren't going to draft you. Everybody knew that. And somebody had told him ... I still can't believe we thought this would work.

We downed instruments and left the house, straight to the store. There we purchased a five-pound bag of white sugar and, back at Billy's, we made a sugar drink that was effectively one full glass of sugar, with just enough water to transform it into a sludge.

Mike downed the whole thing, glass by glass by glass, until the bag was empty. Because he had been told that when he took the blood test all that sugar would mimic diabetes. And guess what? It didn't work. His blood test came back normal. In the end – I don't know why – he never did get drafted. Instead, he set off to spend the summer in San Francisco, checking out everything that was going on there. He returned in full Jim Morrison regalia, and he looked amazing. But The Pox had already petered out.

While Mike soaked in the San Francisco sun, Billy and I had found ourselves jobs.

Billy first. We were spending a lot of time hanging out in St Mark's Place, where some of Manhattan's best shopping was to be found. Back in the forties and fifties, St Mark's – and a lot of the Lower East Side as well – was known for its clubs: places that teetered between incredibly groovy and dangerous, perverted and sleazy, the whole spectrum from the cleanest to the dirtiest motherfuckers you could ever find on this planet.

A lot of them had gone by now, and the stores were what replaced them; even the Five Spot, where Thelonious Monk used to play, was now a $3 clothing emporium called the Late Show, just one of a tangle of boutiques, record and used clothes stores, places like Limbo's and the Army & Navy; McGregor's the barbershop, with the entire building painted like a giant truck; and, like a monarch surveying its domain, the Electric Circus, a huge blue building that became the Palais Royale of the hippies.

There were a lot of late-night coffee houses there as well – Ratner's, which was a kosher place next door to the Fillmore East, and these Russian places that we called the Slow Russians, where you could sit all night talking and drinking, and watching writers and artists and bookworms doing the same thing.

Billy landed in the thick of all this, directly opposite the Electric Circus, in a store that specialised in used furs, Grizzly Furs. We always made a point of browsing in there when we passed, but it was unusual that we could afford anything. But once he started working there, it opened all of its treasures to us: stoles and wraps and all manner of fashions. Billy immediately picked up an American Civil War-style rebel coat; I got a Russian hat, one of the heavy black ones that would open up like an envelope. He landed on his feet and, a short while after, so did I.

Different Drummer was at number 792 Lexington Avenue, and I still remember the day I heard they'd taken me on.

My family and I had moved out of Hillside Avenue by now; home in 1968 was a sixth-floor apartment on 59th Avenue in Regal Park, Queens, right off Queens Boulevard; cross the highway and you'd be in Forest Hills. I'd become friendly with a girl who lived down the hallway. She was visiting one day when the phone rang. It was Eddie, one of the guys who'd interviewed me (the others, his fellow co-owners, were Paul and Todd).

He was quick and to the point – "Come in on Tuesday, you've got the job." And I swear, although I was sitting down at the time, I leaped so high that I touched the ceiling.

I was so happy. I could dress the way I wanted, not like in those other places where I had to wear a white shirt and tie simply to deliver sandwiches. I wouldn't have to comb my hair, I wouldn't have to watch my language (and I don't mean cursing – even slang was frowned upon in sandwich land). I had just been handed the best job ever.

The Different Drummer sold everything. Everything a kid my age could need, anyway: Fillmore East tickets, underground comics, perfumed oils, Nehru shirts, bell bottoms, the most fantastic clothing you could imagine.

It was famous, too. Shortly after I started there, before I was allowed to actually sell to customers, I happened to be in the store when a fleet of limos drew up outside and who should walk in but Brigitte Bardot. *The* Brigitte Bardot ... the one my parents had named my little sister after. And, although she could speak English, she preferred to do her shopping in French.

Which suited me to the ground because I was the only person at Different Drummer who could understand her when she announced that.

What an afternoon, following Bardot around the store, with one of my co-workers staggering beneath the weight of everything she wanted to try on and buy ... all of it in black, by the way, twenty-six-inch waist, thirty-six-inch legs. She would be browsing, and then *that* voice would call across the store, "Oh, Sylvain?" Even when she was in the dressing room and needed help zipping up her Landlubber hiphuggers. "Oh, Sylvain?"

Bardot finished shopping; now one of the girls in her entourage came up and asked me to give her exactly the same clothes, in exactly the same colour, only in her size.

I filled the orders, I made the sale, and I was still in dreamland when I was summoned to the upstairs office and told that from now on I could work the registers. It was one of the greatest days of my life so far – so you can imagine how I felt, just a couple of hours later, when I was called back upstairs and told I was wanted on the phone.

By Brigitte Bardot.

There was a problem. She didn't want to wear the same clothes as her assistant. Would I gather together the exact same clothes as she had just purchased, but *in a different colour*, and she would be in to pick them up the following day?

Of course I said yes, and I hung up. That's when I realised that the entire store was holding its breath. Every eye in the place was on me. What did she want, what did she want?

I smiled. "She asked me out."

Bardot returned the next day, but by cab this time, and without the entourage. I had everything ready for her, and we made the exchange.

Janis Joplin's visit was also memorable.

I was a huge Joplin fan, ever since I saw her with the Dead and Airplane in Central Park the previous summer. She was playing the Fillmore this particular week, and she dropped by to pick up a new pair of blue jeans, smiling, effervescent, a cloud of patchouli oil in those glasses you see on the cover of the *In Concert* album, and those skinny slippers with heels that she always wore.

There was no set store policy about how to behave when somebody famous came in, but of course there was the unwritten law that you don't scream and run around, you don't ask for autographs, you don't do anything that might embarrass them ... or you. So she told me what she wanted and I was on the ladder up to the top shelf where we kept her size, when suddenly the music that had been playing in the store – a James Brown live album, probably; Eddie loved that stuff, and I did too – was abruptly curtailed and replaced by one of Janis's own records.

I cringed; what sort of idiot would even think of doing that? The one who I was working with that day. I couldn't believe it and neither, it seems, could Janis. I turned round to at least mouth an apology, and she'd already walked out of the store.

There's a postscript to this, from a few years later when I told David Johansen the story, and it turned out he had one of his own. David saw Janis on the street once, drinking a can of Coca-Cola. She finished it, turned and tossed the can into the garbage. David promptly sprinted over, scooped it out, and he treasured that can for years.

I usually took the bus into work. Experience had taught me to loathe the subway and avoid it as often as I could. I had a lot of bad times in there; it was one of those places where all the laws of society seemed to have been placed on hold, and even New York's traditional disdain for giving you a little personal space was completely disregarded.

One time, I was sitting on the subway and a man walked up to me, right in my face, and spat, "You know what, even better than youse guys is lesbians." I swear it felt like you only needed to leave the house wearing something other than chinos and a stained wife-beater and people would assume you were gay. More than assume – they'd shout it out. I ignored them. I probably had more girlfriends in tow in one month than those morons would ever have in their whole lives.

Besides, all I was doing was dressing as I liked, in whatever finery I could stitch together (sometimes literally), and I wasn't going to give that up for anybody. So I started riding the bus instead, boarding the Green Line at the corner of 59th Avenue, crossing over Simon & Garfunkel's groovy 59th Street Bridge, and riding as far as the cable car that goes to Roosevelt Park.

Then I'd walk down past Bloomingdales, looking into all the stores, and, just before I reached Different Drummer, I'd pause at Tender Buttons. Which just happened to be one of the greatest stores you could ever want.

They sold buttons. Coat buttons, shirt buttons, trouser buttons, fancy buttons. The lot. Greta Garbo used to shop there; so did Jackie Onassis (Kennedy as was); and so did my Uncle Victor, who was a tailor on Madison Avenue. I used to hang out there as often as I could, lunchtimes especially. It was always a nice walk, smoke a joint, check out Tender Buttons. Sometimes, I'd be in there so long that the owner used to throw me out. But I'd always go back, and she knew it.

I wasn't the only one, either. One day I was on my way there when I saw this guy with an elaborate Afghan bag, fabulous weaves of leather, strips and fringes, really cool clothes, and ever-so-slightly femme. Walking with this absolutely gorgeous chick with bright orange hair. And fuck me, it's Johnny, and guess where they're coming from? Tender Buttons.

I waved him down, "Hey, kid from High School!" We'd scarcely seen one another since I was kicked out, but we caught up quickly and, once I told him where I was working, I knew I'd be seeing a lot more of him.

Johnny was not the only slice of the Different Drummer experience that would soon be becoming a major part of my life, however. Just as significant, if not more so, was one of the store's closest neighbours.

No, not Bachelors Three, the bar that football star Joe Namath and a couple of his colleagues had opened right next door. I'm talking about the business that operated across the street, up on the second level, and whose vast neon sign was destined to haunt my daydreams for years to come.

It was called the New York Doll Hospital. I loved it; it sounded so good. I even pointed it out to Billy and Johnny, and said wouldn't that be a great name for a band?

"What? The New York Doll Hospital?"

No, the New York Dolls.

Chapter 10

LEARNING TO DRIVE GIRLS CRAZY

It was just before Christmas 1968, the busiest day of the year, and I didn't show up for work. I'd had a long, late night the evening before, and either overslept or got too stoned. Whatever, it was my fault, my mistake, and mine to regret for a long time to come. Because when I did make it into the Different Drummer, Eddie took me to one side and told me, "I'm sorry, I have to let you go ..."

And I was gone.

The strange thing was, I was ready for it. Not getting peremptorily canned; that wasn't a part of my masterplan. But finding my way out of the city; making a start somewhere different, that was an idea that had been percolating for a time. Now it started to boil.

Billy, Alphonso and I were spending more and more time in Woodstock. Between the Croner family's regular visits, those occasional trips with Eddie and co. and just hopping the bus to visit under our own steam, we were finding it increasingly hard to stay away. Now that I was without a job to keep me in the city, and no real desire to remain in New York anyway, that little artist colony in upstate New York was looking even more attractive.

We weren't alone. Although the influx had yet to become a flood, and the legendary festival was still a long way from any kind of reality, Woodstock was one of several small, upstate communities that braced themselves every weekend for an influx of city kid visitors, hippies, artists and musicians looking to get back to the country, if only for a few days.

Billy and I were no different. We knew we had to get something together, and find some way of making money. But we were also deep into the hippy freedom thing, make love not war and all that other crap, and a straight job was the last thing we wanted.

An idea began to ferment.

We already had friends in the area. Back at Halloween, while I was still working at the Different Drummer, the owners had persuaded a couple they knew to drive down to New York and set up a pumpkin stand outside the store. I got talking to them and when the woman, Joyce, started a club in Woodstock, Joyce Lake, that became a regular haunt.

There were others, too, mostly girls, so we always had a place to stay if we needed one. But Billy and I had an independent streak as well. If we were going to live in Woodstock, we were going to do it under our own steam. We decided to build a house.

A tree house.

One of our favourite places in the entire town was the Big Deep, a swimming hole in the woods off Casablanca Lane. We'd spend hours there, skinny-dipping, smoking, lazing in the sun, and maybe we'd been smoking a little too much one day because we suddenly got the idea that this was where we were going to live.

Back in New York, we raided Billy's dad's tool chest – a couple of saws, a couple of hammers, a drill, all manner of things – and then back up to Woodstock on the Trailways bus, dragging these bags of tools between us. We got off at the bus station on Tinker Street, the main street in town, and walked the rest of the way: out to the Big Deep and then deep into the woods, in search of the perfect trees.

There they were, a group of four in a near-perfect rectangle. Up we climbed, twelve feet off the ground, chopping down branches from other trees to make a platform, drilling holes in the trunks and then hammering in the branches. Or, should I say, hammering in one branch. It was like trying to fit a giant toilet roll holder, and it took hours to get it done, by which time it was too dark to even think of continuing.

Down again we went, rolling out our sleeping bags and preparing for sleep. Which is when the mosquitoes arrived. Squadrons of the things, all with one target in mind – teenaged New York flesh. We suffered for as long as we could, which wasn't very long at all, then fled to the sanctuary of our friend Jennifer's house and spent the night there. That was the end of the tree house.

From Jennifer's, we went to stay with a couple of other girls we knew, but that lasted only a couple of days, until we discovered they couldn't afford to heat the place, and we were up all night shaking with the cold. It was time to take control for ourselves.

Billy and I were still putting our own clothing together, knitting and sewing the outfits we wanted, but which nobody else was making, and occasionally we'd branch out to make similar items for other people, friends who admired our original handiwork. In fact, that became such a constant soundtrack to our lives – "Hey, love your pants, where can I get a pair?" – that we had long been daydreaming of setting up our own business. Now, we decided, was the time.

Walking up Tinker Street one day, I spotted a "for rent" sign in an upstairs window, over a store that sold infants' clothing. It wasn't a very fancy-looking place, but I walked in and started chatting to the woman who owned the place, Bonnie, and told her what we were planning.

She asked a few questions, and I told her my surname, which Billy always joked was what swung the deal. I mentioned that my father was a banker, and she thought she might know him. I don't think she did, but I wasn't going to disabuse her of the belief. Plus we had enough cash stashed that the $65 a month rent was not a problem.

There were a few things to work around. The space was intended as office space only, meaning no retail, manufacturing or residential use, which were the only things we were interested in. But Bonnie was on the town council, and she assured us that she could pull a few strings. We were in business.

Back to New York. The Pfaff Sewing Company on Fifth Avenue was doing a deal on Passap Duomatic knitting machines – buy one, and they'd throw in free lessons. At $600, they were a little out of our price range, but the woman we were dealing with there was Swiss and welcomed the opportunity to speak her native French with someone. We wound up being offered the floor model for $300. All we needed to do, she explained, was clean it and it would be as good as new.

We bought it, transported it back to Woodstock, set it up and started taking it apart. We were geniuses, after all, Billy and me: young entrepreneurs starting out on the road to fame and fortune. How difficult could it be?

Very. Even though both of us were certain we remembered where every little piece belonged, those babies are as complex as shit. Back to New York, then, back to the nice lady at Pfaff, and the machine was reassembled by the experts. (Today, there are YouTube videos that tell you how to do it!)

Our contact lady was tremendous; she arranged for us to have our free lessons, and also set us up with a yarn wholesaler, the Aberdeen Yarn Co. on 37th Street. They used to buy the cones that factories had left over after a particular production run was done, then sell them by the pound, a mishmash of colours and materials that was perfect for Billy and me.

We named our business "Satcha Knits" after Mike Turby's sister's dog. Another friend designed a logo for us to place in the window – gold-leaf letters that looked like something out of an old western movie, hand carved out of wood.

Inspired by Different Drummer, we set about reworking the decor. We picked up some flat sheets of pine wood, stained them a beautiful brown, and completely reworked the space. We covered the old ceiling, which was horrid, we petitioned off a sleeping area and installed a couple of bunk beds. And I designed our first item, a simple vest, but a striking one. It sold.

Quickly, we moved onto sweaters and more; and, just as we had expected, they sold too. I was making regular trips to New York City with samples, selling them to different stores ... Paraphernalia's, where you could get those plastic dresses that were really popular, Jumping Jack Flash, Limbo's, the New York branch of Granny Takes A Trip, and Betsey Bunky Nini's which was where Betsey Johnson was just starting out. Oh, and Ian's, a really funky store on Grove Street, where my friend Mary Anne Marlow always enthused over whatever we offered.

Soon we were expanding even further. One of Heidi Murcia's friends, a fellow ex-pat Colombian named Margo, had a loom, and she used to send us these beautiful sweaters. She was so talented; when I sent her the design for a knitted bikini that I was sure I could sell to Paraphernalia's, she didn't even bat an eyelid. She made it, I sold it. It was insane, but it was a hit.

Zeroes, a boutique across the road from Max's Kansas City, wanted a consignment of white sweaters – everything they sold in that store was white. We delivered.

Billy had the idea of refurbishing vintage shirts that he'd pick up at thrift stores and selling them to Granny Takes A Trip. It happened. It was an incredible time, and we were doing really well.

Woodstock, too, was picking up. The tickle had become a deluge. Every weekend, crowds of teenagers were coming up from the city to just hang out and whatever, just like Billy and I used to, but in far, far greater numbers. Musicians, too. One day I was looking out of the window down onto the street, admiring a beautiful silver Corvette Stingray that was parked there. I couldn't see who was inside, but then another guy crossed the street going "Hey, Jimmy", and who was it? Not Jimmy, but Jimi! Hendrix! It turned out he had three of those cars, a silver one, a red one and a white one, and he used to take a different one out every day.

Bob Dylan, shy as he was, would be around occasionally; members of The Band, all manner of people. And more and more visitors, piling in from all over, just to hang out.

At first, the locals tried to ignore them, knowing they'd be gone in a day or two. For all its subsequent legend, Woodstock was a very conservative, very uptight, town; it might have been an artists' hang-out in the fifties, but that had been a gradual process. This was like a tidal wave, and, as the crowds grew and the noise increased, they grew bolder and bolder, dancing in the street, screwing in the alleyways, and drugs everywhere. Finally, the council put its foot down.

Police roadblocks started appearing on a Friday evening, effectively penning the incoming tide into the Trailways station. Then the cops would start putting everybody back on the buses; or, if they were at all disorderly, dragging them to the police station. They began enforcing the loitering laws – if somebody was stopped and they didn't have at least a couple of bucks on them, they'd be arrested. If they didn't have the correct papers for the car, or they were caught with any quantity of drugs, off to the slammer.

It was ridiculous, but what could we do? One night, watching as the latest round-up took place, I placed my Bandmaster amp in the open window and started blasting Sly & The Family Stone into the street, 'Dance To The Music' and all of the rest, the most uplifting music you could imagine. Of course the kids all started cheering and dancing, but the cops were glaring up at me and it was no time at all before Bonnie, our landlady, started receiving complaints.

She brushed them off. Our business was doing so well now that we'd rented two other rooms from her, the ones immediately behind ours, breaking down the walls between them and opening it up into a magnificent space. And all for just $120 a month.

Where there's fans, there's bands. Joyce Lake was really swinging now, while the lady who ran the bakery next to the Trailways station started staging concerts in a field she owned. I saw Soft Machine there, and spent the entire show wondering how Mike Ratledge managed to get feedback from an organ.

And then the festival was announced, an extended August weekend of non-stop music that would put Woodstock on the rock'n'roll map forever. Only the council did not want to be on the map. Everything they could do to block the festival, they did. And, of course, they succeeded. Although the event would still be called Woodstock, it ultimately took place forty miles away, on a dairy farm in Bethel.

The entire mood of the town had changed. What Billy and I had seen as a haven, a respite from the cut-throat madness and grind of New York City, had become transformed into a nasty, petty, cynical and, most of all, killjoy community. It was time to leave. We would stay until the festival, sell off everything we could *at* the festival, and then head back to the city.

And that's what happened. We hired a local artist to make us some new signs, "Satcha Knits of Woodstock", and we loaded every piece of stock we had into boxes. A friend who had a van agreed to drive us to the festival site ... and then we hit the traffic.

We knew the festival was going to be big, but nobody – least of all the organisers – realised how big. A quarter of a million people flooded into that field, pouring in from every direction. The fences fell; no matter how many tickets had been sold for the event beforehand, the crush of people wanting to get in overwhelmed any attempt at organisation. Woodstock was barely a couple of hours old, and it had become a free festival.

The roads were total gridlock for miles around. Finally, we got out of the van and walked the rest of the way, found a couple of trees just before the trampled fences, and we set up.

Everything was on sale for $10, and we really didn't do badly. Plus, when the fashion magazine *Women's Wear Daily* published some pictures of the festival, there we were, Billy up in the tree hanging our sign, and me down below, in my seafarers bell bottoms and one of the sweaters I'd designed. Because that's the thing about me making clothes. I want to keep it all, I want to wear it all. The only reason I'm making clothes is because this is what I want to wear. I never cared about what's fashionable, I cared about what I wanted to wear, and if I couldn't buy it anywhere else, I'd make it.

I would take the same approach with me into music. Into the New York Dolls.

We got to see a lot of the festival ... Arlo Guthrie, Joan Baez, Country Joe as the sun was going down on that first day; Sly Stone, Mountain, The Who and all the others over the weekend; and we stayed through to the final morning, long after the crowds had started to thin out, when Jimi Hendrix closed the festival in front of the last few thousand sleepy stragglers, and the beginning of the post-festival clean-up.

Discarded sleeping bags, battered tents, mountains and mountains of garbage. The place looked like a war zone.

Back in Woodstock, our pockets stuffed with $10 bills, Billy and I decided to treat ourselves to some transport. There was a motorcycle shop in Saugerties that we often stopped to browse through, dreaming of the day we could afford one of those fantastic-looking British bikes, the BSAs and the Triumphs.

That day had still not arrived, so we zeroed in on the next best thing, a Jawa, which was a 250cc Czechoslovakian copy. But how to get it home? Forget that we didn't have crash helmets, driving licences or insurance. Forget, in fact, that neither of us had ever ridden a motorcycle before. The only thing we were concerned about was that we didn't have licence plates.

Easy! There was a trashed bike across the courtyard that the shop was fixing up. Nobody was around; it took a matter of moments to run over, remove its plates and, out of sight of the store, install them on the Jawa. Then we wobbled back to Woodstock. I was driving, Billy rode pillion, and somehow, trial and error mostly, we made it home.

Over the next day or two, I practised as hard as I could. I figured out how to make the bike drive smoothly without taking kangaroo hops across the street; how *not* to hit the brake when I was meant to pull the clutch: I even went out and bought a helmet.

It was time to put the bike through its paces. I needed to go down to New York to buy some wool – although we'd given Bonnie our notice, we were still in business for a few weeks more, which meant we still needed stock to sell. So I jumped aboard the Jawa and I was merrily cruising down the New York State thoroughfare when, inevitably, I was pulled over by a policeman.

I racked up the violations. No insurance, no licence, switched plates ... Parking the Jawa at the side of the road, he loaded me into his squad car and drove me to night court, which was held in the judge's own home, down in his basement.

It was an open-and-shut case. Three days in jail and a fine of ... the judge looked at the cop and raised his eyebrows. "He's got $50 cash," the cop told him. A fine of $50. He took my money and the cop drove me to Kingston County jail and threw me into a cell.

I don't know what was going on at that time, but the place was packed. There must have been forty people to a cell, and every ten minutes or so, one of the state troopers would walk up to the bars and start shouting at us.

He took a particular dislike to long hairs. "How long you in for?" he'd ask, and if the kid was only in for a day or two, he'd be hauled out of the cell then returned a little later with a buzz cut. Again and again, hippies were being shaven by this one nasty trooper, and finally it was my turn. "How long you in for?"

"Three weeks."

"Okay, I'll get you later."

A narrow escape.

I did my time. I remained caged up through the weekend; they released me on the Monday morning, and I hitch-hiked back to New York City, got some money from somewhere, and then returned to Kingston to get the bike out of the police pound. The first thing I did after that was get the bike registered.

Then we closed out the shop, left Woodstock, and that was the end of that.

It was time to go back to New York.

Chapter 11

TRUTH AND SOUL KNITWEAR

"Truth and Soul."

I discovered the name on a movie poster. *Putney Swope* starred Arnold Johnson as the sole African-American executive in a top Madison Avenue company, who is elected chairman after all his fellow execs, prohibited from voting for themselves, instead cast their vote for the least likely person to be given it.

It's another of my must-see movies, but what caught my eye at the time, before Billy and I had even entered the theatre, was the poster. "The Truth and Soul" movie, insisted the posters and, just as I had with the New York Doll Hospital, I knew it was a name I could do something with. I just didn't know what.

Not yet.

Back in the city, back at my parents' house but spending just as much time at Billy's, the first few weeks were devoted to reconnecting with old friends. We were back in with the Quintano's crowd, and those occasional classes in Central Park. Johnny, my erstwhile guitar student, was around a lot too, with his friend Gail Higgins. Together, we'd all descend on this little bar we'd discovered called Nobody's, across from the Village Gate at 163 Bleecker Street, just to eat and drink and watch people. We usually aimed for a table up on a little raised platform, commanding a view of the bar and the main door; one night, we saw

Rod Stewart there, wearing his tight red pants. The following week, we all had them.

Another time, Johnny kept pointing out this skinny little fellow wearing a green army-style raincoat, blondish Beatles-y hair and combat boots.

"Hey Syl, you know who that is? It's Iggy Pop!"

Poor Iggy. He sat there for hours, nobody spoke to him, and he left on his own. A week later, Jimmy Page and Robert Plant walked in and every girl in the place left her boyfriend, ours' included, and went to them.

Nobody's was, and would remain, a major part of my life for the next couple of years. But I wasn't finished with the rag trade yet. The success of Satcha Knits proved that Billy and I had what it took to make a go of things. But we also realised that trying to run your own business was itself fraught with difficulties. Our interest was in the design and the manufacturing, not in the buying and selling, the invoicing and wholesaling. We wanted a fashion line, not a fashion business.

To the telephone. Every day, Billy would sit with the Yellow Pages on the table beside him, calling up every knitting company and manufacturer in the book, introducing us and outlining our intentions. And that's how he found Arnold and Charlie Nussbaum's Knitting Mill in Brooklyn, a part of the Monsanto empire.

He talked a sweet game, explaining how we'd come to the city from Woodstock, at a time when that was the magic word for anybody looking to get into "youth culture"; he told them how well we'd done there, and if they had that back issue of *Women's Wear Daily*, they could check out the merchandise in the photograph. We were invited in to meet with them.

They expected us to bring some of our designs. We went one better and took in some actual samples. I never drew my patterns – I knew exactly what I wanted to do instinctively; the entire outfit was complete in my head. All I ever had to do was sit down and actually knit the thing. And *that* would be our drawing.

The brothers were thrilled. On the spot, they offered us a deal – four of our sweaters at $200 per design. It wasn't much by some designers' standards, but it was more, said Arnold, than he'd ever paid before. Even better, he also offered us a showroom on 33rd Street, across from the Empire State Building, on the very edge of the New York garment district. He put us up at the Washington Square Hotel in Greenwich

Village, to save us the commute from Queens to Manhattan; he asked us what we should call the line, and he raved over Truth and Soul. When it came to advertising, he allowed us to call those shots too.

I suggested a pair of what were then ultra-hip magazines, *Eye* and *Avant Garde*, and the next thing I knew, I was at the Cooper Union School, between St Mark's and Broadway, helping dress and pose the models who would star in our first national advertisement, wearing our sweaters and holding aloft protest signs. At least, I thought that's all I'd be doing. Instead, the photographer said, "Hey, you have a great look, too," and roped me into the shoot as well.

I was in my element. Billy, on the other hand, hated it. There's a multitude of downsides to being your own boss, and we'd experienced most of them in Woodstock. But there's a lot of disadvantages to *not* being your own boss as well. Barely had we cashed the first Nussbaum cheques than Billy announced he was going to take his half and go to Amsterdam.

I didn't mind. It was January in New York, and I'd been eyeing a vacation as well, a couple of weeks in the Caribbean sun of St Thomas, one of the US Virgin Islands. And wouldn't you know it, but the first people I met on the beach were a couple of New York fashion designers, named Pinky and Diane. Who would, in years to come, not only rank among the New York Dolls' earliest and most devoted followers, they would also help me put together the group's first LP cover.

They were such fun to hang with. One time, we were out on a beautiful white sailboat with some guys they knew, smoking pot and wetting ourselves laughing when one of them fell into the water. To make matters even more hilarious, as we struggled to turn the boat around, Pinky and Diane terrified the poor man by pretending there were sharks approaching.

Another time, passing a US Navy aircraft carrier that was in the harbour, the girls took off their tops and flashed the sailors. You have never seen so many eyes bulging.

We were all booked to fly home on the same flight, from St Thomas to San Juan in Puerto Rico, and thence to New York. And, because they're all US territories, there'd be nothing like customs to worry about. Right?

Wrong.

One of the girls had a joint on her, the cheapest, cheapest pot you could imagine. But Puerto Rico customs not only found it, you would have thought we were running smack for the Mafia. For suddenly this cry of "Marijuana! Marijuana!" went up and all three of us were arrested on the spot.

Thankfully we didn't have to go to the cells; instead, they put us in a hotel for the night and then escorted us before the judge the following morning – an old Spanish guy who fined us $50 and sent us back to the airport. All of which came back to haunt me a full forty years later, as the new Dolls were on their way from Seattle to Vancouver, Canada.

Crossing the border, I was called into customs, where the officer very politely told me, "If you tell the truth, you will be out of here in five minutes."

No problem.

She asked if I'd ever been busted. Now, Puerto Rico had happened a long time before, and I had never had cause to think of it since then. Plus, I was thinking about felony drug busts – the heavy stuff. "No, never," I replied.

She cleared her throat. "San Juan, Mexico, 1970."

The penny still didn't drop. I shook my head. "No, I wasn't in San Juan, Mexico in 1970." Which was true. But she wasn't happy. She kept repeating it; I kept denying it. And, while I was eventually allowed into Canada, there was a sizeable fee for the visa stamp, we'd been delayed for a good three hours, and I was still protesting my innocence. "If you did that here, you'd get life," said one of the customs officers as they waved me off, and I still didn't know what I'd done!

It was only later that I realised what had happened. There are two San Juans, the one in Puerto Rico where I'd been, and the one in Mexico, where the customs woman insisted I'd been. She simply didn't know her geography, and I was the one who was branded a liar.

Back in New York, back to Truth and Soul, I was now renting an apartment on 88th Street, between Amsterdam and Columbus, working on my next line. Occasionally, Charlie Nussbaum would have me accompany him out to one of the trade shows; there was one in Chicago, and we did a bunch in New York.

Money was no problem whatsoever. I left 88th Street and took a place on the East Side, on 91st Street, paying $200 a month for a newly renovated studio apartment. I was even hiring staff for Truth and Soul – a girl to handle skirts and tops for the female line; a US army veteran, who we renamed Frenchie (his real name was Christian Rodriguez); and some others, too.

By the summer of 1970, Truth and Soul was on $5,000 a line, and that really was serious money. And suddenly I understood why Billy had quit back in January, thrown it all up in the air and gone off to Amsterdam. Success is great; knowing you're good at what you do, too. But it has its own demands, its own expectations and, most of all, its own cost.

We'd named the company Truth and Soul because that's what we believed we were putting into it. But it was also sucking the same things out of me. Billy realised that, and got out early. It was time I followed him.

I invited Charlie Nussbaum over, so I could break the news in person, sitting in my swank studio while he just stared at me in amazement. "Think of the money! You must be crazy!" And maybe I was, but I was resolute. "I love you guys, you know that. You're the greatest, and I owe you so much. But I've got to do it."

I thought first of going to Amsterdam and seeing if I could hunt down Billy. But London was far more appealing, particularly after my mother called and mentioned the full-page ad that Pan Am had taken in that day's *New York Times*, announcing their first cut-price direct flights to London. Until then, I'd been intending flying the same way as Billy had, on one of Icelandair's propellor-driven trips from New York to Reykjavik, and from there to Luxembourg; then making my own way to Amsterdam. Pan Am made my mind up for me.

I'll never forget my first morning in London ... my first morning in Europe since we left Paris almost ten years before. I found myself a little bed and breakfast in South Kensington; I opened the window and on the street below, there was an Englishman sitting in his little Triumph convertible, waiting for the lights to change and shaving at the same time. And while I watched that, the little radio behind me was doing a report on how much bubblegum Americans consume in a year. (A lot.) That was my introduction to English life, and I loved it.

Up and about that same morning, my first port of call was Piccadilly Circus, and the short walk up Shaftesbury Avenue to Rose Morris, the musical instrument store. From the very first time I saw one, on stage with Hendrix in 1967, I had wanted a Marshall stack amp. They cost the earth in America at that time, but in London they were practically giving them away – £300 for a full three-piece set-up. Even with the cost of shipping and storage at the cargo department at JFK in New York, it was a bargain. The entire time I was in Europe, at the back of my mind was the thought of my Marshall waiting patiently for me to return home.

I went to King's Road and visited all the boutiques. I hit Carnaby Street and the stores I'd only heard about in the past. At the Roundhouse in Chalk Farm, I caught Tyrannosaurus Rex; Marc Bolan sitting on his little carpet with a Marshall stack behind him and Mickey Finn battering those bongos as though they had personally affronted him. They'd just brought out the *A Beard Of Stars* album, and the music was amazing. I'd never seen Bolan before that – the only time he'd played in New York was while I was up at Woodstock, the previous summer. But I'd loved the occasional song on the radio, and now I made certain to hear absolutely everything.

From London, I took the ferry across to the Hook of Holland and made my way to Amsterdam, hanging out at the Paradiso, marvelling at all the hippy girls who would strip off their tops and dance to the music. I saw The Who and The Golden Earrings (as they were then called). And I found Billy, when my attention was caught by a busker, sitting on the pavement with a massive bag of peanuts, playing guitar while a pool of shells spread out around him.

He leaped up when he saw me, we hugged and danced around a bit ... the boys were back in town!

Billy had long since blown through his Nussbaum riches; now he was living in a youth hostel right next to the red light district, and getting by however he could. I moved into the same place and we set out to absorb Amsterdam.

We needed transport, and it so happened that Billy knew of someone who was selling an old VW van.

It was a weary creature, that old van. Her owner had used her to drive back and forth with the hashish caravan to the Middle East, so she had some serious mileage on the clock. The guy said as much, too; he warned us that the engine was about to go, so maybe it was the chillum that we smoked beforehand, or maybe the fact that I'd just puked my guts up over the side of his barge, but I didn't care. I wanted that van.

Of course we didn't get far. We were driving through Belgium, Billy, myself, and a French girl named Dominique, and the old girl wheezed her last. Only it wasn't her last, because a local VW dealership had no problem at all popping out the old engine and popping in a new, or at least reconditioned, one, and we were on our way again, $300 lighter but mobile once more.

Reasonably mobile, anyway. The transmission was still very dicey, particularly if you were in second gear. The stick would shift itself unless you physically held it in place, and while we made it to London without too much problem, it was just a few days later that we came to grief, late at night, right in front of Harrods.

I was in first gear, waiting for the light to change so I could make a turn. Then I shifted into second, holding the stick as I turned the wheel, and I couldn't quite make it. My turn was too wide and the next thing we knew, a Rover 2000 came barrelling up the road and smacked into the side of us.

Around and around he spun, before finally coming to a stop, while Billy and I frantically changed seats – I still didn't have a driving licence. And then the other driver appeared alongside us, an older chap, who looked in through the side window and the first words out of his mouth were, "Boys, are you all right?"

What a gentleman! Not a word about the collision, not a word about insurance papers or cops. Just an inquiry about our welfare, and then the polite assurance that he would take care of everything and we should be on our way. I *love* England!

We finally sold the van to a friend in Earl's Court. Well, I say "sold"; in fact, we traded. He was a marijuana dealer, selling it stuffed into Swan Vesta matchboxes. He gave us about ten of them for the van, and we couldn't have been happier. Besides, we already had our eyes on something we'd found in the classified ads – a silver-grey 1964 Jaguar 2.4, red leather upholstery and just £600 from a guy in north London.

Again she had a bunch of miles on the clock, but just looking at that car was like having an orgasm. We didn't even haggle over the price; I just paid him on the spot and off we drove. Some nights we even slept in the car, parked among the taxi ranks at Notting Hill Gate. We'd go to the Chelsea Baths to wash; we'd find a park to smoke a joint in; we could have been in heaven.

Billy's sister Heidi and her friend Margo arrived. They had continued making sweaters long after we left the clothing business, and they carried on in London, selling their wares at Kensington Market; in the end, both stayed on long after we returned to the United States. In fact, Margo married a guy who owned an antiques store on Portobello Road, and England remains her home to this day.

Billy and I were growing restless, though. We were still in London in September when we heard that Jimi Hendrix had died, but the money was finally running out. I paid to have the Jag shipped back to New York, then we decided to have one final fling in Amsterdam before returning home.

We hitch-hiked to Holland and checked back into the youth hostel – and that's where we were the night the police descended *en masse*, looking to bust a couple of Americans who, apparently, were shipping hashish back to the States, stuffed inside clog-shaped boxes of chocolates.

The police got a lot more than they bargained for. There was never more than a fragile truce between the cops and the kids in Amsterdam at that time, as the government tried to play down the city's new-found reputation among cannabis tourists (the first quasi-legal bar, the Mellow Yellow tearoom, had opened earlier in the year), and the law's heavy-handed arrival in the hostel shattered it.

A full-scale riot broke out, not only inside but out on the streets, too ... cops getting pushed into the canals, windows breaking, tear gas being fired. Finally, however, the law gained the upper hand and rounded up who they thought were the ringleaders of the smuggling ring. Which, in turn, meant anybody who said "yes" when they asked, "Are you American?"

Billy was smart; he'd made it outside. I wasn't so lucky.

I'll admit I wasn't completely innocent. When they searched me, I did have a small amount of hashish in my pocket. But who, in Amsterdam at that time, didn't?

No matter. Unceremoniously, a bunch of us were hauled off and locked up in a cell that was nothing more than a cinderblock box with metal bars. No heat, no amenities. Just a box and bars.

We were there for three days, until at last I was escorted to the airport and placed on a flight back to New York City. My papers – which amounted to nothing more than a stateless passport and a permit to re-enter the US – were handed to the captain, who in turn would give them to the authorities in New York; and that was it. I wasn't even twenty years old, and I'd now been kicked out of two countries.

In the end, I negotiated the American customs a lot more easily than I expected; they knew I'd been deported, but I told them it was for vagrancy, rather than anything to do with drugs. They held me for a while, searched me one more time, and I was released.

Straight across to the cargo department to pick up my Marshall, and one phone call later, brother Leon was picking me up and driving me home to Queens. A couple of weeks later, Billy was Stateside as well. We had the Jag, and we still had warm weather. We slipped back into New York life as though we'd never been away.

Chapter 12

UP YOUR LEGS FOREVER

One afternoon, shortly after Billy returned, we were hanging out in Central Park when a long hair wandered over and asked if we wanted to appear in a movie.

That wasn't such a strange request in those days, although normally you'd find yourself hustled off to a decaying tenement where someone was shooting porn. "What kind of movie?" I asked. "A John and Yoko one," he replied and he could probably tell from our expressions what our answer was.

He gave us an address on the West Side and we were there in record time. He'd also added that it was a "legs" movie, but that meant nothing to us. But that's exactly what it was. John and Yoko were filming legs, from the feet to the groin, for what turned out to be a seventy-minute movie, called *Up Your Legs Forever.* Apparently, 367 different pairs of legs are seen, and now you know who four of them belonged to. And, before you ask, I kept my underpants on. Billy didn't.

The room was busy, but we quickly spotted John and Yoko, and May Pang, their personal assistant. Al Goldstein, the publisher of *Screw* magazine was there as well; in fact, after I'd been handed the dollar bill that every participant was paid, Lennon leaped over the desk he'd been standing behind and thrust a copy of *Screw* into my hand. "Hey, there you go."

It was all over in a few minutes, but back in the park, we were telling our friends about it all day.

Central Park was a great place to hang out. Billy and I had started doing stuff with the knitting mill again, just to raise some cash, but we were bums as well, running around in the Jaguar, cruising Central Park Drive with our English licence plates still proudly displayed. But then Billy got pulled over one day, taken to the precinct while the car was impounded, and we had to pay to get it out. That was enough. A few days later, we sold the Jag to one of our friends for $2,000.

We were going to gigs all the time. The Faces, Humble Pie, anything that looked good. The big one, though, was The Kinks at Lincoln Center.

Johnny in particular loved The Kinks – and why not? I wasn't the only person, after all, who heard 'You Really Got Me' with the guitar cranked up to death-ray distortion dimensions and felt their life would never be the same. I wasn't the only one who walked the streets dressed in who knows what while 'Dedicated Follower Of Fashion' echoed ironically in my head. I wasn't the only one who ... well, you get the picture.

When he changed his name from plain old Johnny Genzale to glamorous Johnny Thunders, I never did ask outright if he was inspired by The Kinks' song of the same name, and he'd probably not have told me (although he did admit that the song title 'You Can't Put Your Arms Around A Memory' came from an old episode of *The Honeymooners*). I just remember him calling up one day and saying, "Hey, what do you think of this name, Johnny Thunder?"

"Yeah, that sounds cool."

Ten minutes later, he called back. "I got it, it's even better, Johnny Thunder*s*." And he was right. It's cool, it's biker-ish, it's rock'n'roll, and when you write it down, it looks dynamite. We'd started playing together again, and he was always looking for a good name to use, should anything ever develop out of that. Whereas I once changed my name so I could get a telephone.

Let me explain. In those days, when you needed a telephone, it was the easiest thing. You'd call up the company, and say, "Hey I just moved into this apartment ..." They'd ask your name and you'd tell them. But, if you were wily enough (and broke enough), you wouldn't tell them your real name, because that way, they couldn't bill you. I was Ricky Corvette until they cut off his service.

Anyway, back to The Kinks. They were were ablaze this particular evening, running through all the hits, everything you wanted to hear, and putting on a spectacular show as well. And then they got to 'Lola', and something happened. Ray Davies was beginning to weave a little, unsteady on his feet, rocking a little as he staggered backwards across the stage, back and back and back ... until suddenly he crashed into his brother's Marshall stack and brought the whole thing down on top of himself.

You could have heard a pin drop. The audience held its breath. Even his bandmates looked aghast. Ray was just visible beneath a tangle of amps, lying on his back, completely still. And then slowly, he raised an arm, still holding the microphone, and went "Lo ... la ... lalalala".

The entire crowd went crazy. He jumped back to his feet, The Kinks finished the song, and the place was still going wild. It was like that Bugs Bunny cartoon all over again – except The Kinks could pull it off every night. If I ever had a group, I decided, and I know Johnny was thinking the same thing, that's what it would be like. Not just a great performance every evening. An unbelievable, unrepeatable performance.

We had other examples to follow. One of my best friends, Kenny Aaronson, had put together a band with a drummer named Marc Bell – later to become Marky Ramone. They were called Dust and, for a while, they were widely acclaimed as the Next Big Thing out of New York City.

They were also regulars at Nobody's, holding court before a growing number of fans and hangers-on, all wanting to get in on the ground floor before Dust were signed and whisked away to superstardom. Up at our usual table on the platform, watching all the attention they were receiving, it was hard not to feel a little jealous, or mumble, "Wow, I wish that would happen to us."

But at least we were in the right place: "And look, there's Rod Stewart over there. And look, your girlfriend's kissing him."

One night at Nobody's, our attention was arrested by a couple of guys who weren't at all famous. But they looked like they should be. They were both big tall fellows, which to Billy and I, five foot seven in our platformed feet, meant they were huge. They both had Rod Stewart haircuts and, maybe not on that first night but sometime very soon after, we fell into conversation with one of them.

Arthur Kane lived out on Long Island, and he happened to play bass; his buddy was "Big" George Fodorcik, and he played guitar. Like us, they spent a lot of time jamming together; like us, Nobody's was the place where they liked to hang out, just to see who was around.

The suggestion that we should all get together to jam was probably raised, but, in the meantime, Arthur had other business to attend to.

He'd not had an easy time of things. His father was a heavy drinker and, after one row too many, Arthur went to live with his Aunt Millie. She more or less raised him, but then Arthur and his dad would reconcile, if only until the next big fight. A few nights earlier, they'd had the biggest one of all, which ended with Arthur's father throwing him out of the house. The old man's last words were, "I never want to see you again."

Born in 1946, Arthur was quite a bit older than the rest of us – twenty-four or twenty-five, whereas we were still barely out of our teens. We liked him, though, and when he explained that he was looking for some place to live, as far from the old man as he could get, Billy had no hesitation. His mother had started renting out rooms at the Murcia house ... our friend Rodrigo Solomon was living there at the time. Arthur should give her a call, to see if there was one available.

There was, and suddenly the notion of jamming together became a firm reality, especially after Arthur moved in, with Big George as his roommate. With them in one room, Billy and I already set up in another, and Johnny coming over occasionally, we were down in the basement for hours at a time, just playing together, trying things out, or even simply listening to records.

Arthur had an amazing record collection, stuffed with things I'd never heard of – it was Arthur who introduced me to The 13th Floor Elevators, Roky Erickson and co., although I have to say it was Arthur, too, who turned me off The Who's *Tommy* forever. I know it's great music and all that, but he played it so many times; if I have to hear it again, I'll puke.

For the most part, we weren't as adventurous as when Billy and I had The Pox; that, after all, was mainly the blues, and we were flying, we took solos and really extended ourselves. Our latest configuration was a lot more basic; in fact, I laughed when I read online that we used to play Pink Floyd's 'Interstellar Overdrive'. I don't think we would have even dared.

No, our repertoire was more things like the Stooges' 'No Fun', which was a song Mike Turby introduced me to; '(I'm Not Your) Steppin' Stone'; and lots of Chuck Berry. Oh, and Johnny and I still enjoyed stretching out on those old Ventures instrumentals like 'Pipeline'.

Throughout his solo career, if Johnny ever turned his attention to an old fifties or sixties number, the chances are good that it was something we were playing in that basement.

There was no set "line-up"; jams took place between whoever happened to be around. Sometimes Arthur would be playing bass, sometimes Johnny. Sometimes I would play lead guitar, sometimes both Big George and I would let rip. Vocals were handled by anyone who wanted to try and shout above the rest of the noise.

Johnny had left Queens now, first to a back room in Gail's apartment on First Avenue, between 9th and 10th; then to his own place on Avenue A, furnished for the most part by his mom and his sister Marianne. They gave him an old TV set and some furniture and, the first time I visited him there, he was sitting on the bed, which was another of their gifts, showing me a Marc Bolan song he'd just learned, called 'The Wizard'. Which is another one that he later recorded.

He was always around, though, because he was earning money dealing acid and pills to friends in Queens. And because he loved what we were doing in the basement – not only the musical side of things, but also what you might call stagecraft. Visually, we were already streets ahead, purely because of the Marshall amp and my Les Paul Junior. But now we were having fun with those little moves and antics, or pieces of clothing, that could turn a rehearsal into a show. Soon, we were inviting friends over to watch us rehearse, and I began to realise something else.

If Johnny was still a little way behind the rest of us in terms of musicianship, in terms of looks and what I suppose you'd call "star power", he was way ahead – the sharpest mover, the sharpest dresser. I swear, he could have been the best designer in the world, because the way he was dressing was so immaculate. He would iron his clothes perfectly and arrange them meticulously in his closet. He might have looked as though he'd just fallen out of bed, but believe me, he knew what he was doing.

Even at rest, sitting on the bed or lying on the floor, he looked cool, the only person I had ever met who could do that Keith Richards thing of just pulling on whatever gear he had to hand and looking like a rock star. He'd had it at high school, the very first time I set eyes on him, and he had even more of it now.

I'd look at him sometimes, and the rest of the gang as well, and in the back of my mind, that name I'd spotted three years before, and kept to myself ever since, the New York Doll Hospital ... the New York Dolls ... was buzzing about, trying to get out. I already knew that it was the greatest band name of all time; all it needed was the greatest band. Was this ragtag bunch of buddies in the basement going to fit the bill?

As addresses go, Johnny's new roost on Avenue A was not much better than my old place on Avenue D: just another massive mess of run-down brownstone tenements, high crime and low scruples, and horribly overcrowded as well. In fact, Johnny's place was in a brownstone that was set *behind* another brownstone. You walked through one, out the back, and there was this other one. That's how packed the neighbourhood was. And, if your apartment wasn't broken into at least once a month, then you weren't living in Alphabet City. The only upside to that was that very few of the people who lived there had much that was worth stealing.

Johnny was one of the exceptions. One day, he returned home to discover that someone had been in and out with his bass guitar. He was furious, and he was even angrier a few days later when he was in one of the music shops that then littered Manhattan and saw his guitar hanging on the wall.

He went ballistic, screaming at the owner of the shop, demanding his property back and threatening to call the cops. And guess what? He got his bass back. Everybody knew that half the stuff on sale in the used stores was stolen property; the last thing any owner needed was to have the police sniffing around, particularly if there was someone prepared to make an official complaint.

Johnny was happy then, but I wasn't. It was like I said before, back when I was at school, if you picked on me and I couldn't get you back, I went after your little brother. And I was so pissed off with this particular guy ... there he was, not only buying stolen goods, but stolen from people like us, who were broke and had to deal just to get by. He needed to be taught a lesson, and I intended doing it. I'm a firm believer that you have to take advantage of the people who are taking advantage of you,

First, I sent Billy into the store to get the serial number of the nicest Les Paul in the place. That done, I had another friend make out a receipt saying I'd purchased this beautiful dark sunburst Les Paul Junior from him, with a date, a price and, of course, the serial number. After that, I waited.

A day or two went by, and now it was my turn to visit the shop, to flick through the used records and peruse the instruments – and then, "Oh my *God*! Look! There's my guitar! My lovely, beautiful, stolen, guitar!"

The man behind the counter isn't having it. "Get the hell out of here kid, who do you think you are?"

But I went into the whole "I'm going to call the cops" routine, and I could tell he was getting nervous now. He demanded proof, so I told him I lived just around the corner and I still had the receipt. I told him I'd bought the guitar through the *Buy Line,* which was a newspaper dedicated to buy-and-sell advertisements, and because it was an expensive purchase, I'd had the seller write me a receipt.

I left the store, hung around for maybe half an hour and then walked back in, proudly displaying my "proof of purchase" and that was it. He went to the wall, pulled down the guitar and handed it to me. To which I replied, "What about the case? They stole the case as well."

"Get the fuck out of here."

I got outside and I was physically shaking. I felt like I could throw up and faint right there. But I got the guitar, and later I went back to that same store to buy another Les Paul, a cherry red custom, and what did I do? I traded in the sunburst.

Time passed, and we were still in the basement, still rehearsing. And now Johnny didn't seem quite so enthusiastic. Although he was still with Janice, the girl he'd been dating back in high school, he also had a number of other women in tow and I think the sheer weight of numbers began preying on his time. Whatever it was, his girl problems became more important than the music, he stopped showing up to rehearsals, and finally we threw him out.

He never forgot that ignominy, either. Three years later, during the New York Dolls' first ever trip to Los Angeles, lounging around outside the NBC studios in Burbank, we were recounting the history of the Dolls for photographer Bob Gruen and his little video camera. Johnny even brought it up there!

Of course he didn't stay away for long, but, in the meantime, another face joined our circle. One day as we were rehearsing, our friend Rodrigo Solomon and his girlfriend Consuela looked in. They'd recently moved out of the Murcia household and taken an apartment in Manhattan, on 6th Street, between Second and First Avenue. They stood listening for a while, and then Rodrigo started telling us about this "real cool guy who lives in our building, long blonde hair, he plays the harmonica and he says he's a singer."

There was a theatrical pause. "And you guys need a singer."

He arranged for us to visit ... in the end, only Billy and Arthur went, but they came home raving about this guy David Johansen, how he had this magnificent apartment and his girlfriend was Diane Paluski, who we'd all seen alongside Viva and Ultra Violet and co. in the party scene in *Midnight Cowboy*. They had a kid, too – Merlow wasn't David's, but he was the dream step-father. And Rodrigo was right, said Billy. He was cool. "I think we should invite him over."

David came from Staten Island, but, like us, he'd made Manhattan his home; he worked at Matchless in St Mark's Place, this really stylish place that would make earrings out of beer cans, things like that. And his boss was a set designer for the Ridiculous Theater, so David got tied up in that, not as a performer but as a general do-anything guy; he operated the cassette player when they needed sound effects, he did the lights, he even played little bits of guitar. Anything they needed him to do.

It turned out that I'd already encountered him, too, walking through St Mark's one day, when my attention was snagged by this tall, great-looking dude standing by a lamp post, trying to rile up a protest rally about a friend of his who had just been busted. "Hey, you're the guy ..."

David never did take us up on our invitation to jam; in fact, he never came out to Queens, not once. Which, in turn, means we never really heard him sing. But we'd hang out together in Manhattan, go to clubs and bars, or lounge around at his apartment, where he and Diane would make endless cups of coffee, and the air would be thick with their chain-smoked cigarettes. Because in every way he was the perfect match. He dressed like we did, he liked the same music as we did, and he had the same dramatic effect when he walked into a room as we did. The girls would stare and the guys would glare.

Like us, too, he made his living doing whatever would pay the bills – years later, I discovered he'd come very close to joining the New York Police Department, and all I can say is law enforcement's loss was rock'n'roll's gain. For now, though, he and Diane were just two more members of the gang – Billy, Arthur and Big George, Johnny and Janice, and me and my girlfriend, Valerie.

I met Valerie in Central Park, over by the boathouse; I was wearing a white coat I'd bought at Johnson & Johnson in Kensington Market, and that's why she came over to talk to me. And, from then on, we were inseparable. After years of casual relationships and dates, Valerie became my first serious, steady, love.

Her father owned the Sutain sunglass company; in fact, it was he who invented the heart-shaped Lolita sunglasses, the ones with the butterflies and the sequins. Even better, he used to let Valerie distribute the leftovers and seconds among her friends. Thanks to her, we had shades for every occasion!

She lived with her family up in Yonkers, right by the river, and they were very well to do. Every time I visited, her mother insisted I have a martini, and then I'd dart upstairs and "borrow" some of Valerie's make-up. I'd just seen the movie *Satyricon,* with the men wearing that pale paste spread all over their faces. I'd do that, and then we'd take the train down to NY and go to Nobody's.

Meanwhile, I was still attending occasional boutique shows, representing Truth and Soul, even though I no longer had more than a familial interest in the line. It was doing phenomenally well without me, after all – I later heard that the Nussbaums made $17 million from Truth and Soul, and they even launched a knock-off line, copying our stuff at bargain prices, using the thoroughly reasonable justification that somebody was going to do that so it might as well be the originators.

One of the biggest shows of the year took place at the MacAlpine Hotel, right across the street from the Harold Square Macy's, where my dad worked his second job.

It was the usual set-up. The organisers rented out the first three floors to the shows; every company would have a room in which they could set up their samples, there were more stalls spread across the ballroom, and the buyers and salesmen just walked the corridors, seeing who was there and what they had. All the big companies would be there, and a lot of smaller ones as well; there was even a fragrances department and I remember one guy with a fragrance called Grass High.

One afternoon, as I was walking around, checking out the other stores during my lunch break, this English accent came floating across from the end of the hallway, and I looked up and there was a genuine fifties English Teddy Boy standing there – wiry, skinny, ginger hair, about five years older than me, slouched against the wall at the very end of the corridor. His name was Malcolm McLaren.

He called me over – "Hey mate, come over here" – so I trotted down. "Come on in and check out my shop."

I walked in and was immediately confronted with his partner, Vivienne Westwood, all dolled up, looking amazing, and she was tough-looking too. *Very* business-like. Every time I picked up something to look at, Malcolm would say, "Oh, you like that? Fucking take it, mate"; and, every time, Viv would poke him and mutter, "That just cost me … whatever."

They were on a dirt budget; I think they even slept in the same room that they were selling out of. They didn't have a store of their own either. Later in the year, they would open the now legendary Let It Rock on the King's Road; for now, they were simply manufacturers (also called Let It Rock), selling to whoever wanted to buy their designs. According to Malcolm, they sold old records as well.

I was in paradise. I'd never seen clothes like this before, and Malcolm was the greatest salesman in the world. As I browsed the stock, he gave me a crash course in English Teddy Boy culture; then, when I turned to leave, he told me to come back on Sunday because they'd be selling off their entire range of samples really cheaply, so they didn't have to take everything back to London with them.

Immediately I called Johnny and David – "Oh, you've got to come check this guy out, and don't forget to bring your wallet." That Sunday, the three of us bought a ton of stuff. I still have one of the ties today.

A postscript to all of this. Years later, I read that this meeting didn't occur until August 1973; that both Let It Rock and the New York Dolls were firmly in their pomp when the fates finally conspired to bring us together.

No, it was spring 1971, and here's how I know.

If it had been any later, the band would not have visited their store when we were in England at the end of 1972. Malcolm and Vivienne would never have met Billy; and I certainly wouldn't have been working at a New York boutique show in August 1973, just as our first album was released. Not unless I squeezed it in between however many gigs it was that the Dolls played around the east coast that month.

And finally, Valerie and I wouldn't have visited them in London, when we decided to skip out on another New York summer and go to England instead, just a few weeks after the boutique show.

Chapter 13

THE BUG-EYED SPRITE

Valerie and I stayed with a succession of friends and acquaintances during our time in London. Billy's sister Heidi put us up for a time, and we also crashed at the house belonging to the singer Kevin Ayers, who was one of her friends – she met him, I believe, at Kensington Market, where she now had a stall, selling her own line of fashions.

The house was on Westbourne Gardens, just off the Seven Sisters Road, and we were only there for a short time while Kevin was away in Paris on vacation. But there was another guy from Kevin's Whole World group staying there too, a quiet chap who had filled his one room in the back of the house with an assortment of instruments and a Studer Revox ten-inch reel-to-reel recorder. There he'd sit, crosslegged with his long, long hair, and he'd lay on track number one, track number two, track number three ... he was going nuts.

He could overdub onto one tune for days at a time, building up a labyrinth of sound, but he and I would also sit and play late into the night. I won't swear to it, but I think his name was Mike Oldfield, and my visits may well have interrupted his work on what became *Tubular Bells*. I'm surprised he was so gracious to me.

Someone else we saw a lot of was a French guy named Jean-Pierre, and his Marianne. They were staying at this place above the Wimpy Bar on Kensington High Street, and they insisted that we would be welcome there as well.

I'm not certain that was true. The woman who owned the house was very British, very eccentric, and incredibly domineering. One day, as I was getting ready to go out, she marched up to me, thrust a mop into my hand and demanded, "Go clean the staircase." I wasn't allowed to leave until I'd done so.

Another time, her dog, a huge Afghan hound, ran away and was picked up in Hyde Park by the police. I was sent to collect it. Other people staying there didn't seem to have any trouble; there were some other Americans, and she not only allowed them to henna her hair, she didn't even get mad when they started calling her Carrot Head, after the process went wrong and turned her orange. But she was pretty tough on me; so tough that Valerie and I finally grew sick and tired of her nonsense, and left.

We spent some time in Chelsea after that, staying with a girl we'd met and her boyfriend, a pot dealer. Which was fine until the morning that a silver Jag pulled up outside and these three big men got out and walked in.

It was a bust and they took everything; they took the pot, they took the money, they did everything but arrest us all. And why didn't they arrest us? Because, like the posse that busted Billy and I when we broke into the World's Fair all those years before, they weren't cops. They were rival dealers.

We bought a car, a white two-seater Austin-Healey Sprite, and that got us around for a while; it cost £200 and I remember how impressed we were by the fact that, though the bodywork was well-worn, the previous owner had installed new carpeting. It was only later that we discovered why – the floor was rusted through. It was also strange the way the car started perfectly, first time, when we bought her. After that, not so much.

We didn't care. We had a car, we were running around (we even took her over to Amsterdam for a few days), and if we needed to, we could sleep in the car as well. I still wasn't the best driver, though. Once when I was out with Valerie and Heidi squeezed in alongside me, I accidentally cut off a taxi driver. At the next set of lights, he pulled up next to us, leaned out of his window and said, "You'll never get a licence driving like that, mate." I still use that line myself, occasionally.

It was right at the end of our visit that we finally decided we'd had enough of the Sprite and its habit of breaking down all the time, so I parked her in an underground garage off Sloane Square, placed an ad in the *Exchange & Mart* and sold her to the first person who answered. He offered me £40 for the car and I took it. The parking cost me six.

There were gigs all the time. One night we went to see The Faces, another day we spent at the Crystal Palace Garden Party, with Pink Floyd and Mountain. We'd go to Ronnie Scotts and see all these different musicians playing. We hung out with Pink Fairies, hard-hitting garage rock'n'rollers who were right up my alley. Plus, they loved The Ventures almost as much as Johnny and I, and proved it with a fantastic version of 'Walk Don't Run'. (In later years, Twink, their original drummer, moved to Los Angeles and became close friends with Arthur Kane. Small world.)

Most of all, though, we went to the Roundhouse, the old railroad shed in Chalk Farm where I had seen Tyrannosaurus Rex the previous summer.

I loved that venue. It was the most beautiful set-up, a place where you could do anything you wanted. People were there selling hashish, there was a line of hippies selling food as you walked in, and it felt as though you were taking your life in your hands if you decided to climb the rickety stairs to the even-more rickety balcony.

The show I remember the best, and not only because it was so outrageous, was *Pork*, Andy Warhol's latest production. I went with Jean-Pierre – he'd seen it once before, and was adamant, "Oh you're going to love this." And he was right.

As I said, however, it isn't only the show that I recall. It was the cast – I didn't know any of these people at the time, but it was amazing. Within a year, one of the actors, Wayne County, was opening for the New York Dolls in Manhattan. Another, Cherry Vanilla, was both hanging out and playing at Max's. The stage manager, Leee Black Childers, was a photographer, and he shot us a lot; and, later, he managed Johnny. And all three would work for David Bowie, who became one of the New York Dolls' staunchest supporters. These people would be on our scene, but the reversal was unbelievable. In 1971, I'd travelled 2,000 miles to see them. A year later, they were coming to see us.

We stopped by the Hard Rock Cafe, and the irony made us both laugh so hard. Valerie and I left New York to get away from the burgers; we flew all the way to England and where did we go? A burger bar. We went shopping at Biba on Kensington High Street, another place that would loom large in my near future. And right next door, there was the Great American Disaster – another hamburger place.

I fell in love with Mr Freedom on Church Street, where I'd heard Marc Bolan did his shopping. I used to hang out there just to see who was walking in and out. And, every morning, especially while we were staying in Chelsea, we'd go down to the Cafe Picasso on King's Road for coffee. Then we'd walk a little further down the road to the magnificently named World's End, where Malcolm and Vivienne had finally opened the store they'd told me they dreamed of establishing. It was at 430 King's Road – another address that would become a part of history.

The trip wasn't all a vacation. No matter how much I liked the idea of forming a band with my friends back home, I was also nursing the notion of relocating permanently to London and trying to get something happening there. In fact, immediately before Valerie and I left New York, I'd gathered everyone together and told them outright: I was taking my double cutaway cherry Les Paul Junior with me, and taking my name, the New York Dolls, as well. I really thought things might work out over there and, if they did ... well, see you when I play Madison Square Garden.

In the end, it didn't happen. The London branch of the New York Dolls was a total non-starter. But what did I find when we returned to New York? The New York branch was, if not alive and kicking, at least rehearsing regularly at Rusty Beanie's bicycle repair shop on 79th Street.

To be fair, I'm not sure what I expected the others to do in my absence. I suppose I assumed they would carry on bashing around in Mrs Murcia's basement until either old age or boredom made them stop.

Instead, they organised themselves. Arthur and Big George had moved out of the house by now; Arthur to Manhattan with his girlfriend, George back to his old haunts on Long Island. But Arthur also tracked down a new rehearsal place. Rusty's was indeed a bicycle repair shop, just around the corner from the Natural History Museum, and Rusty himself was a tough old New Yorker who didn't trust anybody as far as he could throw them.

Convinced that anybody who was willing to rehearse in a bicycle shop was probably also intending to steal all his bicycles, Rusty would lock the band inside when he left for the evening, and then come back a few hours later to release them. If there had been a fire, or any kind of emergency, that would have been the end of them.

But they got themselves together, even picking up a tape recorder and laying down a demo of sorts, a collection of songs that would, in later years, emerge as the "Actress Tapes" – Actress, at the time, was what they called themselves.

I was away for all this and, to be honest, nobody ever mentioned either the tapes or that band name to me once I returned. But I can only guess that they listened back to the tapes and realised that what Rodrigo had said all those months before, that we really needed a singer, was true. Johnny was handling vocals, but he was a long way from finding his voice. So they called David and somehow convinced him to join them at the bicycle shop.

I also discovered that they had decided to call themselves the Dolls ... they'd dropped the New York part, but that didn't make me feel any better. That was *my* name – like I've always said, I often come up with good shit, but not always *that* good. In fact, I told Billy straight: "If you're going to call yourself the Dolls, man, you'd better have me in the band."

For now, though, I wasn't. They already had a guitarist in Johnny, and they had a great guitarist in Big George, who played somewhere between Fred "Sonic" Smith of MC5 and Keith Richards. A terrific player. Occasionally I'd go down there to watch rehearsals, and sometimes I'd sit in with them, playing through not only their favourite covers, but also the handful of original songs that they'd written ... a few of which would survive into the New York Dolls' set as well: 'Milkman', which became 'Chatterbox', 'Subway Train', which was called something else at the time, and one or two others.

There was no point in bearing a grudge, after all. I knew Johnny and David wanted to play with me, and Billy of course – we were brothers. And I liked Arthur and Big George; in fact, I remember thinking, this group could have *seventeen* guitarists and it would still be fantastic. So I was happy playing along, making suggestions, and they were happy for me to do so.

We were wrapping up a rehearsal one night when we heard somebody banging on the front door. Rusty had just arrived to uncage us, so he opened up and there were two African-American women, dressed to the teeth, standing outside. Across the road from the shop, on Columbus Avenue, there was a welfare hotel called the Endicott. Tonight, they explained, was their Christmas party. They'd heard the music and wondered whether the band would be interested in performing for them?

Of course they said yes, so everybody grabbed their instruments and, with me trailing behind, they set up on the little stage in the ballroom – Johnny, Arthur, David, Billy and Big George. I don't think they were introduced or anything like that. They just waited for whatever other music was being played to finish, a record or the radio or whatever it was, and then started into the same set of songs they'd been rehearsing.

I'm not convinced that they were precisely what the crowd had been expecting, but they went down well enough, and afterwards they seemed happy. But what could have been seen as their moment of triumph rapidly turned out to be the end. A few days later – and again I wasn't there, so I don't really know what happened – there was a giant spat and George quit. (Years later, he would re-emerge on the scene as Rick Rivets, a Doll for one night only.)

I heard about the news a day or two later, when Johnny called me up. "Hey Syl, we're rehearsing tomorrow at Rusty's, and you'd better be there."

I gave him my answer the following evening as we were waiting for our jailer to let us out. "Okay. But if I'm in the band, we've got to call it the New York Dolls. It can't be just the Dolls."

David looked me straight in the eyes and said, "Exactly."

He knew the power of New York. He knew it gave the name the resonance with which it would rock'n'roll down through the ages.

Chapter 14

WE HAVE COME FOR YOUR CHILDREN'S CHILDREN

It is the same in every art form. No matter what is happening in the underground, in the industry above ground change is something to be resisted, not celebrated. The status quo is all that matters. Nothing can change, nothing can move forward.

And why? Because they don't want to lose their jobs.

In 1971, change was everywhere. You saw it on the streets of New York, in the alternative theatres that were springing up, producing shows that had nothing to do with whatever was taking place further up the street on Broadway – forget off-Broadway, this was off-off-off.

You heard it in the clubs, where Alan Vega and Martin Rev were taking their first steps out with Suicide, a yelping, droning machine that sounded like nothing you have ever described as music before. You saw it on the streets: girls as guys and guys as I don't know what, dressing in the clothes they wanted to, as opposed to those that their parents had worn.

When I first came to America, a decade before, you could barely tell the children from the adults – they may have been smaller but they dressed in identical fashion, wore their hair in identical cuts. Is it any wonder that they viewed the world with identical prejudice? Because they didn't want things to change either.

But they did. They had to. Stagnation is not simply a matter of everything remaining the same. It is everything dying as well. I saw it in Buffalo, and you could see it in every small and medium-sized city across America. In London, however, I caught a glimpse of the alternative, and when I returned to the US, the New York Dolls plunged headlong into its blazing heart.

We didn't do it deliberately. We didn't sit down and map it out, planning some great insurrection to tear the soul from the musical mainstream. We just reacted to, or against, whatever we found.

Music had gone into what we called Opera Rock, mixing classical and jazz and anything else they could think of, technically brilliant, utterly genius, but completely soulless. Whereas we wanted to play the music we grew up with – the girl groups, the pop ballads, mixed up with The Rolling Stones and The Kinks, and then all of that mixed up with The Stooges, MC5 and Pink Fairies. And then we'd make it our own. Three-minute songs with two and a half chords, fast moving and sexy. Back to basics.

Our name was as important as our music. One of the biggest attractions in the New York underground at the time, one with whom we went on to play a few shows, was Teenage Lust, and I cannot tell you how much Johnny and I hated that name. At that age, you can look at a band name, and without even hearing the music, you know you hate them. Or love them.

Names were *so* important back then, and that's what was so magical about the New York Dolls. What a name! It tells you everything. I came up with it, but look what everybody else did with it, at the time and later on. They all decided in their own mind what a New York Doll was, and that's what they lived.

But it was always their own decision. When it came to the acts whom you might call our peers, whose progress we followed and who we admired *as a band*, there weren't any. We hated everything and that's why we turned out to be the way we did.

We were not sitting at a round table saying, "Let's do this, let's do that," or looking at photos and saying, "That looks good." We were apathetic about everything, with one exception.

We were who we were, five friends from the boroughs who united over music, movies, art and lust, and wore the clothes that shouted out that bond, a combination of home-made and store-bought, male fashions and female, vintage and modern, and all topped off with the gear that

Billy and I brought back from London, and Johnny when he went over there too. Thrift shops, vintage shops, mom's closet, and this great place called Transformations on Second Avenue, where you could go in and for $15 come out with a velvet jacket and a hat to match.

The little jacket that Johnny would wear on the cover of our first album, and the sweater I'm wearing, with the cowboy motifs – I found them both in a thrift shop called Love Saves The Day, where Frenchie was working.

The other great thing about boutiques was you might learn something while you were browsing. Barbara Triani, one of the girls who worked at Transformations, and one of David's closest friends, had the greatest record collection and was always playing something you needed to hear.

Sometimes, you'd find things on the street. One of my greatest inspirations was this guy I used to see going out after a rainstorm and looking through all the garbage bins, collecting the umbrellas that didn't make it through the storm. He'd take them home, strip the fabric off the frame, and he would make himself clothes. He wore umbrellas! He was so creative; *people* were so creative. And that was what inspired us.

It is no coincidence at all that the rise of the New York Dolls coincided with the birth of street art, the graffiti tagging that would soon replace all of New York's drab grey and brown with vivid colour and imagery.

Go to Times Square today and it's the mecca for world consumerism. Every sign seems to be advertising something; every store is huge and glitzy, homogenised and sterile; everywhere you look, it's "buy buy buy".

Forty years ago, it was very different. A great movie you have to see is *Midnight Cowboy,* because the scenes in there are exactly what it was like ... like the one where the guy picks up this woman, takes her home, they have sex and then he asks her for money. He's a hooker and she didn't realise. "What? You think I'm going to pay you?" That scene would play out every night there, a hundred times.

Say you were lucky and the pimps didn't get you. Then the food would. There were a bunch of little hamburger stands, one on every corner, selling their burgers two for 50c. But if you ate them, your next stop would probably be the hospital.

I remember once I succumbed to the temptation, and what the fuck? I got so sick, I can still feel the pain. And that's what all the junkies were eating: "Oh that's delicious, man ... hey kid, can you get me some cough medicine? I'll give you a little sip, man."

That's also where you'd go to buy switchblades, which were legal so long as they didn't have the little spring that made the blade switch. Fortunately, there were also a lot of hardware stores around, so you'd buy your knife, then go to the hardware place and buy the spring. You were back in action.

The whole of New York was like that; there would just be different dangers in every neighbourhood. Whatever area you were in, you had to conform to that area's ways, or else people were going to half-kill you. Or, if they didn't, they would completely kill you.

The city was rotting from the inside; the bright lights of the Broadway past had dimmed and darkened; the once proud theatres were now dingy, sleazy strip joints and porn cinemas. I can't remember if we knew it at the time, but New York City was going broke and would soon be bankrupt. Garbage rotted on the streets and people were rotting in their homes.

Great swathes of the city were decaying; some had already decayed. Drug use was endemic; the murder rate was soaring. It was still the Big Apple, but it was livid with maggots.

Then the New York Dolls arrived, plying their trade in those same bowel-like recesses, but doing so brighter than a thousand suns, a riot of sound and vision and the first link in the chain reaction that would ultimately lead to punk rock and beyond. Just like those first tentative slashes of spray paint on walls and subway cars would ultimately flower into a punk art of their own.

Some of us pulled it off better than others. One night at Max's, David and I were picked up by some girls who were staying at the Barbizon Hotel for Women, a block or two away from the Different Drummer. The place was marketed as a safe retreat for young professional ladies visiting the city, models and ballerinas and the like, and its doors were permanently barred to men.

That didn't stop David. Even in my finest finery, I could not get past the entranceway. But David just hitched his hair up into a pony tail and sailed on through and up. Nobody gave "her" a second glance. And I walked away thinking, "Holy shit, I love this guy. I want to hang with him forever."

Nobody's was still our number one nightspot, but we were spending time at Max's Kansas City as well, and that was not exactly easy. Mickey Ruskin's little club had long since won its reputation as the biggest freak show in Manhattan. The legendary home of the (still newly deceased)

Velvet Underground, it was a home from home for the Warhol crowd, but there was no welcoming party for the New York Dolls.

Rather, there was a lot of suspicion, which, I suppose, was natural. After all, we may have *looked* gay, but they were *really* gay, and all they saw when we first started hanging out there was a bunch of straights stealing their thunder. Later, they became friends, fans, the lot. But not at first. We had to earn our place in their ranks.

We were still rehearsing at Rusty's, but we were also spending a lot of time at Johnny's new place. He'd left Avenue A and moved into a little fourth-floor studio apartment overlooking 10th Street, and from one day to the next we'd gather there to work things out, writing songs and playing with ideas.

There were a few new numbers that were already coming together, including three that David brought in with him that were already complete, with words and music – 'Bad Girl', 'Vietnamese Baby' and 'Looking For A Kiss'. One of the first tasks we set ourselves, then, was to rearrange them.

'Looking For A Kiss' was a great song, but it had still to escape the Howling Wolf influence with which David originally gifted it. But it also felt a little like Marc Bolan's 'Get It On' (or 'Bang A Gong' as it was retitled for America). Interesting. I thought about it a little, I rearranged it in my head. Then, as one of the first things I did after I rejoined the New York Dolls, I went up to Johnny and said, "Let's T. Rex the shit out of this thing."

So that's what we did, and not only did it sound fantastic, that became one of the blueprints for a lot of our early songs. We T. Rexed the shit out of *everything*. Including 'Vietnamese Baby', which was our stand against the ongoing conflict. Except it wasn't "make love, not war", it was "fuck everything and get laid". Which was the story of the Dolls.

One other thing about Johnny's apartment. It was perfectly placed to counteract the effects of the midnight munchies. For a couple of blocks in either direction, there was a host of all-night Italian bakeries making the bread for the next day's deliveries.

Every night after rehearsals, Johnny would say, "Hey man, I've got pot, want to come over?" We'd sit around talking and smoking, and, inevitably, we'd get the munchies … in fact, I think Johnny *always* had the munchies. So he'd hand me a few bucks and I'd go down to the street and pick up a sack of hot bread – you couldn't even cut it because it would just melt – and a pot of Philadelphia cream cheese. And that

In my gold Derringer threads, outside Frenchie's apartment.
TOSHI MATSUO.

Lori Lightning and I at the Whiskey, 1973 – the picture that gave birth to Kiss?

David on the stoop outside Frenchie's in the top he bought on 14th Street.
TOSHI MATSUO.

Backstage at Max's, summer 1973. Johnny and his first ever Les Paul Junior, which I traded to him for the Black Beauty. Desmond Sullivan, our roadie, looks on. TOSHI MATSUO.

Jerry, shortly after he joined the band (although it looks like he could have been in Free).
TOSHI MATSUO.

I traded Johnny for the tassled jeans – Vivienne Westwood/Let It Rock originals.

TOSHI MATSUO.

The Dolls at Biba's, 1973.

After Arthur got stabbed in the summer of 1973, Peter Jordan (far left) stood in for him.
TOSHI MATSUO.

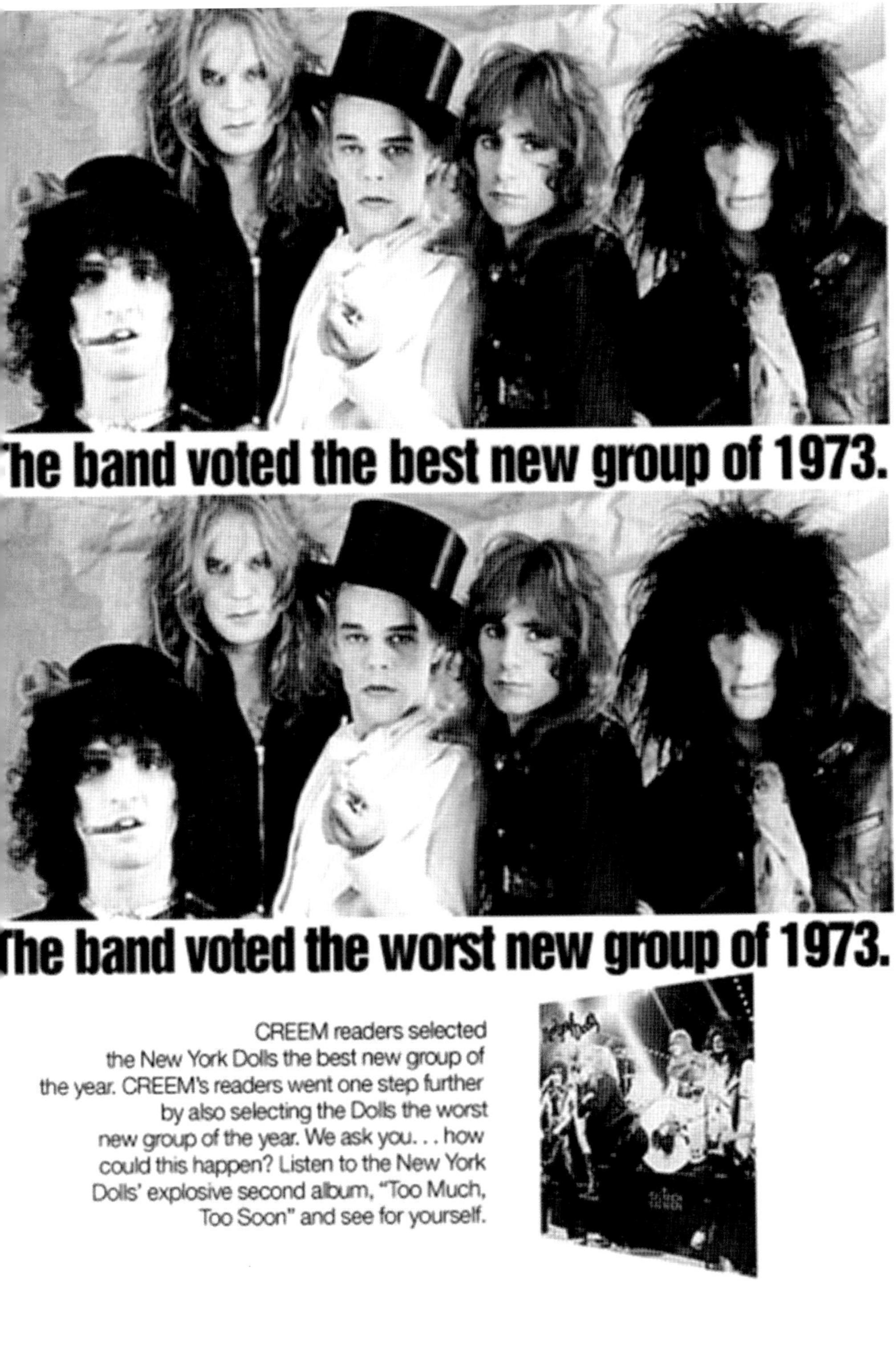

The famous *Creem* magazine advert.

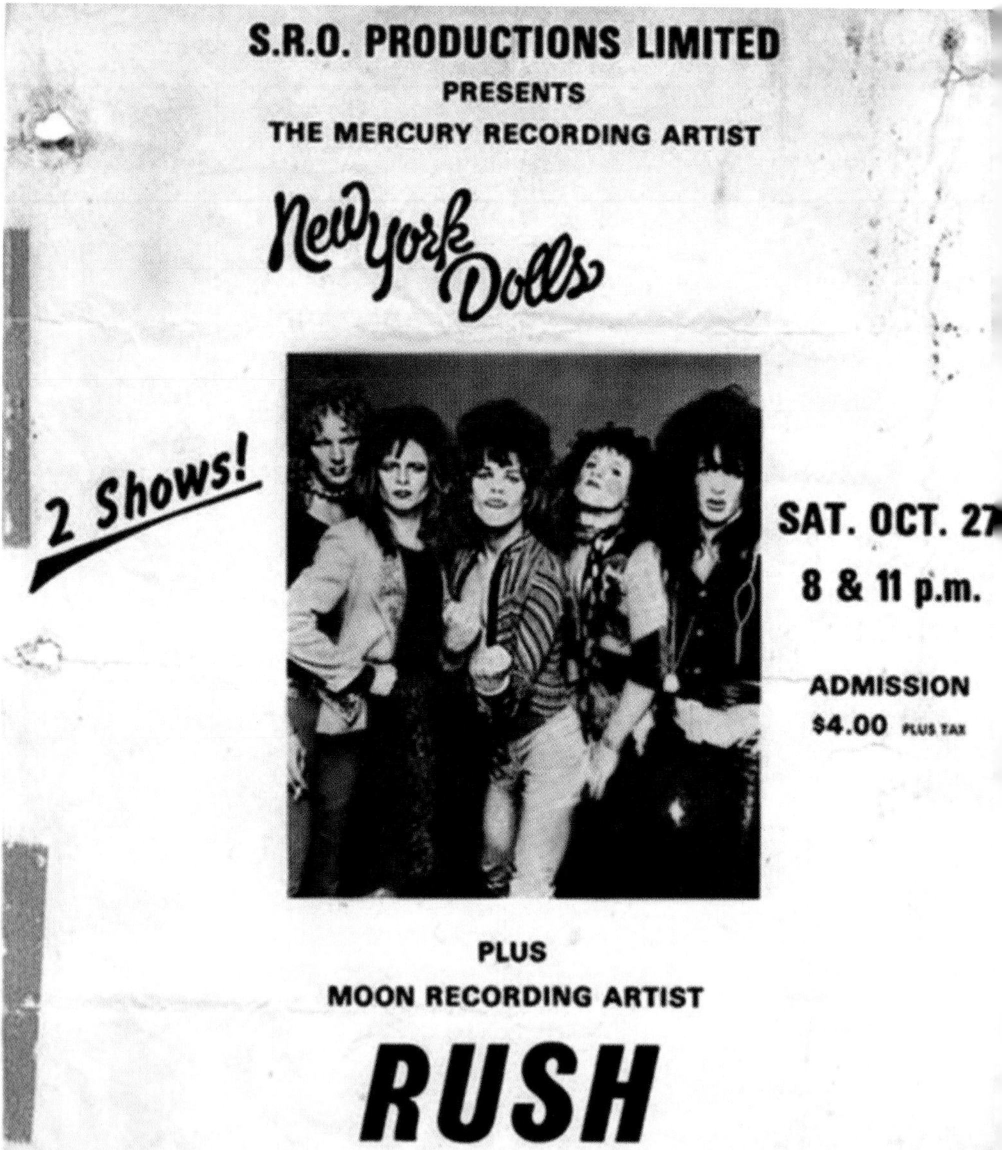

October 1973 in Toronto, the best Canadian gig we ever did – and that despite a fan falling off the balcony, causing us to stop the sho
to save him!

The Dolls arrive in Paris, 1973. Moments later, Johnny will be throwing up on the photographers.

Stop The Presses! Dolls Go Holly-wood

All photographs by Bob Gruen

No this isn't The Dolls' summer cottage in Cherry Grove . . . . our boys have gone all the way to Hollywood, California, U.S.A. to make an appearance on the silver screen. In this picture we see the boys relaxing on the set.

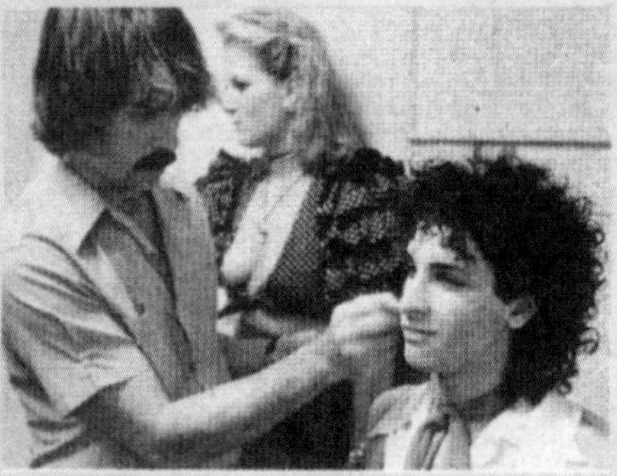

Syl gets his right cheek adjusted by the ever-watchful makeup man. Bet you can't guess what he's going to makeup next.

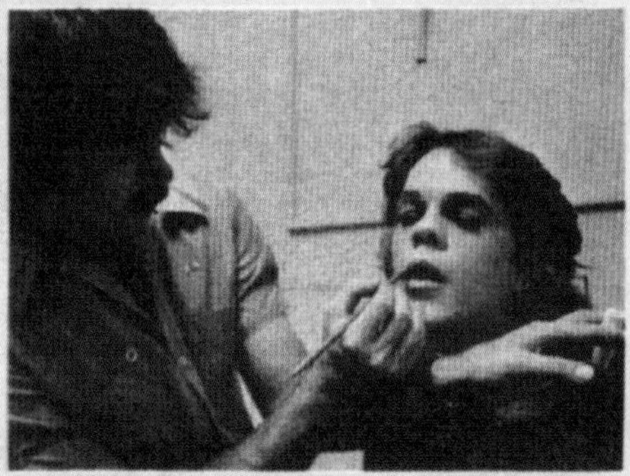

David has his lips touched up by the ever-watchful makeup man.

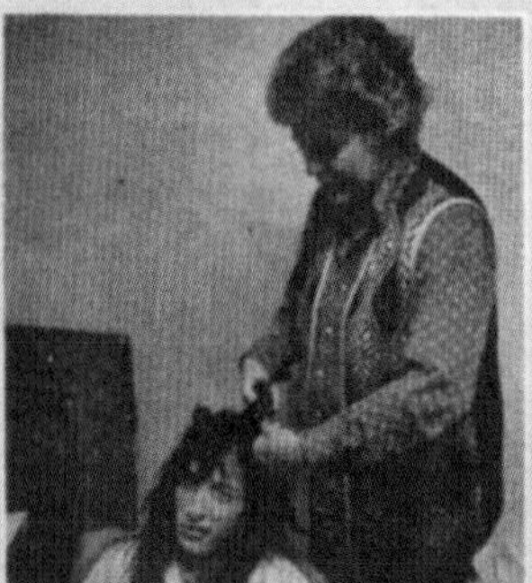

Johnny discovers that things can get pretty kinky in LA.

The Dolls' film debut is in a little epic called Hey Good Lookin'. It is a live and animated feature from the people who brought you Fritz The Kat. Hey Good Lookin' is based on the story of the Amboy Dukes – "the toughest gang ever to come out of Brooklyn," says Bob Gruen.

34

From my scrapbook – the Dolls in Hollywood to shoot our (ultimately unused) part in *Hey Good Lookin'*.

happened so often that one of the shop owners wouldn't even charge me; he thought I had a family to feed, so he'd give me the bread for nothing. Then back to the apartment and we'd listen to records all night long, get high and eat the best bread in the world.

A couple of girls started coming to see us. Jenny and Susan met David at the Fillmore one night, and he invited them along to watch us rehearse. Fashion designers, they were beautiful, but they were *so* tall that Johnny promptly renamed them the Amazon Women.

Susan was especially tall, and I remember the times we spent together, walking down the street, me wearing my black spiked booties with the zipper in the back and my Canali pants, and the truck drivers leaning out of their windows shouting to her, "Don't throw it to waste!" Why? Because she's so hot and I must be gay. "Give it to me, man, I'll show you what I can do with it."

The Amazon Women started making clothes for us. If you ever see a picture of Johnny in the black lamé top with the studs on it, one sleeve and cut down below the nipple, that was one of Susan and Jenny's creations. It was beautiful.

Other girls followed them into our orbit. We'd meet them in different places and, "Hey, I've got a band, you should come and watch us rehearse, meet the others ..." And we were always going to the Fillmore East. Because I used to sell tickets there for Different Drummer, I knew a few of the people who worked there, and I had this thing going. If I introduced one of the doormen to girls, he would let me in. Then I'd say, "How about Billy, how about Johnny," and he'd be, "Okay man, in you all go ... and who's that girl?"

We went to see my favourite group of all time, Humble Pie, when they were recording the *Rockin' The Fillmore* album, with Steve Marriott playing his Junior, and Peter Frampton in black patent leather Mexican Charro boots – man I got a pair of those the next day. (Interestingly, Frampton later married one of Billy's old girlfriends from Woodstock, Barbara Goldberg.)

Humble Pie were a phenomenon live. They had great songs, but you could tell that all they wanted to do was jam ... they'd go out and play and they would just fly. You could go and see them every night they played, and every night would be different.

It was the Amazon Women who introduced us to Deborah Harry. She was working as a waitress at Max's at the time, I believe, but she already looked like a star. We were at Rusty Beany's, sitting around smoking and drinking, and then somebody suggested we head downtown to Johnny's place to see what developed.

It was *not* an orgy. What we would call it was a *scene*. "We're going to have a *scene*." It's still an orgy, but it sounds more polite. And it's sexier. In an orgy, it's all, "Hey, gimme a blowjob, bitch." In a scene, you can't say that; we knew that from experience. There was always somebody who would invite us back to their apartment; there'd be a few girls, and things would happen. As I used to tell people, the New York Dolls were always having sex together. But never with each other.

We got back to Johnny's and quickly paired off. Susan was with Johnny, Jenny was with David in the bathroom, standing up in the shower; and I was in the bathroom, too, not really watching David and Jenny, but Deborah was sitting on the toilet, and I was trying to wash my hands, and, man, she just grabbed my waist, unzipped me and I got the most beautiful kiss I had ever received.

We changed partners. I was with Susan, and Johnny and David were with whoever, but I forgot to mention something. Johnny's friend Gail was there as well, with Oswald Garcia, the photographer, but they weren't having sex. Instead they were walking around going, "Oh my God, I can't believe it ... Can you see what you're looking at, Ossie?"

Plus, Johnny's girlfriend Janice was Gail's cousin, and she *wasn't* there, so Gail was flipping out about that as well. But an hour later, she and Ossie were still there, still walking around going, "Oh my God!"

We were making money however we could. David was doing I don't know what, but Arthur was with Ma Bell, the telephone company, which was great because he could come over and fix us up with illegal lines. I was still doing occasional things for Truth & Soul, choosing colours, adjusting designs, and going on the road to places like Dayton and Cleveland, to visit the garment districts there, or man the booth at trade shows.

Billy was working alongside Mike Turby at a place called Goody Two Shoes, which was making the first platform boots. He hated it, though. Not only did the smell of glue make him sick, he was practically tripping on the stuff as well.

Johnny, meanwhile, was still dealing, and going up in the world too. Moving house again, he teamed up with Billy to rent a loft from the father of one of the girls we'd met in Woodstock – she used to come up there at weekends and occasionally she and her boyfriend would stay with us. Her father was an artist, but he'd started to get into property and he had this place at 119 Christie Street, south of Houston (the area is now called SoHo for that very reason), which he rented to Billy and Johnny.

It was an old factory building; that entire area was factories, going back to the Civil War and before, but slowly, as companies closed down or moved, artists started to move in because the rents were so cheap.

It wasn't a good area; in fact, it was the same one where I got beaten up back when I was still in high school, after I made the mistake of crossing the wrong road while I was out with an African-American friend. A gang of youths came after us; my friend got away, but I still have the tooth chip from where this one guy punched me in the face, warning me, "You run back to the Village and *never* bring that n—— back here again."

Right across the road from the loft, on Broome Street, there was a park and that's where all the hookers used to hang out; the pimps, too, and you could spot them from yards away because they all looked like they'd stepped out of *Superfly*. The movie had just come out, and everyone fell in love with the imagery, Johnny and me included. We went to see it at a midnight showing on Broadway, and, when it was over, we came out and who's standing on the street, picking up chicks? The guy who played Superfly himself, with the same fucking car!

You had the Mafiosi on Mulberry Street killing each other; this was New York at the very peak of lawlessness. You could stand out on the fire escape and watch the mobsters driving around looking for one another, so it was a dangerous neighbourhood, and certainly not a place you wanted to walk around at night. During the day, there were still people, because some of the factories were still going. But after five, when everyone went home, there was nobody there. I had a girlfriend who came to see me; she got mugged and almost molested there.

There was a garage next door, one of the old ones with the tall archway entrance. One summer night I was sitting on the fire escape smoking a joint, talking to Janice, and I saw somebody drive in with a brand new Cadillac. Half an hour later, they wheeled it out again, with nothing on it except the wheels. No bumpers, no engine, nothing. They rolled it out, took it across the way, not even a block away, and then they stripped the wheels off, propped the car up on milk cartons and left it there.

But the loft itself was magnificent. Huge, as well. Johnny and Billy moved in, followed by Frenchie, followed by Janice, followed by Roger

Popeye, who used to give us rides back to Queens in his purple Jaguar. Ossie and Gail were always around, and the rest of the group as well. In fact, that became our headquarters. The very first photographs ever taken of the Dolls happened there, when Ossie turned up with his camera one evening.

We'd hang out there, we'd rehearse there, we'd sleep there. I used to stop there during the day sometimes, and grab a siesta on the couch – and invariably wake up to discover that Johnny had drawn a moustache on my face while I slept. Frenchie went to the army surplus store on Broadway and Mercer, picked up a bunch of tents, and they became the rooms – everybody's room was actually a tent. And the whole kitchen was furnished from the junkyards in Queens and the Bronx; you could buy an entire used fifties kitchen there – the sink, the refrigerator, the stove, everything, for $50.

It's fortunate that the loft was so big, because there were always people around. Which was good for us, the band, because it meant we always had an audience. It was like something out of the old Judy Garland and Mickey Rooney movies, or something the Little Rascals might have done ... David was Butch, Johnny was Alfalfa, I was Buckwheat. Our instruments would all be lying around and suddenly someone would say, "We're bored, man, what are we going to do?" And someone else would say, "Let's put on a show." And we would.

We'd each disappear into a different part of the loft and change our clothes, or put something else on, and it didn't matter to us that we were only rehearsing for a few friends. We were still putting on a show.

Inevitably, word started to spread; friends would tell their friends, who would tell other friends, and we were beginning to pick up a genuine audience. Not only that, we were also beginning to get talked about outside the loft, which is how we landed our very first "paying" gig, on February 4, 1972.

The show was a benefit for Dana Beal, an activist and marijuana campaigner, and was held in the Grand Ballroom of the Hotel Diplomat – the scene of my first ever onstage ovation, back in the days of The Pox.

This was markedly different. For a start, we didn't play long enough to have the plugs pulled on us; it was just a handful of songs, on and off. David Peel was headlining, and there were also sets from Teenage Lust and Uncle Bucks.

But we played our set, and it gave us our first ever mention in the press – "The lead singer of the Dolls just blew everyone out."

Chapter 15

OH SYLVAIN, I HAD SO MUCH SEX IN THAT LOFT

We needed new names, to match the energy of the music and our look.

Johnny already had one; he could never be anything but Johnny Thunders. David opted not to change, but "Johansen" had a certain ring to it.

Arthur Kane – that sounded pretty good already, but then he put "Killer" in the middle (although I thought it should have been "candy" because he was really a sweetheart). And Billy was seriously considering renaming himself Jennifer Woods, which he borrowed from one of his girlfriends, and that would have been great. But Alice Cooper had already done something similar, and much as we loved his music, we didn't want to follow him that far. In the end he became Billy Doll.

That left me. I suppose I could have revived Ricky Corvette, which I still think is a marvellous rock'n'roll name, up there alongside Vince Taylor, Gene Vincent, Billy Fury, Eddie Cochran – the names that hit you between the eyes, which are musical before you even hear the music. Ultimately, however, I decided to simply slap some echo on my first name.

It was right around this same time, too, that we started playing regular loft gigs. I think Billy started it, telling Johnny they needed money because the rent was due, and we should have a rent party. A deuce (two dollars) to get in; Roger Popeye at the foot of the staircase collecting the money, and selling pot on the side; Johnny instructing all his friends from Queens to come over; and then different people from the neighbourhood.

There'd be dealers; there'd be hookers; people who lived in the other lofts on the street – they'd hear our music and they'd want to come and party as well. Drag queens who were doing their own shows, just the coolest of the cool. People were constantly trying to find places to play; it wasn't like it became later – "Oh this is SoHo, let's go there" – in fact it wasn't even called SoHo back then. They'd put on shows to pay the rent, so we were going to those, and they were coming to ours.

Of course, not all of our neighbours were quite so thrilled. The loft faced Christie Street, and we'd set up in the kitchen at the back, overlooking a row of shops selling restaurant equipment. That whole stretch past what became CBGB, up as far as St Mark's, was full of steel tubs, hotdog machines, restaurant tables and chairs, everything.

Upstairs, however, were what they called lie-in houses, Bowery flop houses, and when we played ... we would play all night long, and the down-and-outs who were flopping over there really didn't want to hear us. All they wanted was to crash, and we made that impossible. Soon, every window on that side of the loft had been broken by the bottles and bricks that they threw at us, and even though we tried some soundproofing, tacking sacking up over the windows, I don't think it made much difference.

Those rent parties, although there were only a few of them, were the best shows we ever did. Better than Max's, better than the Mercer, better than London and Paris. When people say they saw the Dolls, I don't care where they saw us, if it wasn't at those rent parties, when we were young and hungry and completely untamed, they didn't see us.

We fed off the audience. If they looked outrageous, so did we. If they behaved wild, so did we. There'd be people fucking in the tents, or sometimes *not* in the tents. There was drink, there were drugs, there were bare tits and full-on nudity; there was everything and anything you can imagine going on, and we'd be playing for hours, every song we knew, and then every song we knew again.

Frenchie would be there blowing his whistle in his fedora hat; Paul and Miki Zone, who would become The Fast, they used to come down all the time.

Deborah Harry was always around. I talked to her recently, asking, "Do you remember the loft?" and she replied, "Oh Sylvain, I had so much sex in that loft!" But so did we all. We were so careless in those days, because you didn't die if you had sex. You might get the clap, but that's what antibiotics were for.

But it didn't take long for the scene to sour. At the beginning, it was a lot of fun, but after a while the parties became really sleazy. People started fighting, and the violence got way out of hand. Every time I visited the loft, I'd have to kick people out who I didn't even know. We kept on rehearsing, but we needed to get out and play other places, where we wouldn't have strangers trashing our home.

Those shows served their purpose, however. They got people talking about us: other performers, actors and artists and musicians. There were so few places that complete unknowns could play in New York at that time that, if you did find somewhere, you were going to be discovered whether you liked it or not.

It was the loft shows that helped ease us into Max's inner circle, because that crowd would come to see us; and it was one of their number, Eric Emerson, who offered us our next paying gig at the Mercer Arts Center at the beginning of May. We made $15, which we split between us, $3 each. Which is how it should have been from that moment on, an equal split between equal partners. But, of course, things change.

The Mercer was like a rabbit warren. It was housed within the University Hotel, which, in a previous life, had been the Broadway Central Hotel. Eight stories high, when it was opened in 1870, back when Broadway and Bleecker were considered "uptown", it was the biggest hotel in America.

But times had changed and, just like so many other hotels, it had gone down in the world. Now it was effectively a flophouse, and the amenities that had once given the place so much glitz had either been repurposed or rented out.

The ballroom, and the rooms that led off it, fell into the latter category; they became the Mercer Arts Center. You'd go in, walk up a dozen steps or so, and the first room on the right was the Kitchen, which was a video workshop, and of course we'd never seen a place like that before. Artists would be there doing the very first work with this new medium, figuring out what they could do with all these new toys. It was fascinating.

On the left, there was the theatre room, where they were putting on all kind of plays and theatrical performances, and that's where we would end up playing, once we were more established. But not yet.

As you kept on going, you reached the bar area, and past that there was the Blue Room, which was a cabaret, really swanky, decked out in silver, with a real stage, and all looking a little like the Milk Bar in *A Clockwork Orange.* Patti Smith played there a few times, when it was just her and Lenny Kaye, a duet for guitar and poetry; and there was a lot of experimental theatre going on, plays that would never have climbed any further up Broadway, but slotted perfectly into the atmosphere of anarchic creativity and madness that sustained the Mercer.

The Blue Room is where I saw Suicide for the first time, soundchecking for their show that evening. Holy shit! Martin Rev in the aviator glasses, hunched over his home-made keyboard, wired up with drum machines and all manner of things, just making this phenomenal noise; and Alan Vega mixing Elvis with all this other weird stuff. It was almost terrifying; I make a joke now that I poked Johnny and said, "Where's the subway back to Queens?"

Then all the little theatres at the back would open, and all the way at the back, the furthest that you could go, that was the Oscar Wilde Room, which is the other room we would go on to play. But again, not yet.

Our show was to take place in the Kitchen. Emerson and his band, The Magic Tramps, were headlining, and there was also an appearance from Satan The Fire Eater, who did exactly what his name said he would, and who rehearsed in the same place as this new quartet who looked like a cowboy outfit, called Kiss. Satan is who they got their fire-eating routine from.

To be truthful, we weren't The Magic Tramps' biggest fans. They were great, but they had a violinist in their line-up, and – at least at that moment – we didn't feel violins had any place in any show that we were a part of. I love violins, but not that night.

They were also very arty, so we knew the kind of audience that would be in attendance. Accordingly, we dressed the way we always dressed; we rehearsed the way we always rehearsed; and we were going to play the songs we always played – 'Subway Train', 'Personality Crisis', 'Looking For A Kiss', Bo Diddley's 'Pills', all the numbers that became the standard early Dolls repertoire.

There wasn't a huge crowd – it was mainly people we knew, and people who The Magic Tramps knew, and people who Satan The Fire Eater knew. But they loved us. Jane Friedman, the woman who would go on to manage Patti Smith and John Cale, was there; and so was a woman who would become very important in my life, named Elda Gentile.

She was one of Eric Emerson's exes, and they always remained friends; he was also the father of her son Branch, who was the most beautiful child you've ever seen. He looked like a California surfer. Right now, though, Elda was free – and, although I was still involved with Valerie, this particular evening, so was I. So one of us picked the other one up, and then she took me home and she screwed my brains out. It was as simple, and beautiful, as that.

For the New York Dolls, a gig at Max's was the peak of our ambition. We thought it was a possibility as well – in fact, Mickey Ruskin told us that if we could prove to him that we'd bring in a crowd, then he'd try us out. Because he needed that. Right now, it was a wasteland: old blues men like Howling Wolf coming in and playing to barely a dozen people, while Mickey was stuck paying them the full rate, feeding them, everything.

We had a goal, then. Make a name for ourselves. Which meant, in turn, taking every gig we were offered. Even street festivals outside St Mark's Church.

Eric Emerson invited us. The idea of the festival was to get local youth involved in something that didn't involve sitting behind a wall sniffing glue. Show them that there was a community, and that could be fun as well. Plus it was a Sunday afternoon, which meant we'd still have the night to ourselves.

Things get a little hazy for me now. Somebody offered me a joint, except it wasn't a joint, because you had to eat it. And it wasn't hashish either. There was a new kind of acid going around, a powder that the street had nicknamed Belladonna, and it was the worst fucking acid ever because it was made from poison.

We were waiting to go on, just one name out of however many were playing this event, and I was beginning to feel really sick; so sick that Elda insisted on taking me back to her place to rest. She was still helping me up the stairs when I started to throw up, and once inside the apartment, I kept going. There was no way I could go and play this afternoon; at one point, there was no way I thought I could even stay alive. That's how sick I felt.

Elda rushed back and picked up the rest of the band, and I received a crash course in street medicine. Nobody knew what was wrong with me, but they all had suggestions – "Hey man, take one of these"; "Now take one of these" ... and so on. And something, probably Johnny's valium, worked. I started to feel better, in as much as I could now move without precipitating another round of dry heaves, so we made our way back to St Mark's, played our show – and hey, that made me feel better too.

I steered clear of taking anything else, though, which means, by the end of the afternoon, I was probably the most sober person in our party. So when Patricia, David's girlfriend Diane's sister, announced that she was too high to drive anywhere, and everyone else agreed with her, I piled everybody into her old Peugeot 504 and drove us back to the loft.

And that's the night the New York Dolls met Frankenstein.

I'd written the song 'Frankenstein' back when I was in The Pox; I had the riff and the melody, but every time I tried to introduce it to Johnny, he'd say, "Sylvain, too many fucking chords."

Tonight, though, I just started jamming it, for the first time in front of everybody, and David not only fell in love with it, he started writing lyrics too, right there on the spot.

Now, the thing with David is, once he starts writing, he just keeps going. So a song that already had too many chords now had too many verses, about 50 million of the things, and it went on for about twenty minutes. But what a night. It started with me tripping and almost dropping dead, and now we're doing a song that I'd almost given up on, and it came out a fucking classic.

David's lyrics were perfect; he graced all of our songs with that wonderful voice of his, which was the most perfect vehicle for rock'n'roll, and he embellished them with those magnificent lyrics. But 'Frankenstein' was one of his best – not because I wrote it, but because it was the story of the New York Dolls.

It was the story of everyone who loved the New York Dolls and everyone who hated them. And that kicked us off. We were having fun, we were having more fun than anyone. Think of The Rolling Stones – nobody could be having more fun than the Stones, right? First they had the best rock'n'roll, then they had the best drugs, then they had the best chicks.

Well guess what? We had all those things as well, only we did it backwards. First we had the best chicks, then the best drugs and finally we had the best rock'n'roll. And that started with 'Frankenstein'. Because that's the way to do it – you build the legend first, and then justify it. Like David sang, "Do you think you can make it with a Frankenstein?"

That's when we started taking things seriously. We were playing the Mercer Arts Center more and more, and one-off shows at other places; and one day Jane Friedman came to us with the offer of a gig, and where was it? A bath house!

We weren't sure. But Jane was adamant. "It's really good money and I want you boys to take it." And it was good money, $400. At the Kitchen, we'd made $15. So we agreed.

We were scarcely strangers to bath houses. There was one uptown called the Continental, where we saw Bette Midler with Barry Manilow as her pianist. I know they're gay baths, all men, but an audience is an audience. Also, did I mention that $400?

Man's Country, out in Brooklyn Heights, is a gorgeous place on the main drag, at the back of an old hotel. Jane assured us that we only needed to transport our instruments; the venue would supply all the amplification. We did pack up one of our practice amps, just in case we needed a spare, but we didn't think any more about it until we got there and asked about the soundcheck.

"Ah, don't worry," came the response. "We don't have a PA; you're going to use the mike that goes into the whole system, through the showers and everywhere else."

There was no stage either: just a circular area in the centre of the room, with chairs arranged all around it, in this great round room with Roman-style pillars and western theme decor – old horse saddles, bridles, and things like that. There wasn't much of an audience either, maybe fifty men all clad in bath towels and nothing else. Whereas we're dressed the same as we always are.

David loved it, he was totally hamming it up. But Johnny, forget it. He spent the entire set sighing and groaning and making faces. I cannot imagine what the rest of us sounded like either – two guitars and a bass plugged into that little amp, while David was making do with a mike that actually had an on-off button; you had to turn it on in order to be heard.

Those mikes pick up everything around them; the guitars were leaking through, Arthur's bass, Billy's drums, Johnny's groans. But we were doing our best when one of the managers, dressed all in white, approached the "stage".

"Stop the music, stop the music, you guys are playing way too loud for us, we don't like it." We'd seen people leaving the room, but because they usually went in pairs, we assumed they had business elsewhere. Maybe they did, but now it appeared that our volume, too, had contributed to their departure.

We knocked it down a notch, went into our second song, and the manager reappeared. "Boys, you're still way too loud." By that time, however, David had removed one of the saddles from the wall, jammed it between his legs and now he was riding that fucking horse. Arthur and I, on our side of the stage, were cracking up.

Meanwhile, Johnny was growing more and more uncomfortable, because he'd noticed that all the men who weren't staring at David were staring at him instead. He was accustomed to getting that kind of response from the girls – he was the best-looking boy in the band, after all. But now he was getting it from a roomful of men, and just to increase his discomfort, those bath towels did not leave much to the imagination. He could see things *moving* beneath them,

Back came the manager. "Come on. I've told you three times, boys, this is way too loud, and David, please put that thing back on the wall." To which David replied, "Make me."

Now we understood. We turned the volume down to zero. All you could hear was David through the PA and Billy on the drums. We played the rest of our set without any complaint and, when we finished, we received a standing ovation. People even emerged out of their private rooms to congratulate us. "I could hear everything you boys were saying." They loved it! We got our $400, we returned to Manhattan, and we were feeling great. At least until Jane called me up and said, "Guess what? They're not inviting you back."

I think that was the one and only gig we ever did for Jane.

Chapter 16

SUBTERRANEAN FLASH, SLEAZOID ROCK

Things were happening quickly. We *were* the Little Rascals, putting on a show, and we kept putting it on. Just like those early days with The Pox, everything was exactly as I thought it ought to be. Form a band, play a show, make a splash ... get signed.

Already people were approaching us, people we'd never met before, asking, "Do you have a record deal? Have you made any albums?" Fans! Not friends, not fellow performers. Honest-to-goodness genuine fans. Other musicians too. We were the It Group, the Next Big Thing, and everybody knew – if the New York Dolls didn't get a record deal soon, nobody would.

They understood what we'd known all along. We were real. We didn't take everything off when we got home, hang it in the closet, and slum around in jeans and T-shirts. We lived it. It was really upsetting, years later, when I saw Tom Verlaine talking about the early days of Television in a documentary and saying, "We didn't want to be the New York Dolls, wearing costumes."

It shocked me, because we weren't doing that. We're not Kiss, mister. These aren't costumes, this is what we wear. This is how we go to the supermarket, this is how we go to visit our moms, this is what we take off when we're going to bed with another beautiful chick. This is who we are. I suppose some people just don't get it.

Or they didn't have the balls to do it.

We landed a write-up in *Interview* magazine, which was a very big deal because of its association with Andy Warhol. It wasn't an interview, just a write-up, but the headline said more than we ever could. "Subterranean Flash, Sleazoid Rock" – those four words *made* us, they cemented our reputation, and once the other papers saw that, they couldn't wait to start writing about us as well.

Yet it was a double-edged sword. All this while, we were being absorbed into that whole world of Warhol, the superstars and the freaks, and in our little corner of New York City, that was the perfect place for us.

What we didn't comprehend was how the rest of New York, and the rest of America, would interpret that. Because that world was one that everybody else was shunning, because they thought it was weird and degenerate. Therefore, we must have been weird and degenerate too.

It's called guilt by association and, ultimately, that's why the Dolls were never going to make it. Because a lot more people have closed minds than open minds, especially in America.

In Europe, particularly in the UK and France, people were more open – they accepted what we were. Not in vast numbers, but enough to make waves and, in the end, make a difference.

In America, however, the places where we would be the biggest were the places where that kind of scene had already taken hold; where people *wanted* to feel threatened, or dangerous, or out on the brink, and where you didn't have to soften the edges and add a pile of gimmicks in order to convince them that you were simply putting on a show.

We gave it to people raw. Right in the face. In those earliest interviews, when the inevitable question about bisexuality came up, it was David who declared we were *tri*-sexual, meaning "We'll try any sex". So many people at that time were asking themselves whether they were straight or gay or bisexual or whatever; so many other people were deciding for them – we were called queer even before we ever went on stage, just because of the way we looked. So we played up to it by not denying, or specifying, anything … we'd try it all!

We were the biggest thing in New York, no question of that. But all we had to do to remind ourselves of how little that meant was walk to the Mercer.

It was a fair distance, largely winding through a very Italian area, the best of all the cafes and coffee houses, the greatest bakeries, some terrific stores. So long as you were there during the day. Walking through these neighbourhoods at night, however, the whole macho Mafioso culture came into play, and they didn't like to see fags, or what they thought were fags, strutting across their turf.

Every cafe we passed, guys would cat call this and that, and yell all manner of abuse at us. Sometimes, I felt as if we were lucky to have even reached the Arts Center in one piece.

Once we got there, of course, you were safe. You were among people who were kinda like you. What you maybe forgot was that they, too, had run the gauntlet of hatred as they made their own way to a safe haven. You forgot, once you were in a crowd, just how small that crowd was in comparison with the rest of the city.

I was making that journey more and more as summer dawned. We had graduated to the Oscar Wilde Room now, and with that came our biggest piece of press yet, a write-up in the *New York Daily News*, accompanied by a terrific picture of Barbara Triani dancing in the crowd. And this was important because now we were being recognised by people who hadn't heard our names before, like the men who ran the coffee houses. "Hey youse guys are getting really famous; free cannoli for youse."

The Oscar Wilde Room was where things really started taking off. We didn't make much money – although we were told we could charge whatever we wanted on the door, usually two or three dollars. It was usually one of our girlfriends who was in charge of collecting the money, which of course meant all her friends came in for nothing – you wind up with $10 at the end of the night, "Ah, Brenda, great to see you, come on in ... hey Michael ... hey, drag queens, come on in."

The word was spreading, though. Just like at the loft, kids would tell other kids, and that's how you do it, you build your name from the ground floor up. We didn't know that at the time though; we were flying by the seat of our pants, and some of us weren't even wearing pants.

All we saw was this gaping void in the kind of music we wanted to hear, and because nobody else was filling it, we had to do it ourselves. There were so many people who were unhappy with what was happening in music, and suddenly here was a band who weren't going to spend half an hour tuning up and expect to get a standing ovation at the end of it; and who weren't then going to launch into a version of some classical piece that went on even longer.

A band who dressed like you wish you could, and who sang about the things you wished somebody would sing about. I don't know if people could even hear the lyrics when we played live, but David's writing was so incisive, and so direct, and it mattered because he was writing about our lives and the audience's lives. Of course people related to it.

The first night at the Oscar Wilde Room, the audience was largely people we either knew or had seen at the loft or wherever. Plus the Mercer's own regulars, and people drawn in by the ads in the *Village Voice*.

So, hot chicks, hot guys, drag queens, this huge mix of people. The Zone brothers were there, still a couple of teenagers just hanging out, a long way from forming their own group. But week after week the crowd grew, and by the third or fourth week of our residency, around the end of June 1972, we were selling out the Oscar Wilde Room, and they were thinking about moving us to an even bigger space. Because people didn't only want to see us. They wanted to be seen seeing us.

Our audience was beautiful – women like Bebe Buell and Cyrinda Foxe were coming to see us, and it pisses me off when I hear them described as groupies because, basically, they were among the most beautiful women in the world. Of course they wanted to be with the most beautiful men, and who were the most beautiful men in the world at that time? They were rock'n'rollers.

Girls like that were not going to settle for any old schmuck; they were going to go where the action was, and when you look at the relationships they are best known for – Bebe with Todd Rundgren, for instance, or Pamela Miller with Michael Des Barres, they were *not* one-night stands. For as long as they lasted, they were long-term, committed relationships.

It was not only gorgeous women coming to our gigs, though. Every time we played, someone would tell us, "Oh, so-and-so was checking you out tonight"; maybe a famous musician, maybe a well-known manager.

I have no idea today of the chronology, if indeed I ever did. But Billy Gaff (who managed Rod Stewart and Long John Baldry), John Reid (Elton John), Shep Gordon (Alice Cooper) and Tony Defries (David Bowie) all came to see us, or sent one of their hirelings to do so, at different times.

Shep even invited us to the brownstone where the Alice Cooper Band all hung out to meet him – I remember Alice coming down stairs with a bottle of Michelob beer. From what I gather, some of the band members' girlfriends were already coming to see us (apparently, Johnny had even sampled some of the goods); they told their boyfriends, who told Shep, so he invited us over.

Paul Nelson, who was an A&R man at Mercury Records, was a fan. He first saw us at the Mercer at the beginning of August, and would come and see us whenever he could. He even tried to interest the label in us, although they didn't bite.

Billy Gaff offered us a gig opening for Long John Baldry at My Father's Place in Long Island, and that was the night we hired a roadie for the first time, a friend named Tony Machine. Apparently, his most lingering memory of the evening was me giving him a lesson in "how to survive a night in jail" – which involved walking up to the biggest guy in the cell and punching him in the face. Because, if you do that, he's going to fuck the shit out of you, and you're going to be his bitch forever more. But that's better, because then you don't have to fuck anybody else.

And no, I didn't gain this knowledge from personal experience.

The New Yorker was writing about us, followed by this magazine and that magazine; we were getting press out of the wazoo. *Rock Scene* magazine, run by Lisa and Richard Robinson, was covering us. And late in June, we met Marty Thau, who was to become our manager.

A big wheel at labels like Cameo-Parkway and Buddha back in the sixties, Marty was now head of A&R at Paramount Records. But he was also scouting around for a new act to work with, and he'd noticed our name in the *Voice* or whatever. So he and his wife Betty came down to the Oscar Wilde Room and he couldn't believe it. As they were walking out, he turned to Betty and said, "I don't know if I just saw the best rock'n'roll band in the world or the worst, but I'm going to sign them."

Not to Paramount, though; he knew they'd not want a band like us. He was going to manage us, and he'd give up his day job to do so.

Those other people were still interested, but Marty was determined to become the main man. He even invited us to the mansion where he lived in upstate New York. We were puzzled, for a while, as to how we'd actually get there, but then Deborah Harry stepped in, volunteering to drive us in her old Camaro – the same one you see in one of Blondie's very first videos.

Of course, Marty only wanted us there so he could impress us with his gold records, and (of course) it worked. There was the 1910 Fruitgum Company; there was this, there was that; and *there*, so close that I could reach out and touch it, was his gold disc for '96 Tears' by Question Mark & The Mysterions.

That, to me, was "wow". Although Marty was never my first choice as manager – Shep Gordon, Billy Gaff and Tony Defries were all higher on my list – I could see that he had something. Besides, he was a fellow New Yorker; *plus*, David and Johnny were really keen on him because they knew, if he signed us, he would devote all his energies to us.

Those other names may have been bigger, with more industry contacts and so on, but they also had bigger artists than us, and that's where the bulk of their energies would be channelled. Marty didn't have any ties, but he was already planning to put together a team to work behind us, and it was he that we signed with. Although, if we were at all superstitious, we might have taken heed from the journey back to the city. Deborah's car broke down on the freeway.

We always looked on the bright side, though. Somehow, we crawled over to the nearest exit, where we found the only garage that was still open. He agreed to fix the car, and while we waited, he pointed us towards a bar where we could get something to eat – an all-black after-hours club whose menu comprised nothing but fried chicken and whiskey. We played pool until the car was repaired, and then we crawled back to New York.

Gigs were coming faster, chicks were coming, songs were coming. One night at Max's, David was so transfixed by a girl he saw on the dance floor that he immediately re-dedicated 'Looking For A Kiss' to her. Her name was Cyrinda Foxe, an Armenian Texan (she was born Kathleen Hetzekian) and, as David's relationship with Diane began to fade, so a new life with Cyrinda came into being. They were destined to become *the* superstar couple of the Manhattan rock scene.

'Looking For A Kiss' was a special song, but so was everything that poured out of the loft. One of the best, to me anyway, was 'Jet Boy'. I walked in one day and Johnny was playing with this riff that stopped me in my tracks.

"Hey, we can write a song around that."

"Oh yeah, Sylvain? Show me."

So I changed the riff a bit, then came up with this little lead that could go with it. Then, when we introduced it to David, his face lit up and he said, "I've got the best lyrics for that," and he just spilled them out – "Jet Boy stole my baby". A few days later, Marty took us into Blue Rock Studio to record our first demos. 'Jet Boy' was one of them.

It was the last weekend of July and Johnny was buzzing. The latest Rolling Stones tour was set to end at Madison Square and, of course, he had tickets. Later, when the concert film was released, you could see him in the crowd, when Mick Jagger has the house lights turned on. There's Johnny, unmistakable, atop his friend's shoulders.

Before that, though, there was business to attend to. Roy Hollingworth, the New York correspondent for *Melody Maker*, one of the biggest London-based music papers, wrote about us. That alone meant a lot to me – I'd loved England on my past visits there; now it almost felt like England was visiting me in return, and I just hoped the affection would be mutual.

It was. Hollingworth's piece, when it appeared in the paper a few weeks later, was everything an unknown band could hope for because it ensured we were no longer unknown. It took a while for copies to make it to the States, but *Melody Maker* had dedicated readers on both American coasts, and in all the big cities in between. Even more importantly, just as Hollingworth's column let the Brits know what was happening in America, *Melody Maker* let Americans know what was happening across the ocean. And this week, although we'd never played there and they'd never heard a note of our music ... this week, *we* were happening. The New York Dolls were happening.

Everything about the article was a dream come true, from the writer's enthusiasm to the photographer's pictures; David in polka dots, with the house key round his waist, me in glasses and one of Janice's striped knitted sweaters, and behind us, the closet full of clothes, rock'n'roll animals to the core.

And who was the photographer? Leee Black Childers, the stage manager of the Warhol play, *Pork*, that I'd seen in London the previous summer. I couldn't believe it. He, too, had an engagement with the Stones that weekend, but he later confessed that his time with us was far more fun. He was doing a lot of work for teen magazines at that time and usually, he said, the hardest part was trying to arrange the idol's pants so his cock wouldn't scare all the teenyboppers. With us, it was the other way around, trying to rearrange us so we all looked like we had enormous ones.

The article ran at the end of August, and Marty's phone started ringing immediately. Everybody wanted a piece of the pie. Everybody wanted to make money from the New York Dolls. Including the New York Dolls themselves.

It wasn't immediate, but very quickly money did become an issue. When we first signed with Marty, all five of us were on a flat $75 a week. Somewhere along the line, however, that changed; suddenly, some people were living in a penthouse, and others ... Arthur and I, for example ... were so broke we couldn't even afford fifteen cents to ride the bus to the management office to pick up our money in the first place.

Once, we even leaped aboard a passing flatbed truck, as it slowed down for traffic, then bounced and bumped across some of the biggest pot holes in Manhattan until it was time to get off. But you can't pull the cord and ring the bell on a flatbed, so we had to wait for another traffic light. Then, once we got up there and asked for our money, we had to wait while management went through their own little routine of "What? What are you talking about? We gave it to you last week."

"Yeah, but that was last week."

They always want to make you beg. And later, we discovered that one of the first things the new management team did was divide the band, in their own minds, between the stars – Johnny and David – and the schmucks ... Billy, Arthur and myself. Soon, they were on $200 a week, although the rest of us didn't know that, and there really wasn't time for us to think about it.

We were playing two or three gigs a week now. We broke into Max's with a couple of try-out gigs in July; then, at the end of August, Mickey handed us a five-night residency – in the midst of which Billy and I got ourselves banned from Max's.

One of Mickey's staff, a wormy little man who was always looking for trouble, caught the two of us in one of the bathroom stalls together, snorting coke. We were hauled out of there and lectured about how the club could have lost its licence if the cops had chosen that moment to raid it, and that was true. At the same time, though, the back room was awash with illegal substances of one kind or another, and the air thick with the aroma of the poppers that the Warhol crowd were cracking everywhere.

There was a real double standard at work, then, but it also presented Max's with a problem. How could we be banned at the same time as we were supposed to be playing a five-night residency?

Easy! Every night for the rest of the run, Billy and I were expected to arrive as close to showtime as we could, and march straight upstairs to the dressing room. We weren't allowed to enter the bar, or the back room, or any other part of the club. The only places we had permission to be were the dressing room and the stage.

Luckily for us, you can get up to an awful lot of things in both places.

Chapter 17

BE NICE TO THE PEOPLE ON YOUR WAY UP, COS YOU'LL MEET THE SAME PEOPLE ON THE WAY DOWN

I don't recall the first time I heard David Bowie. I know Johnny had his *Man Of Words, Man Of Music* album, with the blue cover and the mass of curly hair, and *Hunky Dory* was always playing in the loft, long before *Ziggy Stardust* came to join it, and we played the shit out of that as well.

New York radio seemed to like him too, and his upcoming American tour – his first ever – would see him play, and sell out, Carnegie Hall. Like us, he wasn't yet a star in America. But he sure behaved like one.

It was Leee Black Childers who told us that Bowie wanted to see us, at the Mercer one Sunday in September. It was one of our first performances in the main ballroom, the Sean O'Casey Theater, which was a beautiful room: the walls were all black and there were couches and stools strewn over the floor. We weren't yet filling it up, though, so while the show wasn't *officially* a special presentation for our illustrious guest, in our minds, we were playing directly to him.

Bowie was fresh off the *QE2;* famously afraid of flying, he crossed the Atlantic by boat. Just like I had. Then, once in New York, he and manager Tony Defries set about assembling the entourage that would help him break America – and guess what? It was the *Pork* crew – Leee Black Childers, Tony Zanetta, Cherry Vanilla and co. – and of course they came to the show with him. Defries, Bowie's wife Angie, guitarist Mick Ronson and Bowie's bodyguard Stu completed the party, and even in the midst of our usual crowd, they stood out. Especially Bowie, who was wearing the same suit you see on the cover of *Ziggy Stardust*, with the flame red haircut as well.

We did our best to compete – I'd combed my hair back and drenched it in gel, so it lay flat and backwards, and pulled out my favourite black and yellow chequerboard pants. We knew he'd seen our pictures in *Melody Maker* and fallen in love with our look, so no way were we going to disappoint him.

I'll admit, we were nervous. 'Suffragette City' was in constant rotation at the loft; 'All The Young Dudes', which he'd written and produced for Mott The Hoople, too. All those incredible songs that you could listen to all night long, and when you woke up, they were lodged in your heart. And now he was coming to see us? Holy shit, this is amazing.

We didn't see him before the show, but once we'd finished our set, he was waiting on the steps that led into the room. We chatted for a while, then we asked if he wanted to join us at one of our favourite bars. Yes, so we all piled into the big black limousines, and we directed them to – of all places! – the Canal Street Center Rest, a funky Bowery bar where you could get a dozen small beers for $2.

Bowie was terrified. He probably thought we'd be going somewhere uptown and swish. Instead, we're in this seedy joint where the regulars have been sitting in the same seats for 100,000 years, and there were all these teenagers from New Jersey coming in through the Holland Tunnel because the drinking age was lower in New York than at home.

The decor was pieces of paper with different visitors' names written on them, and I don't know how many years' worth of Thanksgiving wishbones, hanging there with cobwebs all over them. The brightest lighting came from the neon signs advertising the different beer companies. Poor guy – he'd come to Manhattan to play Carnegie Hall, and here he was in a Bowery bar, squeezed into one of the little vinyl booths, with Stu wedged in tight alongside him.

So yes, he was terrified. "What? They brought me here?"

But he was fascinated as well, constantly looking around, listening to snatches of conversation as they floated around the room. He was also getting ever deeper into conversation with Cyrinda, and Billy and Angie appeared to be hitting it off as well. I don't think any of us were surprised when the pair of them left with the Bowie entourage, while the rest of us made our way home, and we didn't see either Billy or Cyrinda for a couple of days after that.

No, they were partying at the Plaza with Bowie and his people, and a few months later, there was Cyrinda, vamping it up in Bowie's 'Jean Genie' video. Which, I'd like to point out, utilised exactly the same riff as 'Hoochie Coochie Man', which we'd performed the night he came to see us. I'm not saying the two had anything in common – a lot of other songs used that riff as well. But I doubt it was coincidence.

Bowie became a real friend to the New York Dolls. Whenever he was in the US, he would come to see us play, and years later he was still talking about us, saying things like this, from 2002: "I remember I was knocked out by the Dolls. My first impressions were that they were the early Stones in strippers' clothes. Fabulous early R&B sound, but much sloppier and more vital. It was the humour, the fun and drunk 'don't give a shit' attitude of the band that was intoxicating."

Of course, his was one of the names being circulated when it was time for us to record our first album. The timing, unfortunately, was wrong – he was in the midst of a world tour at the time. But think about it; he'd already produced Lou Reed and Iggy Pop. With us, he'd have completed the trilogy. Classic American Gutter Rock.

Look carefully at some of the photographs, though, and you'll see his influence regardless. That pair of blue satin overalls I had, with the tiger on the leg – they were his. He'd picked them up in Japan when he was there, passed them onto Cyrinda, and she traded them to me for an English dandy suit I'd bought in London when I was there with Valerie – the same suit, incidentally, that she's wearing in pictures from our Club 82 gig in 1974, the ones where David is wearing her dress.

For the next few weeks, we concentrated all our live attentions on the O'Casey Theater, playing two, three times a week and, every night, the crowd was bigger than the one before, until we were packing the place to the rafters. Even the bar area was wild; in fact, some nights, it was as much of a party as the gig itself.

The most amazing people were coming down – one night I found myself seated between Truman Capote and Elton John. And there was always this guy who had clothes pins on his nipples, like that famous shot of Joe Dallesandro, but this was how he always dressed. A tight black leather jacket, no T-shirt, and these clothes pins. He had the hots for Johnny too, so every now and then I'd say, "Johnny, Clothes Pins is here for you," and he'd be, "Oh fuck you Sylvain."

Every night was like that.

Every night, too, we'd head home laden down with gifts from the fans – clothing, photographs, pieces of art. I still have a set of paper dolls that somebody sent us, all these figures in beautiful dresses and underwear and stuff, and they'd stuck our faces on each one. Like us, our fans were having the time of their lives, and they reflected that in their presence at our shows, and their presents to us.

But the bigger you get, the smaller some people want you to feel. The folk who liked us called us a vision of the future; the ones who didn't said they hoped the future never came. People had always disparaged us, even The Magic Tramps – "You guys don't know how to play." We could accept it from them, though; they knew us and they understood us, whether we were competent instrumentalists or not.

Other musicians, however, seized upon us for other reasons: jealousy, maybe, that we didn't even have a record deal, yet were getting more press than many superstars. Prejudice – that we could get so much attention when we were clearly a bunch of degenerate slobs. And fear. The knowledge that we represented the destruction of the cosy world that they had erected around themselves.

It might not happen immediately; it might not happen next year ... and, in fact, it didn't truly happen until 1976, 1977, when punk rock grasped our intentions like the flamethrowers they were, and laid waste to the entire musical landscape.

And where did it start? Not in New York, but in Britain.

David Bowie was not the only person who picked up *Melody Maker* and fell in love with the New York Dolls. From the moment the issue hit the news stands, Marty's telephone started to ring. A lot of the callers didn't interest him. But one, an English promoter named Roy Fisher, made sense.

His deal was simple. He'd fly us to London and take us into the studio. He'd also set Marty up with some other promoters who wanted to work with us. He was the sweetest guy as well, a total gentleman. He even agreed that whatever we recorded would remain our own property. He simply wanted to license it.

I'd invited Valerie to come with us, but while she made the flight, I didn't. On the eve of departure, I realised that my visas to visit the UK had expired, and I had to hang on for another couple of days while they were renewed. So I missed the reception that awaited everybody else, a horse-drawn carriage that would take them for a few photographs, before they were driven to their hotel.

All I was got was a car and driver.

We were recording at Escape Studios, a sixteen-track set-up in Egerton, Kent. It was owned by a pair of brothers, Richard and Ted Roffey, and had been built into one of the old oast houses where they used to store hops for making beer.

We recorded four songs, 'Personality Crisis', 'Looking For A Kiss', 'Bad Girl' and 'Subway Train', and listening back to them today, maybe the versions are a little slow compared to what came later. Billy was really into playing a groove thing, which was perfect for us at that time, and maybe if the studio engineers had given him a better sound, you would hear that. Unfortunately, they'd never seen us live, they'd never heard us; instead, they were trying to get us to sound like Alice Cooper, because that's what they knew, and that really wasn't us.

In fact, when it came to the music that was on the radio, we really couldn't identify with any of it.

We arrived in England that November, 1972, to discover that glam rock had completely taken over. Back in New York, Bolan and Bowie were seen as isolated phenomena. Gary Glitter and The Sweet had had hits, but we didn't actually see them or hear anything else. Now we got over and everybody was dressing up, wearing make-up, talking about bisexuality and, superficially, you could say we had something in common with that.

Were we glam rock, though? In British eyes, probably. We dressed the part, we sounded the part. In our eyes, no. We came from a different world, and we came from different influences – as I said before, girl groups mixed with the Stones and The Kinks, and then merged with The Stooges and the Fairies. Whereas a lot of what passed as glam rock sounded more like bubblegum pop to us.

We were shocked by the synchronicity, though; and we understood how glam, in as much as it revolved around a succession of terrific-sounding singles, was as much a reaction to what was happening in British music as we were a reaction against James Taylor, Foghat and all the other stuff that was so huge in America at that time. Forget concept albums and endless LPs. The 45 is the ultimate rock'n'roll art form, and glam rock shared our belief in that fact.

But it was just a label. Glam was what the British industry had decided was hip, and so everything that could be saddled with the term was. It's the same in every industry – a word becomes "current" and suddenly it's being applied to everything from washing machines to shoes. They have nothing in common; there's not a single thing that links them. It's the word that sells.

We emerged from the studio and a string of gigs awaited. Billy Gaff had offered us a berth at a huge charity show being given by Rod Stewart and The Faces; and we had one-offs lined up with Kevin Ayers, Status Quo, Roxy Music and a few other people, as well as a few shows of our own.

The biggie, though, was a handful of dates with Lou Reed, beginning at a boxing arena in Liverpool.

It was a long drive, and a difficult one. Billy was starting to suffer from stomach problems, and the switch from American to English cooking set them off. Especially English motorway cooking. So he was already feeling down before we started; by the time we reached our destination, however many hours later, he was in a really bad way.

So were we. Liverpool was cold, grey and rainy; we were tired and hungry; and our budget barely afforded us a bed for the night. Then, when we turned up at the gig, Lou Reed cancelled us. Straight up – he announced that he didn't want us on his stage; didn't even want us in the same town.

We couldn't believe it – it broke our hearts, and it was all down to the rivalry, jealousy, fear and politics that I mentioned earlier. "Who the fuck do they think they are?" Reed had come all the way to England to get away from the New York Dolls, and now here they were again.

So we didn't play any shows with Lou, and that includes all the ones that different websites say we did. Our name was left on the bill for whatever reason.

Hardly surprisingly, the show that sticks in my mind was the charity gig with The Faces. It was at Wembley Pool with us as "special guests", in between The Pink Fairies and the headliners, and as we walked on stage, you saw the whole audience standing with their mouths wide open, not even clapping, because they were in so much shock.

But we played a phenomenal set; it was the best sound we'd ever had, and one of the best shows we ever gave. The biggest audience we'd ever seen was about 500 people. Suddenly we were in front of 12,000, and we killed them. I remember Marty having a tape of the show, and it sounded so perfect – we did a monstrous 'Frankenstein'!

We really gave it our all – we were just a bunch of kids, suddenly playing with these professional musicians who'd been doing it for years and years and years, whereas we were still learning our craft, but we were up there with them and afterwards we were introduced to Princess Margaret, who was the patron of the Spastics Society charity.

The other shows were a mixed bag. The Kevin Ayers gig in Leicester was a good one; the audience was very different to what we were used to, but they knew about us from *Melody Maker*, and they seemed intent upon enjoying it. But the Speakeasy in London wasn't so enjoyable; the audience was primarily drunken journalists and industry suits, whose attitude seemed to be "What the fuck is this?" It was a struggle.

We played with Status Quo at Imperial College, and that's where Mick Jagger came to see us, scouting us for the Stones' own label. We looked fantastic that night; I remember I was wearing the white pants with the red polka dots, but he passed on us with that famous quote, "Their lead singer, I saw 'er and I just didn't think much of it at all."

I think he just didn't like David. The guy's not mimicking him, but they looked similar, and the press were calling David the new Mick Jagger, so two performers like that on the same label would never have worked. I remember Marty being very distraught; he'd spent a lot of the evening talking with Jagger, and now – "Oh shit, there's another one that's passed on us." It would have been a blast to be on Rolling Stones Records.

We did get a few offers. Marty went to meet Richard Branson who was just getting Virgin started; they sat around on Branson's boat, wining and dining, smoking cigars and sipping cognac, and Branson offered him $4,000 for us. Marty turned him down.

The Who were also interested, but they didn't offer too much either, and if you had to pick a moment in the Dolls history when things went wrong, that was it. If we had had a British label, and maybe even based ourselves in London, things would have been very, very different. But Marty and his partners saw us as the golden goose – $4,000 to them, as David would put it, was "chump change". They were holding out for a hundred times that amount. At least.

The irony is, of course, that six months later Branson had a shit load of money coming in from *Tubular Bells*, and we'd have been in on the ground floor not only for everything that happened once punk started, but before that as well. I'm not saying we'd have been welcomed into every home in the country, but I guarantee we'd have got into more than we ever did in America.

All the while, though, poor Billy was getting sicker – he actually threw up on his drums during the Kevin Ayers gig, but he kept going, so it was a relief for all of us when we found a break in the schedule, during which we could just relax before the last few gigs.

We attended a few parties, we saw a few shows, and we did an awful lot of shopping. One afternoon we descended *en masse* on Malcolm and Vivienne's shop; Billy and I spent some time with Margo and her new husband. And one of The Who's managers, Kit Lambert, wrangled us invitations to a massive society party being thrown by Lord Montagu at his stately home in Beaulieu.

David was the star of the show; His Lordship even dispatched a chauffeur-driven Rolls-Royce to collect him. Unfortunately, David was still getting ready when it arrived, so Johnny and Janice, Billy, Arthur, and myself and Valerie piled in instead, and left our singer to make his own way down there. Which he did, several hours and a fuming temper later. In fact, I'd never seen him get so mad.

"That was my car! How dare you?"

Of course, we laughed him off. "Fuck you, we're all in this together." But he wouldn't let it go, and what it confirmed to me more than anything else was a subtle shift in the dynamic of the band. Once, we *had* all been in this together. But now, in his mind, and maybe management's too (in fact, certainly in management's), that was not the case any longer. In other words, "It doesn't matter what I say in front of you. *I'm* calling the shots."

Well, not on this occasion.

The party was out of this world. The gardens were gorgeous, the house was amazing, and the guest list was spectacular. Liberace was there. Rod Stewart. Sal Mineo, who has to be one of my favourite movie stars ever. I can't even begin to tell you the ones I didn't recognise, but they were the best of the best, the richest of the rich.

So we're drinking, smoking, saying hello to people, and there were drugs everywhere. People wandering around practically naked. And everything lit by candles, hundreds and hundreds of them. What a night. Even Billy seemed to have perked up.

It was the lull before the storm.

Back in London, we were all sitting down for breakfast when Billy and David suddenly got into an argument – I think David was laying down the rules a little bit too strongly, and Billy wasn't having it. To make matters worse, he was with a couple of girls he'd met, and David knew as well as the rest of us, you don't lay into somebody like that in front of strangers. Yes, shit comes out of everyone's mouth, that maybe they learned on the streets of New York, but do us a favour. Leave it there.

Billy had had enough. He got up and walked out; I followed him, trying to calm him down, when he turned to me with a big grin and pulled a handful of pills out of his shirt pocket. Apparently, all night long at the party, people had been handing him Mandrax. "But I was smart," he laughed. "I only took half of them." And sure enough, each of those tablets had been broken in half.

That night, Billy Doll passed away. And something went out of the New York Dolls too.

Of the five of us, Billy was probably the one who kept things together. He had a very sharp sense of business, and he had a spot-on sense of right and wrong, too. He was also the shyest of us all, although that didn't stop him from having a constant stream of the most gorgeous girlfriends. But there was also the belief that, if we were talking about something and Billy didn't say anything, then it meant his opinion was probably worth listening to.

Another thing. Billy was not a big drug user. None of us were at that time, unless you count marijuana and alcohol (which we didn't), but Billy less than anybody.

There were drugs all over the New York scene, but we weren't interested. We'd been smoking dope since 1964. We'd taken acid. Cocaine occasionally. But we never touched downers or uppers.

Speed? No thanks. The occasional sniff of coke notwithstanding, I hated anything that made me feel nervous. Johnny dabbled in downers, but they just made you sound dopey – we used to call them goofballs, because that's what they turned you into. There were a lot of people around us taking things like that, and a lot of people trying to get through to us by offering us all manner of stuff. But we always turned them down because they make you miss out on everything else that is happening. Who wants to hang out like that?

What I'm saying is that what happened to Billy was not a part of his lifestyle.

His stomach was still bothering him, I know that. His argument with David, too. I also know that Mandrax is a sneaky bastard of a drug, hanging around in your system long after you think it's worn off.

Whatever happened, Arthur, Valerie and I were up in my hotel room when we got a call from Roy Fisher. Meet everybody down in the lobby right now.

We got there and everyone was waiting – Marty, David, Johnny and Janice, everyone except …

"Something's happened. It's Billy."

We were given an address, right off the Cromwell Road, behind the Royal Albert Hall, and somebody hailed a couple of taxis; Johnny and Janice and some of the others in one, Valerie and I in the next one.

We pulled up at the address just as Johnny came down the stairs. He blocked my path. "Sylvain, don't even go up there. Don't go up there."

I wouldn't listen. "No, I have to." Billy was my brother, my best friend, my only friend. I'd known him for what felt like my entire life, and several lifetimes beyond that. For fuck's sake, we learned 'Wipe Out' together!

Johnny wouldn't let go. "No, please don't." He just held me and that's when we both busted out, we just cried and cried and cried.

Roy Fisher arrived. David, too. None of us could believe it.

What had happened? Billy had passed out. The girls he was with tried to revive him, but they couldn't. It wasn't their fault, it was nobody's fault. It was just a terrible, terrible accident and, for me, it was the worst thing ever.

An ambulance arrived. They took Billy away. I never even saw his body. Then Roy gathered us all together, took us to his house, and he got us drunk. I swear to God, we walked in and Roy busted out this unopened bottle of whiskey and bang. In about ten minutes that baby was gone and he was going out to get another one. We all hugged each other, we couldn't believe it, it was so devastating, and we were so far from home …

First thing the following morning, Marty put us on the first plane back to New York. Scotland Yard was starting to ask questions, and though we didn't have the answers … nobody did, because there weren't any … he didn't want us put through that mill.

We landed; we went home. And that was the end of that. Except it wasn't.

Somebody had to inform Billy's family. I said I would do it, because I'd known them the longest, and that was just as devastating as his death. Billy's mom had come all the way from Colombia, only to lose her youngest son. He was laid to rest up in the Bronx. His tombstone says "Billy Doll Murcia, drummer with the New York Dolls." It has a pair of drumsticks on it.

David's page from my scrapbook.

Johnny looking sick of it all, as the Dolls wash up at a bowling alley near Detroit, 1974.
DON SORTOR.

Johnny and I in the third floor dressing room at Max's, summer 1973.
TOSHI MATSUO.

The Dolls' last ever New York shows, 1975.

The Flying Machine, Florida, where the Dolls played in 1975.

In A&R Studios recording *Too Much Too Soon* in 1974. Johnny had been trying to get his hands on my Gretsch 1959 white Falcon for months, and the moment I went to the bathroom, he pounced. I'm telling him it's way too much for him to handle.

David and I in Kyoto, Japan, 1975. My guitar became known as the Lawsuit, after Gibson sued over the Flying V design.

BOB GRUEN.

David and I flash our tushes to Toshi, shortly after returning from Florida in 1975.
TOSHI MATSUO.

FOR IMMEDIATE RELEASE
FROM THE PEOPLE WHO BROUGHT YOU
"TOO MUCH TOO SOON"

WHAT ARE THE POLITICS OF BOREDOM? BETTER RED THAN DEAD.

Contrary to the vicious lies from the offices of Leber, Krebs and Thau, our former "paper tiger" management, the New York Dolls have not disbanded, and after having completed the first Red, 3-D Rock N' Roll movie entitled "Trash" have, in fact, assumed the role of the "Peoples' Information Collective" in direct association with the Red Guard.

This incarnation entitled "Red Patent Leather" will commence on Friday, February 28th at 10 P.M. continuing on Saturday at 9 and 11 P.M. followed by a Sunday matinee at 5 P.M. for our high school friends at The Little Hippodrome--227 E. 56th St. between 2nd and 3rd.

This show is in coordination with The Dolls' very special "entente cordiale" with the Peoples Republic of China.

NEW YORK DOLLS
produced by Sex originals of London
c/o Malcolm McLaren
New York--212-675-0855

New York Dolls

OVE: Malcolm's infamous Politics of Boredom manifesto, 1975. I didn't agree with a word of it.
LOW: The red vinyl pressing of the *Red Patent Leather* live album. SYLVAIN SYLVAIN

Between songs at the Radio Luxembourg Paris performance of the 1973 New York Dolls European tour.
VEUIGE/DALLE

Chapter 18

IF YOU DON'T BELIEVE ME, ASK THE MONKEY

There was never any question about whether or not the New York Dolls would continue. We had to keep on. Billy would not have had it any other way: "I didn't devote two years of my life to the group for you to break up the first time something goes wrong."

Insanely, he and I had even talked about something like this happening … not in some deep, profound way, and I'm not saying he came over all prophetic one night. But we were chatting about musicians we knew, and people we liked, and players we admired, and it was in that context that Billy told me exactly what we needed to do.

"If I ever die," he told me, "Jerry Nolan is the drummer."

Everybody loves you when you're dead. Before Billy died, yeah, they wrote about us here and there. After Billy died, forget it, we were all over the place. And now we were definitely going to get signed.

There was a lot of beautiful, beautiful things said; Ray Davies in, I think, *Melody Maker*; and, of course, David Bowie in the song 'Time', on his very next LP, *Aladdin Sane*.

Things like that, too, told us we had to keep going.

We closed 1972 with auditions. Marc Bell of Dust was one we tried out, and Peter Criss, of Kiss. But Jerry Nolan was always at the top of our list, even before he came down to play with us and blew all the competition away.

We already knew him. His band Shaker had been on the bill when we played the opening party for Jackie Curtis's *Invitation Beyond The Valley* at the Hotel Diplomat, back in May. But even before that, the first musician Billy and I ever played with, who was destined to become a New York Doll, was Jerry Nolan, back in 1965 or so.

Jerry and his bass-playing best friend Gregory, a Haitian guy, lived in Queens and they were a lot better than us; even then, Jerry could have been in any group he wanted. He was the perfect session musician; he knew his shit, and he had been out there already. But I know he loved Billy and me. We may not have been as talented as Jerry and Gregory, but the thing with us was we could invent. We would improvise and we weren't afraid to enter the danger zone.

And guess who Jerry was going out with at the time? A young upcoming singer, a student at the music and arts school, name of Bette Midler. And a few months after Jerry joined the Dolls, we were at the NBC Studios in Burbank to play *The Midnight Special*, when suddenly somebody started calling Jerry's name from the other end of the corridor.

He turned around and it was Bette, on her way to do the Johnny Carson show that same night. She came hurtling down the hallway, threw herself into Jerry's arms for a huge hug and a kiss, and we could hear Jerry chuckling from where we were standing.

Even stranger; later that same day I bumped into Ellen Croner again. Her boyfriend was in Bette's band.

I was the one who called Jerry to tell him he was in the New York Dolls, a few days before we played the Mercer on December 14, 1972, and he was so happy. So was I. Jerry was left-handed, which meant he always played a little behind the beat, and I loved that. Even today, I ask my drummers to play just a little behind, because it sounds so sensational.

Of course I still missed Billy, missed knowing he was behind us no matter what we were playing or doing. But Jerry was the next best thing, and he took the New York Dolls into a whole new dimension.

'Trash' was the first song I wrote after Billy died. David did the lyrics, of course, but, for me, that song epitomised both what we had lost and what we had gained. The New York Dolls had always looked towards the future. 'Trash' was the sound of looking towards *our* future, in the belief that the two things were one and the same.

We still had the playing field to ourselves. A lot of the history from this period has been telescoped – people think of Max's and they think of all the people who appeared on those *Live At Max's* albums, people like Cherry Vanilla, Wayne County and The Backstreet Boys, The Fast, Philip Rambow and the rest of the crew.

But they all came later. Wayne was already doing a lot of DJ work, but now he had Queen Elizabeth as well, who opened for us at the Mercer's New Year's party, alongside Ruby & The Roughnecks, The Magic Tramps and what was then an unknown Boston band called The Modern Lovers, with the young, wired and weird Jonathan Richman already writing songs like 'Roadrunner' and 'Pablo Picasso'. But when we first started playing Max's, and for a long time afterwards, we were it as far as local headline material went.

That's why I say we opened the door to all that was to follow – people came to see us because we were the only thing to go and see. Suicide were playing around a little more, but even that was down to us because, beforehand, nobody beyond the Mercer would touch them. Or afterwards, for that matter: it would be 1976 before Suicide were picked up by a label, by which time we'd been gone for two years. And who signed them? Marty Thau.

We inspired so many people to start their own bands, and I'm not being conceited when I say that. The history books agree with me. They'd see us and think, "Well, if these schmucks can do it, anyone can." In fact, the future Tommy and Joey Ramone came to see us when we played at the Hotel Diplomat; they were just a couple of high school brats from Queens, but someone overheard Tommy talking: "See these guys? Look at them! They can't fucking play and that's why we can do it too."

On the other side of the coin, of course, there are the groups who saw what we were doing and decided that they wanted to grab a piece for themselves, and the biggest examples of that are Kiss and Aerosmith. Make-up was the hot new thing, and suddenly industry people were picking up these bands and saying, "Hey, you got to wear the make-up, it'll get you in *Rolling Stone*."

Todd Rundgren, for instance, when he appeared on *Midnight Special* looking like I don't know what. The Edgar Winter Group, too. Our song 'Frankenstein', if you look at the album jacket, is called 'Frankenstein (Original)' and that's because the Edgar Winter Group came up with their own song, 'Frankenstein', and didn't even write any lyrics to it! It was an instrumental that they could have called anything on earth. But then you look at the album cover and there's Edgar looking supremely awkward with the make-up and the clothes, and what's the title of the record? *They Only Come Out At Night.*

So no, it didn't always work. You'd see photographs of different bands and they would be looking so ashamed of themselves. But they still did it. In fact, I can imagine them sitting in the office, with management telling them, "If you go gay, you'll be the big thing."

"But I'm not gay," they'd reply, but management would just shrug. "Don't worry, we can make you look like you are." Which is how Kiss started; they wore the make-up but they took out the sex, so people didn't feel threatened by them. But I will never forget going to see them at the Hotel Diplomat and overhearing Peter Criss's mother asking him why they wore all the make-up.

"Because of the New York Dolls," he replied.

Valerie and I had broken up by now, and I was back to playing the field, as my mom might have put it. So when I bumped into Elda again one night, my only thought was to get her into one of the telephone booths and have sex. Well, from what I'd heard, everyone else had.

Instead, with a quick hug to say hello, she said, "I hear you write songs?"

"Yeah" ... not quite the reunion I was expecting, but no matter.

"I write as well," she continued, and proceeded to tell me that she'd just finished a new song called 'I Left My Wednesday Panties In Passaic, Passaic, New Jersey'. How could I resist? "Well, let's have a look at it." *Then* we had sex in one of the telephone booths.

Back at her apartment ... I think she may have sung me the song that night. But we had a lot of other catching up to do too, and when she heard that I was basically homeless at the time, she thought nothing of inviting me to stay.

She lived in what was called a railroad apartment, way up on the top floor of a brownstone on First, between 11th and 12th. It was perfect, especially during the summer – we were just a short flight of stairs away from the flat roof, where we used to go to sunbathe. Johnny called it Tar Beach, and that was appropriate. On a hot day, everything you put on the ground would wind up with little black spots of tar all over it.

Railroad apartments are so called because the rooms just follow one after the other, like a railroad carriage. In this one, the first room you came to was the kitchen, and that's where the bath tub was as well, with a metal plate on top so you could use it as counter space.

I cannot begin to tell you everything Elda taught me. She was working at Warhol's Factory at the time, over on Union Square Park. It was an interesting job because Warhol never paid anybody a wage. Instead, if they complained, he'd give them one of his art works. I think his attitude was, I'm making you a star, that's enough; and, looking back, I wonder if a little of that magic didn't wear off on Elda. Because she completely reshaped my brain, and the way I looked at the world. Not just because she introduced me to The Velvet Underground; I mean everything about life and art and New York.

It was Elda who taught me to get up early on Wednesdays, because that was garbage day, and you needed to check out what people were dumping. You could find all manner of things – clothes, furniture, good shit that people were throwing out, so we'd be out at 7.30am, just gathering stuff, and there'd be people from the antiques store, and vintage places, and they'd be out as well. Later on, this would become eBay!

It was Elda who introduced me to The Velvet Underground. I'd been aware of them in the past, but now I came to truly love them. She had a funky little record player in there, and that's all she ever used to play. The Velvet Underground: the first album, the second, the third, the fourth, and then back to the first.

And it was Elda who really immersed me in Max's. Of course we were already playing there, but there was also the sense that we were still finding our way, gatecrashing somebody else's party. Billy and I being banned proved that; the prohibition had since been lifted, of course, but it would never have fallen in the first place if we'd not still be seen as outsiders.

But Elda was a part of the scene, and now I became a part of it as well. We'd start the evening sitting and listening to The Velvet Underground; and, when it was finished, we'd play more Velvet Underground. Then, when we were done, we'd go to Max's, and straight into the back room where all the action was. Sometimes Warhol would show up, but not really ... the whole thing was, "He might come tonight." Lou Reed would be there, but of course I'd already met him, Iggy Pop, John Cale, whoever. But it wasn't the "stars" who made the back room what it was; it was the sheer freedom that it represented.

The back room was everything you have ever heard, with all manner of crazy things taking place. Crazy, but beautiful. And very, very innocent. Not crazy to be crazy.

Eric Emerson would be there, wearing the silver hot pants that Iggy Pop later borrowed. Up he'd get, dancing on the table, and then down would come his pants and he'd whip it out and begin masturbating a big hard-on.

There were people having sex in the phone booths; in fact, I'd got good at that myself. But that was out of sight, in a way. The real action took place in full view of everyone, including a lot that you could probably only ever do in the back room.

Max's was paradise, and it was a wonderful place to eat as well, especially if you were a starving musician. Every day at happy hour, Mickey Ruskin would bring out a couple of trays of barbecued chicken wings, place them on the bar, and everything was free so long as you were drinking.

Two bucks would buy you a beer, and I used to go there with Arthur Kane all the time, because boy, he had an appetite. We'd get there as early as we could, and there were some days, even weeks, when we ate nothing but Mickey's barbecued chicken wings.

Elda knew everybody. She had the most amazing circle of friends; the entire Warhol circus was forever in and out of the apartment – Jackie Curtis and Candy Darling, Joe Dallesandro and my favourite of them all, the most wonderful person I ever met, who I remembered from the movie *Trash* which I saw back in 1970 … Holly Woodlawn.

If you haven't already, read Holly's book *A Low Life In High Heels.* It's incredible. If you look at the struggles that the gay community has today, back then it was far, far worse. They were shunned by everybody, from work, from stores, everywhere. But Holly just brushed it off, and I cannot stress how amazing she was, how intelligent, how creative, and what a survivor.

Holly, her friend Douglas and her brother Eddie would come over; we'd sit in the kitchen listening to records, and I was like a sponge in the bath, absorbing everything they said or did, and then that would feed back into our music and stage show. For example, if I thought we, the Dolls, were flamboyant, Holly taught me that we'd not even got started.

In later days – say Arthur and I needed to go out to the supermarket – we would take hours getting dressed up first. Holly is who I learned that from, because she was incredible, and the most unbiased, uninhibited person I have ever met. And believe me, you need an example like that in your life, somebody who is forever screaming "You gotta do what you want" when you're standing at the deli counter buying some soup, and the guy behind you says, "The things you see when you ain't got a rifle."

The other thing about Elda was that she had a heart of absolute gold. She was always willing to do favours for other people. Such as the time another of the Warhol crowd, a big guy named Tony, all beard and Hawaiian shirts, asked if she would mind taking care of his dog while he went on vacation. He offered her $25 a week.

Naturally, she said yes, and that is how we wound up with the Beast.

The Beast was an enormous black and white Great Dane, who looked more like a pinto horse than any dog I had ever encountered. He was big enough that when Elda was at work, sometimes, I'd dress little Branch up as a cowboy and sit him on the Beast's back, clinging onto the dog's collar while the Beast growled and bucked and shook his head, sending waves of saliva lashing around the room and smacking you in the face.

He was the most playful dog, but because of his size – he could barely get down the stairs – he'd fall half the way and drag me with him. When he wanted to go out, everybody knew, because if he took a shit in the house you'd have to fumigate the entire block. And once, when he got excited, his tail was wagging so fast and so hard that he actually broke the glass in one of the windows.

We wrestled him to the vets, which was an experience in itself, then back home he came with his tail all bandaged up – which meant it was even heavier and harder now than before. It was like a vast white mallet and when he swung it at you, bam! He'd hit your knee and you'd be down on the floor, with a monstrous mouth breathing dog breath in your face and half-drowning you in slobber.

I loved that dog. But we weren't too sad when Tony returned home.

We had other guests, but human ones this time. Most of the Max's crew would wind up crashing at Elda's for a night or two; several times, I'd get home from somewhere and Patti Smith would be sitting there, reading poetry to whoever was around.

Holly and Douglas even moved in with us for a time – a period which included the night that Elda and I were awakened by voices and laughter coming from the kitchen. We walked down there to discover that Holly and Douglas had dragged Nureyev, the ballet dancer, home with them!

The New York Dolls audience expanded with our name – if you watch Bob Gruen's home movies, which have been released on DVD, 1973 is when you start seeing a lot of very straight-looking people coming to our shows. The freaks were there still, but they were getting sidelined by the people who didn't dress up so much, but still wanted to have a good time. We gave it to them.

We were *the* Max's band, the biggest draw Mickey had seen in years. We were even hanging there when we weren't playing, and that became a draw as well. When I first started visiting the club, the question on everyone's lips was always, "Do you think Andy will be here tonight?" – meaning Warhol. Now it was, "Do you think the Dolls will show up?"

In fact, when people started complaining that Max's was changing, I have to hold my hand up and accept at least a little of the collective responsibility.

The "rock stars" started coming in and the drag queens left, because it was getting too lame; and, in a way, it was our fault, the Dolls' fault, not because we broke up their monopoly by bringing in the next generation that was going to make it, but because it was now our name that gave Max's its public notoriety. Suddenly all manner of people – trash-hungry journalists, sensation-seeking hangers-on and camera-toting tourists – were pouring in there, simply to see (or participate in) the outrage. It was like any scene that explodes into the public eye. The original purity is crushed beneath the weight of the common herd, and it can never be restored.

While it lasted, though, we felt like kings, and these people were our subjects. Of course they wondered if we were there. To them, the New York Dolls *were* Max's Kansas City.

We rarely disappointed them, either; or, at least, Arthur and I rarely did, although you might have to turn up early to see us. Every happy hour, there we'd be, with our $2 for a drink, to devour those stupid chicken wings. But the chances were we'd be back again later, because that's where all our friends were. Maybe, this is another of those moments that we can all look back on and think, "If only things had been different."

We were gigging a lot. But we were also partying a lot. So when did we rehearse? When did we write songs? Looking back at our repertoire, at least so far as our two albums are concerned, and with the exception of 'Trash' and one or two others, every significant song we recorded had already been written before Billy died.

One song that did emerge from this period was 'Lone Star Queen', although I have to confess, it was something of an accident.

If you listen to one of our live shows, and there's a lot that were taped, you'll realise that Johnny spent an inordinate amount of time tuning his guitar. Ba-ding, ba-dong, he'll be going, trying to get it right, but the G is in and now the B is out, then he realises the G was a little high, so he goes back to the D, and on and on and on.

Which is where David and I would start jamming on other songs, me improvising a riff, him making up lyrics on the spot. And one night we came out with what became 'Lone Star Queen'. Listen to the tape and you can hear Johnny in the background, still tuning. There's also a recording up on YouTube, and the whole thing is Johnny tuning up. It's funny as shit.

The thing with Johnny, though, and I've mentioned this before, is that he wanted everyone to think he was the Jeff Beck of the Dolls and he wasn't, and it confused him. But his ego was so big – if someone congratulated him for a solo, he'd take the credit, even if I was the one who played it. Even if I was sitting right next to him at the time.

Just like he said way back when, he was the lead guitar player, and I was the rhythm, and people went along with that. Not the rest of the band so much, but fans, journalists, the reference books.

That chipped my confidence. It really hurt when I realised it didn't matter what I played, or how well I played, Johnny would be the one who took the credit. Just like it didn't matter what I wrote, he and David would get the songwriting credits, *not* because they demanded them but because, when we gave a new song to management, whatever we said about its authorship would fly out of the window, and they'd credit it to Johansen/Thunders.

Occasionally I'd speak out, but to no avail; in management's eyes, and maybe even my bandmates, I was being a troublemaker, and my own questions and objections would be lost beneath the most irrelevant details. Or someone would turn around and say, "Forget it, you're going to be so rich!" And that gets to you after a while, until I wouldn't say something because, if I did, I felt like I'd be kicked out of my own group. It was only much later on, in the eighties, that Johnny started telling people I taught him everything he knew, and even then, people would march on up and ask if it was true, as if they knew for certain that it wasn't.

The band was folding in on itself, but it is only with hindsight that this became apparent. At the time, we were too busy *being* the New York Dolls to even begin to worry *about* the New York Dolls. We didn't even notice that, no matter how much press attention we were receiving, we had only ever played in two cities. And one of them was on the other side of the Atlantic.

Yes, we did Long Island and Brooklyn and places like that, but the furthest afield we had ventured, in early 1973, was Boston. America is a massive country and it didn't have a clue about us. Our pictures were in the magazines, *Rock Scene* and *Creem* and so on, but unless you'd ever visited Manhattan, you wouldn't have a clue what we sounded like.

Even in New York, our circuit was limited. The only places we played regularly were Max's, the Mercer and an Upper East Side club called Kenny's Castaways, where we headlined twelve nights in succession in January/February 1973, and where Bowie dropped by to see us again.

But I wouldn't change anything that happened, not in the studio, not on the road, anywhere. Because, if I could have changed anything, then everything else wouldn't have been allowed to happen. Throughout the time we were together, and particularly towards the end, people constantly tried to change *us* – management, from the moment we signed with them; our record label, once we finally found one; even some of our fans, they all had ideas of what we should do.

Everyone had an agenda, a business angle, a get-rich scheme. "Don't be this fruity." "Don't take that drug." Girlfriends who would walk out, saying, "Well, you were hot last month, but now you're not," or "You were hot last year but now your guitar player is hotter." And all the while, the press were telling us how badly we sucked, and how we shouldn't be playing, shouldn't be writing, shouldn't be tuning up for half an hour. *Creem* magazine once voted us the best new band of the year and the worst new band *in the same poll*! So we took out an ad, same picture above and below, one captioned "the best" and the other "the worst".

Johnny's apartment was our go-to place after an evening at Max's. We'd left the loft at Christie Street by now, so Johnny (and Billy at the time) found a two bedroom on 14th Street between Second and Third. After Billy died, Johnny stayed on. That's where we used to watch the late-night movies, and the early ones too, and he always had pets around. Dogs mainly, but he was very open to other things as well – we all loved animals, but Johnny being Johnny just had to take it to the next step. He decided to get a monkey.

New York was littered with pet shops at that time, mostly selling fish because they were probably the easiest creature to look after in the city. But there were exotic birds and other things, and this one store had a spider monkey. And that beast was really clever.

The first cage Johnny got for him, the monkey figured out immediately. We all grew quite accustomed to waking up in the morning, with whatever guest we might have come back with, and there'd be the monkey watching everything we did. So Johnny went down to the hardware store and picked up a big roll of chicken wire and a couple of two by fours, and he proceeded to rig up a cage, right next to the kitchen.

But the monkey figured that out as well. While Johnny was asleep, he got out, and when Johnny awoke, "Where's the fucking monkey man?" The next thing we knew, the monkey was coming down the fire escape into the apartment and in each hand he had three eggs. He was balancing them and making his little monkey noises; he went straight into his cage and started eating them.

Bang bang on the front door. Johnny opened it and was confronted by the Asian woman who lived upstairs. So far as any of us knew, she didn't speak a word of English. But we were wrong. "You little motherfuckers, your monkey broke into my house and stole my eggs!"

Johnny apologised profusely, paid her for the eggs, and swore he would make certain that the monkey never escaped again. Back to the hardware store, more rolls of chicken wire, more two by fours. And out goes the monkey once again, only this time he was found by a couple of Latino kids who demanded $15 before they would return him. Johnny paid.

In the end, Johnny gave the monkey to a friend, and it lived happily ever after. But there was one final drama that played out, the night the car we were in was stopped by a cop. He was just about to launch into his spiel, demanding insurance and licences and so forth, when suddenly he saw something on Johnny's shoulder.

"What's that?"

"It's a monkey."

The cop looked at us, looked at the monkey, and stepped away from the car. He let us go. He didn't want to be the guy who dragged in the kid with the monkey.

One last memory of that apartment: that's where we were first introduced to Miss Connie, who claimed to be a former member of the GTOs, the infamous groupie girl group that Frank Zappa championed, and a whole new piece of New York Dolls folklore was born.

It was the night she and Arthur first met; he brought her back to the apartment, and whatever he intended to happen it somehow got delayed because, first, we all got dressed up in the most ridiculous clothing imaginable, just a bunch of crazy whores who were running around like madmen.

Miss Connie had been wearing a tutu; now Arthur had it on, and that became his signature thing. For a long time, he wouldn't even go on stage unless he was wearing his tutu, and the sight of him cracked the rest of us up for a long time too.

Listen to the one song he wrote for the Dolls' *Private World*, all droney slide and low, deep notes, and now picture him wearing that tutu. He wasn't a small guy, after all, and he wasn't a gentle bass player either. He played with three metal strings and one nylon one, which gave him such a weird sound. And he could break them! You never hear about bassists breaking their strings, but he could. He'd hit them with such conviction that they would just pop. But he wouldn't care; he'd just go further down on one of the others and hit that note anyway.

He always had that expression on his face, too; the one that said, "It is taking everything out of my soul to manufacture that one note for you, ladies and gentlemen."

In a tutu.

A few years later, Captain Sensible of The Damned also took a fancy to tutus, so maybe it's a secret bass player obsession. But I swear, the Captain looked positively balletic alongside the full Killer Kane experience.

Chapter 19

CLOSE YOUR EYES, COS THIS IS GONNA HURT

Management was losing patience; not with us, but with the industry. Here we were, the most talked about rock'n'rollers in the country (even if hardly anyone had heard us), but beyond that couple of offers in England, and some tentative interest from elsewhere, they had yet to receive a single concrete offer for the services of the New York Dolls.

It was time to put on a showcase. Every record company in the country would be invited – and not only that, but the *heads* of every record company in the country. Ahmet Ertegun, David Geffen, Clive Davis, the biggest wheels in the industry would be crammed inside the O'Casey Theater, and all we had to do was put the fear of God up them; or, at least, the knowledge that if they didn't sign us immediately, then somebody else certainly would.

We, the New York Dolls, were dubious, but management laughed our concerns away. The following morning, we were confidently informed, you wouldn't be able to move in the office for offers. Back when Paul Nelson first saw us, a figure of $250,000 had been bandied about – by management, I should clarify, not by Mercury. That, we were assured, was now the minimum they would accept.

It looked like the strategy was going to pay off, too. Everyone accepted their invitation; they all settled into their seats; and, watching from afar, it was clear that they weren't paying their surroundings the remotest attention. Instead, they were all eyeballing one another, to see how they reacted to us.

Badly. Worse than badly. We were dreadful that night, turning in one of the very worst shows we had ever played.

It started when we were in the dressing room. Every show we had ever played in New York – or at least every one we'd played in the last nine months – we'd been dragged to the stage by the sound of the crowd, that hum of expectation that rose to a roar when the audience thought that showtime was approaching, and then erupted as we stepped out on the stage.

Tonight – nothing. Silence. We took the stage. Not a murmur. David said, "Hello." No reply.

We froze. We literally did not know what to do. Every show we had ever played, to friends or strangers, to princes or paupers, and everything in between, we fed off the audience's energy as much as they fed off our's. Just one cheer from the darkness would have made all the difference, but no. So confident was management of making a million bucks, they had forgotten, or neglected, to invite any of our fans. Maybe our girlfriends were there, but of the people who should have been there, the real fans, not one.

It was like playing into a vacuum, an army of middle-aged men in expensive suits looking at us, looking at each other, sniffing cocaine, whatever. Another thing. Most bands when they go on stage, they're fine-tuning their performance. With us, we were just trying to find a tune, and that was a part of our act. That was when the craziness happened. But it only worked if there were people there to go crazy.

These people didn't go crazy. They went, "What the fuck?" You could almost hear their minds working: "They're tuning up? Deep Purple didn't tune up when they auditioned for us." These people were used to the good life. They were already feeling awkward, south of 14th Street; they had probably never been that low before – they'd probably brought their passports.

We started to play and there was nothing. You could hear a pin drop. Somebody moved out of their chair, and we heard it squeak. We'd been nervous to begin with; now we were scared. This was not good.

We kicked off with 'Pills'. Now, the PA at the Mercer was a good PA: Voice of the Theater cabinets and Baldwin amps. But it was intended for a theater; it was not built for a rock'n'roll band to blow the shit out of it.

Which didn't matter if you were playing to people who knew the songs, or wanted to get off on the atmosphere.

It *did* matter in front of a room full of stiffs.

We finished and there was not a single clap. They didn't get 'Pills', they didn't get 'Personality Crisis', they didn't get anything we did. We played all our hits and the only sound from the auditorium was the squeaking growing louder and louder as guest after guest walked out. And that was it. We didn't even need to play any more. They'd all gone.

The only guy left was Paul Nelson from Mercury, and that was no surprise because he was at all our shows, and we knew that he'd tried and tried to persuade the label to pick us up, but they wouldn't. In fact, he was the only person from Mercury who even showed up; nobody else at the label even bothered.

So that was it. We'd played to every record company in America, and every single one of them hated us. Management called us up the next day, and they didn't even need to speak. But they did, anyway, listing everybody who had passed on us, which was everybody in the room. Every single one of them. Three hundred people had been invited to the show, and not one of them liked us.

And then Paul Nelson called. Like I said, the head of Mercury was the only record company chief who didn't show up at the Mercer. Which meant he was the only one who didn't know how awful we were. But Paul had lunch with him that afternoon and I don't know what he said to him. But one of the worst days of our careers so far was suddenly one of the greatest.

The New York Dolls were Mercury Records recording artists.

The first order of business was to record a fresh set of demos. We used a few studios: a disused church on 57th Street, a converted basement in the old fur district; Mercer Street Tapes (nothing to do with the Arts Center); another on Green Street; and maybe more. The CDs that have since been released of those sessions usually credit them to Planet Studios alone, but I'm sure a few tracks came from those other places.

We played everything we knew – all the songs that Johnny and David had written; the ones I'd put together; the ones David brought along when he joined. We played blues songs and oldies, the stuff that I loved, 'Showdown', 'Don't Start Me Talkin'', 'Hoochie Coochie Man'.

We nodded towards the MC5 with a steaming version of 'Back In The USA', a song we only started playing when Jerry joined; and when I heard David kick off 'Looking For A Kiss' with the opening lyric from the Shangri-Las' 'Give Him A Great Big Kiss', I thought, "Well shit, this is perfect," and brought that song into the repertoire as well.

Not everything was intended for immediate use. Paul Nelson wanted to get an idea of what we'd be recording for our first album, but there were songs there that would be held over to the second one, and some we never released during our lifetime. We taped everything.

There were tensions, but they didn't seem that awful. David and Johnny were still working out their star stuff, but they hadn't yet adopted the lifestyle. Hard drugs hadn't raised their heads yet; the serious arguments and overwhelming jealousy were still kept in check. We hadn't yet separated and become isolated. But the tape does capture one telling moment, and I don't even remember what sparked it. It's the sound of David telling Johnny not to be so "attitudical".

The tape was everything we'd hoped for. It was just a take or two of each song, but you could really hear us putting it all together. It wasn't New York's answer to The Rolling Stones any more; we were New York's answer to itself. David and Johnny were just sparking off one another; everything they did was gold. If they had an idea together, they'd fly, and the rest of us would just inject what we could to make it better. The songs were strong, the performance was perfect, everything we had learned had come together.

We had found a new rehearsal space, too, although it was not destined to remain long in our lives. Baggies was on Wooster and Grand, which was almost opposite another loft I had, and it was run by a couple of guys named Night Bob and the Hamster. At least, that's what we called them.

The space was upstairs, and you reached it via one of those old hand-operated elevators. There was a larger room on the floor below, but it was more expensive; plus, upstairs had a billiard table, and downstairs didn't. No decision!

One day during rehearsal, we took a break and an elevator ride to the floor below, where there were some vending machines. We grabbed a beer, grabbed some food and then went back upstairs to discover all our guitars had vanished. Including the Les Paul Custom which I had traded for the Junior that I got from that music shop.

We flew at the Hamster and Night Bob, but they were totally non-plussed. Somebody must have ridden the elevator up and grabbed them, then ridden it back downstairs again. They shrugged, as if to tell us it was our own stupid fault for even bringing our instruments into a district like this.

What could we do? We looked around the place a while, but there were no hiding places that we could see, and we discussed calling the cops, but what would they do? In 1973, the law was too busy busting musicians to worry about them being ripped off by other people. Finally, we left, and we never returned to Baggies. But perhaps I learned one lesson, as the free guitar I got way back when came back to bite me hard. So stay straight, boys and girls.

We were booked to begin recording our first album in earnest in April, and conversation turned to producers. Bowie was mentioned, of course, because he'd seen us so often, and management threw a few other names at us. But it always comes down to who is available, and we were lucky. The best guy for the job had both the time and the right attitude to do it.

Todd Rundgren was one of those people who were captivated by the New York Dolls, and who got caught up in that whole scene, hanging out at Max's almost every time we played; in fact, that's where he met Bebe Buell.

He also knew our material inside out, and he knew the songs were hits. We were adamant that whoever we worked with had to capture the sound of the New York Dolls as we were, not as he heard us, or someone said we should be, and Todd got that.

He even mixed it as though we were on stage; myself on the left side, and Johnny on the right, because that's how important that dynamic was. I don't think he did the best job with the sound on the drums, which was a complaint that Jerry often brought up, and there were other things that could have been done differently as well.

But he encouraged us all to do what we wanted and, for me, that was the piano rhythms and rolls with which I embellish 'Personality Crisis' and 'Private World' (and a few others as well), and the backing vocals, the ooohs and aaaahs that I lifted straight out of the Brill Building sound. We spent so much time on those, bringing them out and up, layering them into a full Wall of Sound.

He also knew the songs that we should present to the world; if you compare the tracks on the final LP with all that we recorded for the demos, we did not take a single false step. Every song on that album was a drop-dead classic, at the time and today. I don't think you could ever have sat the five of us down together and compiled a list of five albums that we all agreed were the finest ever made. But there was one thing we all agreed on. We'd just made the sixth.

Now we had to decorate it.

Mercury had very firm ideas of what the album sleeve should be. One afternoon we were scooped up, made up, and driven to one of the local antique stores, a dark and dusty place full of old furniture, vintage knick-knacks and, absurdly, a lot of moose heads. A photographer was on hand to capture the scene and, a few days later, Marty called me up to his office to look at the proofs.

They were terrible. Somehow, they had contrived to take the most exciting band in the world and drop them into the most boring setting on earth. As much as everyone wants to complain about the album cover that we did eventually use – "And that's why they didn't make it, because they were in drag on the album cover," which I hear over and over again – the cover that Mercury wanted was even worse. To me, later on, it would be like Aerosmith's *Toys In The Attic*, which is not a bad cover for them, but it's not a New York Dolls cover.

I flipped out. "We can't use this, it's horrible!" And poor Marty didn't know what to say because Mercury had spent a fortune on this sleeve, between the photographer and the cost of renting the store for the shoot. But I knew what to do. "Listen, hold on a second, let me make some calls."

I rang Pinky and Diane, the two girls I got arrested with in Puerto Rico. They loved the New York Dolls almost as much as we did, so I explained the situation and they got to work making calls of their own.

They rang back that same afternoon. "We can do it, but we're going to need $1,000." Toshi, a fashion photographer who'd done a string of *Vogue* covers was going to take the pictures in his third-floor loft on 29th Street and Park Avenue South. He, in turn, hired a hairdresser, Shin. A guy named Dave O'Grady was in charge of our make-up, and Bruce, a really flamboyant drag queen who Pinky and Diane knew from somewhere, was handling set design.

Now this sounded more like it.

I called Marty and extracted the promise of $1,000 out of him. Then set out to meet Pinky and Diane.

The first thing we did was sheer good fortune. As we were making our way to Toshi's, we came across an old couch that somebody had dumped on the sidewalk. It looked perfect.

We wrestled it up to his studio and started draping stuff over it – fabrics, scarves, anything we could lay our hands on. Then the others arrived and we started dressing them – I'd bought a bunch of clothes with me ... Jerry, in particular, always needed help getting Doll-ed up, because left to his own devices he could have passed for a member of any band from Foghat to The Faces. He wound up in a sequin jacket that I traded from one of my girlfriends, Lynette Bean.

Arthur wound up looking like the scariest hooker in the world; I was wearing my cowboy sweater and roller skates, and between shots, I'd be skating across Toshi's beautiful hardwood floors. That sweater is now in the Rock and Roll Hall of Fame, by the way.

Johnny looked incredible as usual, and David? Years later, David asked me, with genuine bemusement, "Why did people think I was gay, back in the New York Dolls?" Well, apart from wanting to be the first male rock star with tits, in my silent scream I replied, "Haven't you seen all the pictures, and the Bob Gruen videos?"

We were playing Max's when Toshi arrived with the finished photographs, and immediately Marty knew we'd done the right thing. Everybody loved them, management, the band ... even Mercury were really good about it. Of course, I didn't get the $1,000 they'd promised; they only gave us $900, and that's what I gave to Toshi. He was fine with it, though, and the following day we went down to the Gem Spa to take the back cover shot.

We'd made the album we wanted; we had the sleeve we wanted. Now we had to wait and see if we were what America wanted.

Management decided we needed new equipment. With the album imminent, we had a string of prestigious gigs lined up.

Mott The Hoople were about to launch their latest American tour, and we'd been tapped to open for them. The first show, at the Felt Forum, Madison Square Gardens, was just days away.

Yes, we needed new equipment.

First, Jerry got a new drum kit, the legendary pink kit with matching stool, with the biggest bass drum we had ever seen in rock'n'roll, a twenty-six-inch monster. Then Johnny and I were told to pick up new guitars. There was just one catch. Because Johnny was the lead guitarist, he had $800 to spend. And because I was "only" the rhythm, I had $300.

I confess, I was furious. But I made the most of it, a yellow Les Paul Junior single cutaway with two P-90 pick-ups, which looked and played like a dream. Johnny didn't do too badly either – he went straight down to a store on 48th Street and picked up a Les Paul Black Beauty.

We were rehearsing just down the road from there, at Carol's Music. I was already there when Johnny walked in, trying out my gorgeous new toy, putting it through its paces and revelling in its tone. It sounded so cool, so nasty.

Johnny arrived, watched for a bit, then plugged in the Black Beauty. Still watching me, still trying to figure out how I was getting this amazing sound. Because, try as he might, he couldn't. I don't think he'd been there ten minutes before he finally came out with it: "Sylvain? I'll trade you right now." And that's how I wound up with an $800 Black Beauty, and he went home with a $300 Junior.

The big day arrived. August 3, 1973. The New York Dolls at the Felt Forum. It was the biggest show we had ever played in America, and how did it begin?

The Mercer collapsed.

The place had been teetering for a while; the walls were sagging and there was a huge crack in one of them, which was regularly being plastered over. Then a second crack appeared, and people walking through the place insisted the walls were groaning. Literally groaning.

Builders came in to try to shore it up, but they also removed some of the beams that held up the ground floor. And when one of the express subway trains that passed beneath roared through, the sheer seismic shock of its passage was too much for the old facade.

It was five o'clock – the height of the rush hour – and it took just seconds for all eight floors to be reduced to rubble. People were killed, dust choked the air, Broadway was blocked by bricks and masonry. And I think all of us wondered, privately at least, was it an omen? The Mercer had made us what we were. What would we become with it gone?

Mott The Hoople were the best, not only as a band (that goes without saying) but as people too. Ian Hunter, their singer, in particular became a good friend of the New York Dolls, although the first time he saw us – after the tour had been arranged – he admitted he was glad that we were what we were. "They had songs, they had everything, and they were scary to look at! The first time I ever saw them, I just thought 'Jesus, if they play like they look, they'll destroy us.' Fortunately they didn't, but they weren't far off it."

The first Mott shows were terrifying for us, even more than the Wembley show. Hunter, again, remembered, "Even at the Felt Forum, people were looking at them going, 'What the fuck is that?' And then when we took them out to the Midwest, I remember them actually huddling together, physically, they were fucking scared, they really were. It was difficult for them.

"They were a great band, but their manager let them out of the house too soon. He should have kept them in the house another six months, because they could have been huge. But the manager wanted money, and it was difficult for them, because they were so totally different. Anywhere north of the Bowery even."

We revamped our live set for the tour, kicking off with our arrangement of the theme from *Courageous Cat*, which was a cartoon I used to love when I was a kid. In fact, our version had very little in common with the original; it was a melody I came up with during a rehearsal, and Johnny just took off on it. But it had the same feel, so we thought, "What the hell?" *Courageous Cat* was fabulous.

We were not playing the full Mott tour; we had a bunch of our own shows that we were already committed to and had to fulfil those instead. Not that we were complaining, though. First up was a six-night residency at Max's, and then we were off to Los Angeles to play another five at the Whisky a Go Go. Except it wasn't six gigs, followed by five gigs. It was two shows a night for six nights in New York, and then a further two a night in LA. With two days off in between, that made twenty-two shows in two weeks.

That business about omens, though, was hard to ignore. I forget which night it was, but we were in the midst of the Max's run when I received a 2am call from Mount Sinai Beth Israel Hospital on the Lower East Side. Arthur had been stabbed.

He was still with Miss Connie, the girl who introduced him to his tutu, living in an apartment upstairs from a bar. Home from the gig, and both very drunk, they got into an argument over the upcoming Los Angeles trip – Miss Connie was a native Californian and she wanted to go back there to visit. And, maybe, show off her superstar boyfriend.

Arthur said no. For a start, we were on a tight budget; and besides, you don't take your girlfriend on tour. Well, not unless you were David and Jerry, both of whom would be accompanied by their ladies. But Arthur and Miss Connie went back and forth on this, until finally he fell asleep. At which point, Miss Connie stabbed him in the thumb ... his playing thumb. She severed a tendon and she fucked him up good.

First thing I did was call David: "You've got to come with me." We waited while Arthur was sewn up and his hand was placed in a cast, then we took him back to his apartment.

Miss Connie was smart. She'd split, and now the police were looking for her, because the moment Marty got wind of what was happening, he was straight on the phone to them. Even the hospital had been demanding to know who did it.

But clearly Arthur couldn't play that night – or for a lot of nights to come, and we were so, so fortunate that one of our roadies, Peter Jordan, was also a brilliant bassist. Better than Arthur, in fact. That night at Max's, Peter took the stage with us, and he'd remain on board for the remainder of the New York shows, and then the full California trip too. He's even playing on the *Midnight Special* performance, although you can't see him. Arthur was with us as well, of course, and we weren't going to deprive him of his national television debut. So he stood at the front, still wearing his cast, and did his best to pretend to play, and Peter was behind the amps. He was as much a New York Doll as the rest of us.

The Max's residency was an amazing experience, the peak of our relationship with our home-town crowd. But even while we were on stage, we couldn't wait to get it over with. California occupied our every waking thought. David alone of the New York Dolls had been out there in the past, back in 1967 when he visited San Francisco. For the rest of us, it was uncharted territory.

We had a good idea what we were looking for, though.

In the same way that *Rock Scene* was the big New York music magazine, *Star* was the epitome of LA. We were constantly checking it out, not only to see what groups might be worth paying attention to (of which there really weren't many), but also looking at the girls – again, I suppose you'd call them groupies – who were as big a part of the scene as any musician. And one day Johnny looked up from the latest issue, pointed to one particular beauty, and announced, "When we get to LA, she's going to be my girlfriend."

Her name was Sable Starr.

Star magazine was another friend of the New York Dolls. Our pictures were always in there and, as the gigs grew closer, the magazine went out of its way to prepare Los Angeles for our arrival. All we could talk about was how much LA was going to love us, and first impressions did not let us down.

The welcoming committee was not huge, but it was certainly impressive. Bearing gifts and flowers, we were met by Rodney Bingenheimer, whose already legendary English Disco was one of the first places we wanted to visit, and a handful of girls, including Lori Lightning, whose past conquests allegedly included Jimmy Page and David Bowie … and Johnny's dream come true, Sable Starr.

A couple of limos waited to take us to the Hyatt House hotel and, all the way there, we were like children at a birthday party, pointing out all the sights we'd heard so much about – Tower Records, where the covers of every month's new releases would be painstakingly painted onto the walls, *New York Dolls* included. Grauman's Chinese Theatre. Hollywood High, where the young Phil Spector was a student. The Hollywood sign up in the hills.

It was like an episode of *The Jetsons*, only this was real life. All these places you've heard of all your life, and seen in all those movies, so close that you could touch them. But it also reminded me a lot of Cairo – the weather and the swimming pools and the desert and the big cars … I thought about my mom a lot while I was there.

We'd already started fooling around with the girls in the limos, and once we arrived at the hotel, we paired off – "This one's with me, that one's with you" – and, inevitably, "Sable's with Johnny." And that's how it stayed, the whole time we were out there, to the point where not only were they inseparable, the rest of us referred to them as husband and wife.

They bought each other gifts; the first thing that Sable gave Johnny was a Bohemian doll, with a string coming out of her back. When you pulled it, she said, "Oh, where we going tonight, darling?" He loved it; every time I saw him, he'd be saying, "Hey Sylvain, check out what my doll says."

Meanwhile, the girls were taking us out around the thrift stores and the swap meets, and we picked up so much shit – clothes, records, everything. Johnny bought a load of blue Boy Scout shirts, so short that his belly button was visible; and Sable found me a pair of pink women's knickers with a feather on them. I wore them on stage a lot; I'd put on my tights, then I'd put on the underwear, and I'd top the look off with my black shotgun leather chaps with zippers all the way down.

We went to the English Disco, although it was something of a disappointment; the photographs and articles made it look and sound so glamorous, whereas all it really was was a storefront with darkened windows and one disco ball. But we hung out with Rodney, and we were introduced to Kim Fowley ... oh, and we did some work as well.

The Whisky shows could not have gone any better. For a start, the place was packed every night – it's not huge, but it was big enough, and we didn't simply sell out all ten shows, we could have sold out another twelve on top. At some point during the run, the club's owner told me that the last group who did this much business was Chicago, who had nothing to do with us musically or in any other way, but hearing that made us feel so good.

A lot of the audience had already bought our album so they knew what to expect. But even people who'd not heard us, they'd seen the album and that cover told you all you needed to know. These guys are going to be a good time. And we were.

We crammed so much into that week in LA that it feels as though we were there forever. And life was only to get even better after I discovered that the maid had forgotten to lock the connecting door between my room and the suite next door. A full suite, with a living room, a bedroom and two televisions!

I immediately moved in and made myself completely at home. Poor Paul Nelson, who was also in LA that week, was mortified when he came to my room one day and found I had moved next door. "Holy shit, this has *got* to be illegal." And maybe it was. But I'll tell you this. When we got kicked out of the Hyatt House, which happened just a day or two later, it had nothing to do with me switching rooms. Something else happened, and I never did find out what. Although I doubt that it was as sensational as the reason we were evicted from our next port of call, the Ramada Inn just down the road.

As rock'n'roll party places go, the Ramada was certainly a few steps down from the Hyatt House, which was not nicknamed the Riot House for nothing. In fact, it's more the sort of place you stay when mom and dad are taking you on a road trip some place. Staid, quiet, comfortable.

Exactly the sort of place that would not want the New York Dolls moving in *en masse*, and converting a little corner of Hollywood into a slice of New York ... namely the Chelsea Hotel, at the height of its decadent infamy.

Our entire stay was a non-stop party, and one of the wildest, craziest, that we ever had. Our entire entourage was placed on the ground floor, right beside the swimming pool, so all night long we'd be running from room to room, slamming doors, leaping into the water. With hindsight, it really was only a matter of time before somebody, and I'm thinking now of Arthur, wandered into the laundry room and emerged with as many boxes of detergent that they could possibly carry. All of which were then emptied into the pool.

There were bubbles everywhere, particularly after we all jumped in and began splashing around in the water. I heard later that they had to drain the pool and give it a thorough cleaning. But we'd been evicted long before that.

We did not party alone, of course. Any number of people were invited along to join us, Kim Fowley among them, and Shaun Cassidy, younger brother of teen idol David, too. Sable brought her sister Coral along, and she brought along her boyfriend, Iggy Pop.

Iggy wasn't having a good time of things back then. His new album, *Raw Power*, had just been released, but it had already sunk like a stone, and though he and James Williamson were looking for gigs, they weren't finding any. They had a place on Mulholland Drive, paid for by their management (Tony Defries), and Leee Black Childers was staying there with them, as a kind of babysitter.

They were so bored, though, which means we were like a beacon in the darkness. And each of us, in turn, went home with a favourite Iggy anecdote.

Mine ... well, I'm not sure that it is a favourite. But here goes. One evening, Arthur and Iggy got together, and the next morning he's telling me how Iggy taught him this new thing called a plate job ... which he then proceeded to explain to me in vivid, lurid detail.

What he didn't know was that I had already encountered such a thing – it was performed on stage in *Pork*, although there, I believe, the link between the naked man with a plate on his chest, and the woman crouching above him was some well-positioned dog food. Arthur's experience appears to have involved something far more organic and, having said that, I never want to talk about it again.

Something else happened in Los Angeles, though, that would have far greater ramifications for the New York Dolls. The night Coral, Iggy and maybe one or two of their friends gathered together in Johnny's hotel room and ... .

I didn't see it, I wasn't there and, to this day, I don't know what happened. But Johnny walked into that hotel room completely clean, and he came out with a needle. And Johnny being Johnny ... I flashed back to the first time he tried some pot, and how the next day he had a pound of the stuff. Or the first time he experienced acid and the same thing. He was an instant convert.

It was the same now. Only heroin isn't acid or pot. They give you a high; heroin gives you a lifestyle and it's not one you would wish on your worst enemy. It became his first love and only love. Not music, not clothes, not girls. All he cared about was chasing the first heroin high he ever experienced, which of course is an impossible dream. But you keep on trying, regardless.

After the New York Dolls ended, I'm the only member of the band who played with all of them ... I played with David, I had a group with Jerry, I worked with Arthur and produced a couple of records for him, and I played with Johnny. And I could see the difference heroin made.

For a while he had that junkie cool thing going, and he still does as far as a lot of people are concerned. But starting that moment in Los Angeles, things began to change. They began to get dark, and they began to get a little more egotistical: "I can do this on my own, I don't need anyone to tell me what to do." Heroin changed his lyrics, it changed his performance, it changed his time-keeping, it changed his mood. Everything.

It changed a lot of people's lives as well, the ones who saw him and wanted a piece of whatever he had. Because, like Johnny and – soon after – Jerry, many of them are no longer with us.

Chapter 20

WOULD YOU DO THIS TO ELVIS?

From Los Angeles, we travelled up to San Francisco to play the Matrix, with a new local act called The Tubes opening for us.

What a performance! They just blew me away; they were so tight and so inventive and they put every other showman of the age to shame. Even today, I regularly visit YouTube to watch vintage film of them performing 'White Punks On Dope', and though neither their music nor their act had anything in common with what we were doing, I know there was a common lineage, the same love for theatre and sixties pop that set us on our way.

There again, San Francisco itself was like that. Los Angeles is the most glorious playground in the world, but you need to dig really deep to discover its true self, past the layers and layers of glamour and sheen that have been plastered across it over the years.

In San Francisco, the underground was above ground, in the stores and clubs, the restaurants and the night haunts. True rock'n'roll takes root where life is at its sleaziest, and walking down Broadway – that was sleazy. Our first day there, we had just finished the soundcheck and walked out onto the street and directly in front of us was a freaky-looking long hair, dressed as a wizard crossed with Jesus Christ. He looked like he'd been living in the woods for a week.

"Johnny Thunders!" he was shouting. "Sylvain Sylvain!" We looked at one another and said, "Shit, is this our audience?" Then we looked back at the venue, which was also a Chinese restaurant and said, "And is this where we're playing?"

I love that city.

Back to Los Angeles for more madness. We'd been booked onto the *Midnight Special*, which was probably the biggest music television show of the time. I'm not sure how much I enjoyed it, though, because sometime between landing in LA and arriving at the studios, I'd come down with what I liked to call the Hong Kong flu … the sexual Hong Kong flu. And to make matters worse, I'd only been with one or two girls.

Sable, I think, pointed me towards a doctor on Wilshire Boulevard who was familiar with both my profession and my complaint – which may or may not explain why the first thing I saw when I walked in there was a signed photograph of Michael Jackson. The kid had only just turned sixteen at the time!

Sable was right, though; the doctor knew exactly what was going on. In fact, the first thing he said to me was, "Why didn't you ask her to just give you a blow job?" Then he jammed me up with so much damn penicillin that by the time we got to Burbank I felt as though I was dying. Either that or going through the menopause. Cold sweat, hot flushes, the lot.

Literally, I was begging for mercy, and Frenchie, who we'd hired as our valet, was an angel. He found me an empty dressing room so I could rest undisturbed; he brought me blankets, he massaged me, he saved my life … but if you watch that performance, I look like I haven't washed or changed clothes for days, and that's why. I swear I grew a beard in about half an hour.

I was playing the Flying V guitar, and it looked good. But in truth, the New York Dolls were down two men that afternoon; first Arthur, nursing his thumb, now me, and in a way, that's *why* I was playing that guitar. It used to be Johnny's, and, as usual, I got it through another of our trades. And the only reason I wanted it was because it looked so good. A lot better than it sounded, anyway.

It didn't matter what you did to that instrument – and Johnny did a lot, including having a third pick-up attached, which cost more than he'd paid for the guitar in the first place. You could not get a decent sound out of it to save your life. I, on the other hand, felt as though I was barely clinging onto life that afternoon so we made a good match.

We would do one other TV show while we were in Los Angeles, and that's an important one too, because it's where the sleeve to our second album was taken, us in mid-performance. *The Real Don Steele* show was a local programme, broadcast on KHJ-TV and fronted by a fast-talking veteran DJ from the Murray the K generation.

One of the features in the show was a news segment, with each headline punctuated by the sound of a massive gong being struck. So he would announce that "LA's own" Sable Starr was now dating Johnny Thunders – GONG! – and I was so glad there was no chance of Janice ever seeing the show, back in their apartment in New York on her own. Then we lip-synched to 'Trash' and 'Personality Crisis', roared on by a bunch of the fans who we'd got to know from the Whisky shows. Some were stoners, some were arty types, and some were there to be seen seeing us. But they had poured in from all over California and they were at every gig. That felt good.

We hit the road, four nights each in Houston and Dallas, and then slowly back to Manhattan via Memphis, Detroit and Milwaukee, before we rejoined the Mott The Hoople tour at the beginning of October. The thing is, the moment you leave the coastal cities, you start running into a whole new demographic, one that I always called the Black Oak Arkansas crowd – straight ahead rockers who hated Mick Jagger because they thought he was a fag, hated David Bowie because they'd read he was a fag ... and they *really* hated us, because we dressed like fags.

We weren't running into too many of them at this stage, mainly because the clubs we were playing were barely large enough to contain the people who genuinely wanted to see us. But they made their presence felt regardless, and I couldn't help thinking, if we'd been topless with washboards, like Black Oak's Jim Dandy, we'd have been fine. Or if we hadn't used the men's bathroom. We scared so many macho dudes like that; they'd walk in and see what they thought was a woman standing there having a pee.

Some of the shows went really well. There were places where we could get away with anything, and there were places where they weren't going to give us a chance.

A lot of it depended upon who we were billed alongside. Fortunately, we never did gig with Black Oak Arkansas. But Lynyrd Skynyrd was a difficult ask, particularly in Missouri, and Rush, up in Canada, was scarcely a blend we'd have chosen for ourselves.

The Mott tour was perfect, of course, especially with Aerosmith along to make up the numbers, although even there, promoters were capable of shooting themselves in the foot, by billing the gig as a Glitter Rock festival. That was a turn-off for a lot of people.

But in Houston on our own, we played a former drag club and the audience was as amazing as you'd hope it would be. The moment we landed in Dallas, however, there was trouble.

To nobody's surprise, Sable left LA with Johnny, and they intended continuing their relationship in New York. The problem with that happy scenario was that she was still underage: just sixteen. The moment Sable left the state, her mother called the cops, and they were waiting for us when we arrived in Dallas.

What they didn't realise was that Johnny had thought ahead, and – with Valerie suddenly out of the picture – sent Sable straight back to New York. The only woman with us was Cyrinda, who certainly didn't take kindly to a phalanx of Texas policemen descending on her, saying they were taking her back to momma.

Our reputation preceded us in other ways, too. In Denver, we were greeted by a dozen or so women waving placards and insisting that the New York Dolls were making fun of women, and dressed the way we did to demean them. But we thoroughly enjoyed being there, wandering around the stores picking up cowboy boots and ten-gallon hats that really could hold ten gallons. And, when we got to the show, there was a bunch of chicks from the local Playboy Club that Frenchie personally invited to the after-show party at our hotel.

In truth, the place wasn't much better than the cheapest motel management thought they could get away with ("It's okay, boys, it's only for one night"), but Frenchie made it sound as though they were going to Paris.

Of course, a wild time promptly ensued, with the usual high spirits, slamming doors and loud music, until hotel security called the cops and the party was closed down on the spot. The police even searched our luggage, but thankfully they didn't find anything. But, as they were leaving, this one crew-cut bulldog turned to me and asked what I played. I told him guitar.

"Yeah, well I play the walls."

We got the hell out of there.

Iggy joined the tour, not just as a friend but as a performer. He and Williamson had finally got onto the road for a meandering six-month outing that would end in the brutality and violence of their *Metallic KO* album.

Our tours intersected in Memphis on September 21, 1973, and tensions were high from the outset. There was so much local opposition to us playing, apparently, that the local newspaper was reporting that the vice squad would be attending the show, and they were itching to bust these big-city sleazoids.

It was a peculiar situation. Iggy at that time had a reputation for onstage violence and lewdness that most performers could only dream of; he certainly left us in the shade. But the cops didn't even watch his portion of the show. They only had eyes for us.

The venue was an auditorium; the sound wasn't ideal, but the crowd was reasonable, and they gave the Stooges a fair hearing. Then we came on and a few kids got up to dance. Then a few more, then a few more. By the time we were into our second or third song, there must have been a couple of thousand people up on their feet, so David started to invite a few up onto the stage.

It was something we'd done on a number of occasions at the Mercer; it makes the audience as much a part of the show as the band, and it can lead to some really exciting performances. Unfortunately, it can also lead to the Memphis vice squad cutting the sound, stopping the show, and then arresting David for inciting a riot.

I'll never forget the sight of these burly cops dragging him away, David in this long, white, one-sleeve glitter creation with "New York" written on it, shouting, "Would you do this to Elvis?" And a cop replying, "Damn right we would."

We had another brush with officialdom on our way back from a radio interview in Windsor, Canada.

One of the most pressing problems the New York Dolls ran into was airplay. New York and LA weren't bad at all; we had friends at most of the local stations. But out in the rest of the country, we couldn't get a spin for love or money. Even in Detroit, where we were big enough to sell out the Michigan Palace, there was no interest.

Across the river in Windsor, Ontario, however, there was a DJ named Legs who adored us. Even better, the station he worked for could be heard all over Detroit and was, in fact, many people's preferred listening. That played a big role in our local popularity, so the morning after the Michigan Palace, Johnny and I piled into a black limo and set off to be interviewed on the station.

The journey there was fine; the interview was fine. But driving back across the border, we were stopped. Down came the window, in popped the customs guy's head and you could see his nose wrinkle as he detected the tell-tale smell of pot.

"Everybody out of the car."

They took us into their little building and announced we were to be searched. One guy took my arm, and the other – who looked a little fruity, even to me – tried to take Johnny's.

Johnny flipped. "Fuck that! I ain't going with that fucking faggot." He completely let rip, every homophobic slur he could think of and a few that I'd never even heard came tumbling out of his mouth, all leading up to his final shot. "I am not having that guy look up my ass."

Any place else, I imagine the two officers would just have been told to switch places. But Johnny's rampage completely unsettled everybody, to the point where the chief told us to get back into our car and get out of there. Which, very gratefully, we did.

One final road memory from fall, 1973: it was October 10 and we were on a plane flying to Chicago, one more stop on the Mott tour, when the announcer came onto the speaker and said, "I'm sorry, ladies and gentlemen, but I have some really terrible news."

He paused and the entire cabin was silent, everybody sitting there looking shocked and thinking, "Oh God, we're going to die." Because what other "really terrible" news is there, when you're cruising at 20,000 feet in an aluminium envelope filled with jet fuel?

Then he came back on. "Vice President Spiro Agnew has just resigned."

Immediately, David was out of his seat. Nobody else, row after row of businessmen in their suits and ties and briefcases, had even had a chance to react, but David was dancing and clapping, "Yeah, yeah, yeah!" Then I joined in, and the others too, and you could feel the loathing radiate from the rest of the passengers. "You fucking hippy bastards."

The final stop on the Mott tour was Radio City Music Hall, back in New York, and at last, the end was in sight. Just a couple of Canadian gigs with Rush, then down the east coast via Connecticut and Rhode Island, to be back in New York for Halloween, and another of the all-time most memorable New York Dolls performances.

We took over the grand ballroom of the Waldorf Astoria for the occasion, a massive Halloween party dreamed up by promoter Howard Stein. There were bands, there were DJs, there was even a costume contest, with the grand prize of a free stay at a motel close by Newark airport, and a bottle of Taylor New York State champagne. Which, you might think, doesn't sound like much of a prize, and you'd be right. But it was very, very campy.

Wolfman Jack, the host of the *Midnight Special,* was one of the judges, and we even made the local news – something along the lines of "The Dolls are bringing in 10,000 tons of equipment and they don't even know how to tune up."

Up in the suite that was doubling as our dressing room, we resolved to dress as crazily as we could. I was Charlie Chaplin, the Little Tramp, complete with moustache and morning stripe trousers. David had another Barbara Triani triumph – white tails and tux. Arthur had his tutu, and even Jerry looked good. Now all we had to do was wait for Johnny.

We saw Sable first: black face and Afro wig, Johnny's leather jacket and a cigarette. Her face was set in a permanent snarl; she looked amazing.

Then Johnny. Black tails, high heel sneakers ... and a swastika armband. We didn't say anything; we knew he wasn't a Nazi, or showing support for their creed. It was simply a rock'n'roll thing to do ... a biker thing, to be more accurate. It wasn't even for shock value, because that wasn't what we were about. If anything, he was wearing it because he'd spent the last however many years of his life living with a poster of Brian Jones, done up in full Nazi regalia.

It was total innocence, then, but it was a bad move all the same. On the tape of the show, you can hear people asking him to take off the swastika in between songs, although by that time, to be truthful, there were other things to worry about.

The venue had been completely oversold, and the people locked outside were not going to take it. With a crash, the massive glass doors at the front of the hotel were shattered, and the crowd just poured in. The place was already packed; now it was packed even more. People spilling out of the ballroom into reception, onto the stairs, everywhere.

News cameras were capturing everything: people like Liza Minnelli and various other big stars sat stoically at their tables, with the plush white tablecloths, and the candles and canapés, while a full-scale riot went off all around them.

We played; of course we did. Even though we had to fight our own way through the melee in order to reach the stage, we knew that if we didn't show, the riot would be even worse. And the next day, of course, the news was full of people demanding to know how a monstrosity like the Dolls was actually permitted to enter the Waldorf in the first place. But it was a brilliant idea all the same, and a genius move by Howard Stein.

We didn't stay home for long. A few days later we were back on the road: five nights in Athens, Georgia; one in South Carolina; and a handful that were at least within driving distance of New York.

But, just like the Max's residency back at the end of August, our eyes weren't really focused on what we were doing in those particular moments. Because as soon as we got the last of these shows played, we were going back to Europe.

Chapter 21

BLACK BIBA LIPSTICK

Europe was where we should always have been. Europe was where we should have been born. The UK, France, Germany, Scandinavia, they all understood the New York Dolls. Even in Spain, where the record had to come out without our picture on it because the Franco government banned it, the boys and girls got it. They saw the humour, they saw the excitement and they saw the sexuality. All the things that Americans didn't want to be bothered with, or backed away from, the Europeans gobbled them up.

Our first stop was in London, holed up at the Blake Hotel, right off the King's Road. It was a gorgeous place, old and overflowing with character. We all had fantastic rooms and that first evening, back from the inevitable (if jet-lagged) shopping spree at Malcolm and Vivienne's, Mercury's UK office staged our record release party in the basement.

The album was just out in the UK and was already picking up speed; the party reflected that, a room full of journalists, a succession of interviews, endless drink and laughter. Malcolm and Vivienne were there, of course, and they'd brought along their own coterie of supporters – Ian Dury, from the band Kilburn & The High Roads, Brian Eno and an Ohio girl who was working at the store named Chrissie Hynde.

We had a couple of days off, and then hit the road: a short tour of universities, and they were okay. A little reserved, though, as if people really didn't know who we were. Later, someone told us that a lot of university gigs were like that. People went because they got a discount at the bar; it doesn't matter who's playing, it's cheap beer.

It's a shame, too, that somebody in Leeds decided to rip us off – a couple of acoustic guitars went astray when our backs were turned, and we had to have new ones sent over from New York.

Back in London, we played two nights at Biba, the boutique that had fascinated me the first time I visited England, although it had certainly gone up in the world since then. Once a simple storefront on Kensington High Street, it now sprawled across an old department store, with a ballroom perched at the very top of the building.

The Rainbow Restaurant wasn't the biggest place we'd ever played, and the stage was especially tiny. But it was a lovely room with a PA to match, and the soundcheck left us all feeling good. So Arthur went and got himself arrested.

We had finished the soundcheck and Arthur and I wandered downstairs to look around the store. We were already broke; we'd spent all our money at Malcolm's. But you can't keep a shopaholic down, and we were always on the lookout for bargains.

Unfortunately, Arthur decided to make a bargain of his own. He'd found a really cool black jacket with faux leopard collar and trims, but it was priced way outside his budget. So he switched the tags.

The lady at the cash register barely even blinked. She looked at the price tag, looked at Arthur, and immediately called security. Arthur was arrested, and it took all of Marty's charm to get him out of it. We still made the evening news, though, busted for stealing from the very venue we were supposed to be playing that night. Of course, they didn't ask why we were so broke that we had to steal clothes in the first place.

There was such a buzz around those two London shows. Mercury had produced these little round stickers with our name on them, and walking down the street, I saw a bicycle absolutely festooned in them. There wasn't a piece of frame, handlebar or saddle that wasn't covered in these stickers, and I have to say it made me feel good. Almost as good as hearing our record blasting out of the different stores I passed.

The audience was wild. They weren't loud, though; they were absorbing, as though the entire room was a sponge, just soaking up our attitude, our music, and our very existence. In the years since then, I have met so many British musicians who say they were there that night, it almost reminds me of that famous remark Eno made about The Velvet

Underground. "Not many people saw them, but everyone who did formed a band." A band that was for real.

The first night was fantastic; the second promised to be just as exciting. In-between times, however, we had another engagement, filming our spot on television's *Old Grey Whistle Test*. Which also meant it was time for me to really show off my latest pride and joy, the one guitar that everybody associates with me. The Gretsch White Falcon.

I found it at Alex Music on 48th Street in New York, and it wasn't cheap. Nor should it have been. A pristine white body, gold-plated hardware, gold sparkle binding. It was the most beautiful thing I had ever seen. But, again, it was expensive; the guy wanted $800 for it – which, to me at that time, was a fortune. The days of the Nussbaum knitting mills and my $5,000 a line were long over. I'd have had to sell everything in my apartment, including my girlfriend, if he'd held out for cash.

Fortunately, he was willing to trade, so the next day I was back with both the Flying V *and* another guitar I had, and not only did I get the White Falcon, he threw in its original case as well.

I'll never forget introducing it to the others. We were back at Carol's Music, rehearsing for the European tour, and everybody was there – Arthur, Jerry, David, Johnny, Cyrinda. I walked in, lay the case down and opened it. And everybody in the room went "Wow". Followed by "Holy smoke", "Oh my God" and, from Johnny, "I'll trade you for it now. I'll give you everything I own."

But it was Cyrinda who said the most magical words. "Sylvain? That's not a guitar, it's a Cadillac." And she was right.

Johnny didn't do so badly, though. Up in Leeds, Arthur was poking around a pawn shop when he came across a Vox Teardrop guitar for £20. Johnny had to have that as well, and Arthur let him.

Of course, there was a reason why those guitars was so inexpensive. They played like shit. They looked cool as hell, but they sounded horrible, and you're probably thinking that's a strange mistake to make when you're appearing on the most important rock TV show in the country. The most important *live* rock TV show. It was years before I discovered that every other guest who performed on the *Whistle Test* plugged in and played live, because we certainly didn't. Instead, they cued up 'Jet Boy' … and not even the album version of it; they chose the single, which had been edited down to three minutes something, and had us lip-synch to it.

Then, when it was over, the show's host, Bob Harris, turned to the camera and mumbled, "Mock rock." So maybe that's why they made us lip-synch. "Their record sounds plenty bad enough. Can you imagine what they'd sound like if they were actually playing?"

I loved it, though: firstly because, when Mercury did the edit, they took away Johnny's solo but left mine intact; and secondly, because that song could be very hit or miss with Johnny. Some nights, we could take off on that solo and really fly – there were times when it went on for ten minutes or more, the two of us just rocking our tits off. But some nights, not so much, and we were almost grateful when it dribbled to a halt.

As for the mock rock remark – it was probably the smartest thing that guy ever said. Because the length and breadth of Britain, kids who watched that show just lapped it up. Joe Strummer – "The great thing, the Dolls were on TV" – Graham Parker, Morrissey. In the early nineties, Arthur and I were invited to see the latter at the Santa Monica Civic Center, and he told us about the first time he ever saw the Dolls, sitting in the living room between his mom and dad, watching us on *Whistle Test.*

We didn't stay at the Blake the entire time. One night David asked Frenchie to draw him a bath. The water was still running when we called to do a soundcheck … and Frenchie forgot to turn it off. David's bathwater inundated not only the bathroom, but the entire room and out into the hallway, too. We got back and we were politely asked never to come back again.

From London, we flew to France, and that became another page in the legend of the New York Dolls, the story of how we landed at Orly to a welcoming committee of journalists and photographers, all vying to catch our attention. And Johnny threw up on them.

Even before that, Johnny fascinated them, so everyone was calling his name as he came down the steps in the terminal. He turned to look at them … and bleaugh! He threw up, all the way down the staircase, all over the cameras. Then he smiled and just kept walking. But later in the day, he was so poorly that Peter Jordan had to stand in for him when the photographers descended again.

A press conference awaited us at our hotel, the Ambassador, which our fans promptly renamed the Ambassadolls, but for me, simply being back in Paris was such a rush.

I went back to the street where we lived when we were exiled; to the flea market where dad used to take me shopping; all the places I'd known and loved, and a few I'd completely forgotten. Every street, every sign, they all brought back memories, but the biggest treat was still to come.

Throughout the time we lived in France, the biggest thing in Paris was L'Olympia. It was *the* concert hall, the place where only the grandest stars could play – Piaf, Brel, Bécaud, Aznavour, all the legends headlined L'Olympia. And now we were adding our name to that role call.

It wasn't strictly as grand as it sounds; for a start, we were playing a specially arranged matinee show, at 3.30 in the afternoon. But I don't care. We played L'Olympia.

The show itself was everything I had dreamed of. We were using The Rolling Stones' usual sound man, and somehow he'd got us their back line to use, these huge Ampegs that, normally, I wasn't crazy about, but on this occasion … my God, they even had confetti in them, left over from the last time the Stones played a gig.

The concert is a blur. I remember Arthur standing on the edge of the stage, resplendent in his huge glow-in-the-dark white parachutist boots, and some kid scrawling "LSD" on them in black marker. I remember Johnny suddenly announcing that he had to go pee, laying down his guitar and walking off stage, while David and I vamped 'Lone Star Queen' to cover his absence.

And I remember the dogs.

We were back at the Ambassadolls, the adrenalin still pumping from an amazing performance, when Johnny walked in with this absolutely gorgeous French girl whom he'd met, and two massive Great Danes.

I don't know how they got past the desk clerk and up to Johnny's room, because, like food, dogs were distinctly forbidden in the rooms. But all night long, we could hear these two dogs barking, and ever more desperate cries of "*Ou sont les chiens?*" as the hotel staff and security tried to find the source of the noise. They never did, though; not until morning, as we were preparing to leave, and Johnny came down with his coterie of guests.

The bellboy flipped out completely. "I've found them! They're here! *Les chiens*!" But it was too late. Johnny kissed the girl goodbye, patted the dogs on the head, and we climbed aboard the bus.

Malcolm and Vivienne were in Paris as well. They'd come over specifically for the Olympia show, but we also visited some people they knew, including a designer friend who threw us a spaghetti party – the main meal was spaghetti. That was the night, incidentally, when Vivienne told me,"You boys look so much better in women's clothing," because everything we'd ever bought from her store was for chicks. It wasn't always the best quality back then. Her vinyl leather line had a terrible habit of disintegrating after time. But it looked so good, you really didn't mind.

We played a few shows in France, out in the country, and like the gigs outside London (or even beyond New York), they were little more than space fillers between the more memorable events.

Back in Paris, though, we recorded a terrific performance for Radio Luxembourg, in front of an invited audience of industry and radio people. I've read that we were extraordinarily drunk by the time the recording began, and maybe we were. But it was a cool show, and a really funny one as well. Especially when David tried to address the audience in French.

Poor thing. He had learned a bit in school and thought he could get by. But he couldn't. "Ding dong," he'd go, "*ou est la bibliothèque*?" when he meant to say, "*Dites-moi*" [tell me] where is the library?" That's what he'd learned at school in Staten Island. "Ding dong." I can still see the audience cracking up laughing.

Of course, it wouldn't be a Dolls tour without a riot of some sort, and sure enough, there was one still to come. We were playing at that other world famous Parisian concert hall, the Bataclan – famed now, of course, for such tragic reasons, but equally renowned back in the seventies, too.

The gig itself was sponsored by the government, part of a scheme to put on cut-price events for kids who couldn't afford to go to regular concerts. Normally, such events attracted a healthy crowd, but they were never particularly swamped.

Tonight, though, even from our dressing room, overlooking a little alleyway at the back of the theatre, we could see masses of people converging on the place. It was like The Beatles or something; in fact, I said as much to Johnny. I had never seen that many kids come to see us, never. They were packed together in a wave, just pouring in, and they had really made an effort. From Arthur's and my side of the stage, we could even see a few guys in drag, very young, very cute.

Johnny's side, though, was weird. It was as though every street kid in Paris had gravitated towards him, real tough cases, the way I remembered them from my childhood, in leather jackets, with their short hair combed back. Bikers, rockers, call them what you like. There they were and, as soon as we started to play, a few of them began spitting at Johnny.

He ignored them for a while; at least for a couple of songs. But then he snapped, picking up his microphone with its solid metal base and throwing it right into this one guy's face.

The fan fell back, blood everywhere; but his mates poured forward, scrambling onto the stage. My side, the crowd was still calm and beautiful. Johnny's side looked like something out of *West Side Story*, with Johnny swinging his guitar by the neck, batting them off the stage until we could pull him away

We fled, off the stage, out of the club, into our bus and away. Next stop, Germany.

That show, by the way, was being filmed; a French woman director shot the whole gig – or at least as much as we played of it – and interviewed us in the dressing room as well. As far as I know, the film has never been shown; in fact, I don't know anyone who's even seen it. I hope it surfaces soon.

Marty had accompanied us so far on the tour. Once the final Paris engagement was out of the way, however, he bailed back to New York. We were left to our own devices, but, worse than that, we were thrown back on our own hazy understanding of economics. When we came to check out of the Ambassadolls, it was bad enough that we'd run up a bill of $3,500 in phone calls, bar tabs and other expenses, but far worse was the realisation that we had no way of paying it. I don't remember exactly how we got out of that, but I'm sure it was simply added to our ever-expanding debt.

There were no gigs lined up for the German leg of the tour, just a performance on the *Musikladen* television show and, the following day in Hamburg, another industry bash, this time at the Star Club, the place where The Beatles started.

It had fallen on hard times since then, though. Now it was a strip club, specialising in stunning Vietnamese girls, which is why we were playing the afternoon matinee. No club owner in his right mind would cancel their performance for ours!

I don't remember the gig itself, but the dressing room is engrained in my mind. It was the one the girls usually used, a fabulously styled room, all crushed velvet wallpaper and a big sign on the wall saying "boudoir". We used a picture that was taken there for the back of our second album, David in the blue jean jacket with a picture of Cyrinda painted on it (although everyone thinks it's Marilyn Monroe), and the rest of us looking so sharp and relaxed. Hand-painted by a New York artist, it's one of my favourite Dolls photographs.

The days were crowding in on one another. In Holland, we did the *Top Pop* TV show and we definitely played the Paradiso in Amsterdam, where I met my old friend Dominique again. There was more television in Belgium, and there may have been a few more gigs as well ... every so often I'll read something online, "The Dolls played here, the Dolls played there", and maybe we did and I've just forgotten it, or maybe we didn't and somebody got their wires crossed in a book or a magazine article, and it's now accepted as gospel.

For example, despite what you can read elsewhere, I'm fairly certain that we didn't appear on the *Russell Harty Plus* TV show in England, because I would remember that – it was on this show that Keith Moon removed his own trousers on live television one night when The Who were Harty's guests. We'd probably have gone without trousers to begin with.

It's the same as when someone comes up to me at a concert to announce they've seen pictures of the New York Dolls having sex together on the internet. Really? I'd like to see those.

You can't even say it didn't happen, or the pictures aren't real, because sometimes the fans know more than you do, and sometimes they just think they do because they heard or read something so long ago that it's almost become a part of who they are. We're like Elvis: there's been a lot of real sightings, but there's even more fake ones.

Chapter 22

Y'ALL DON'T KNOW HOW TO PLAY, BUT Y'ALL BOOGIE LIKE HELL

We got back to New York and went straight into another round of shows – Boston, Cleveland, Washington DC. No time to adjust, no time to process what we'd just experienced.

What we did know was that things were changing. We still had our supporters, the people who'd been behind us all along, but our American audience wasn't getting bigger, and may even have been shrinking as the old fans drifted away, convinced we'd become too big for them.

The fate of our second album, *Too Much Too Soon,* would do nothing to disprove that. The good reviews would come from the writers we expected to get good reviews from; the bad ones were from those who'd never paid attention. It went into the charts at number one hundred and something, but it never climbed higher than number 116, and within two or three months it was forgotten. *Billboard* have this thing where a record goes into the chart "with a bullet", and our album was always associated with a bullet. Unfortunately, I think they were aiming at us.

But really, that's not such a bad thing. After all, that's when you know you've made it, when the newspapers start attacking you. It means you've annoyed or upset them. If you were genuinely crap, they wouldn't mention you.

However, there was also an inescapable sense that management really didn't know what to do with us. We knew there were several places where we were actually doing well: Canada, for instance. But management was so focused on breaking us in the United States that they never took advantage of it.

It was the same now, when we returned from Europe. They must have seen the response that we received there, but it was still back on the road in America immediately afterwards, because that's where they thought the money was.

Meanwhile, Johnny and David were furiously running their own personal agendas, not only planting the seeds for the future, but also setting up their own later clashes, because they were both running around with the same girl, and the animosity was growing. And at the same time, management was taking each of them to one side and whispering, "Hey, you're the front man, you're the big star, you're the one that everyone wants," and that was turning their heads too. David even went through a phase of either not answering when you spoke to him, or simply saying "yes".

Then you throw the drugs in.

We were going separate ways.

Right now, we still felt like big stars, and we were still in demand. But there's another side to becoming "popular", which is suddenly that the kind of clothes that we used to find in thrift stores and reinvent were beginning to appear in stores.

I won't say designers and outfitters were copying us, but we opened a door there and a lot of very smart business people burst through it: "Oh, this is what the kids are wearing ... I'll start selling it."

Outfits that we'd thrown together could now be bought, ready-assembled, in St Mark's Place and the Village, and I have to agree that it's flattering. But the co-opting of your "look" has other consequences too, in that you're having to push harder to keep ahead, at the same time as not wanting to do that, because what you're wearing is who you are, and trying to go beyond that doesn't work. It's artificial and fake.

Our look was making a million dollars. Our record was in the dollar bins. Can you wonder that tempers were fraying and moods were growing darker? Sometimes it felt as though we didn't even need to make records. We should have just had our photos taken early on, played a bunch of shows, and we'd have made as much of an impact as if we'd made a hundred LPs. Which is hardly the kind of attitude you need when you're going back into the studio in a couple of weeks.

At the same time, though, you *want* to make a record; you *need* to make one. I kept thinking of the Stones' *Gimme Shelter* movie, which I was utterly addicted to – the part when they go in to record 'Wild Horses'. They just wander into a studio, record the song, and wander out again. They were dying to do it; everybody was excited; and that's exactly how we felt when we went in with Todd Rundgren.

But now? Daffy Duck. It's a great act, but what do you do for an encore? Back in New York, back to the grindstone, and it really started feeling too much like a job. The last thing rock'n'roll should ever become is a job.

Of course, management didn't see it that way. They were paying us a salary, they had money invested in us, and they wanted a return. So they kept us working, kept us gigging, and it didn't matter to them that one day we were headlining the Michigan Palace and the next time we were in Detroit we were playing a bowling alley. Every gig we played was money for them, but the less money they received, the less was doled out to us.

It happened really fast as well. Suddenly David and Cyrinda were no longer living in the duplex penthouse at 65 East 11th. They had a one-bedroom apartment on 17th Street. I was in an apartment at 9 Charles Street; Johnny and Sable were still together, living on 24th, but the honeymoon was beginning to wear off, and they were starting to feud. Things were changing, and one of the reasons for that was we had finally realised what we were missing. It was the success that we had been promised.

Of course there were still good times. Amazing times. That Michigan Palace show for example. New Year's Eve in Motor City – how can you go wrong? Even when the power cut out a couple of times during the show, we kept everybody on their feet; stopped them from getting pissed off. "We came a long way to rock'n'roll and that's what we're going to do," I shouted, and the whole place roared right back at me.

But it wasn't really an exciting time, and it was about to start getting a lot worse.

At the end of January 1974, we headed up to A&R Studios on West 48th Street, to begin work on our second album. We didn't even demo it first. That was a warning sign, right there.

I have no complaints about the studio – it was one of New York's finest, and might even have been a step or two above the Record Plant, where we recorded the first album. Plus, right next door was Mr G. Banks, purveyor of theatrical footwear, and Cyrinda and I were in there whenever we had some down time, browsing the stock or getting boots made. But the highlight of the entire month we were recording, at least as far as she was concerned, was the day James Brown walked into the studio. She ran over and got his autograph.

Once again, various names were being bandied about as producer, and I was firmly in favour of bringing back Todd. He took us to where we needed to be, capturing our live performance, except with a bigger sound, a cleaner this and a dirtier that, so basically there was no production at all. I was convinced that he'd be able to make the second album even better than the first. Capture our signature sound.

Marty had other ideas, though. He came up with Shadow Morton, and you would think I'd have turned somersaults to celebrate. Shadow, after all, was one of *the* legends of my beloved early sixties sound, and the mastermind behind all those glorious Shangri-Las records. David was thrilled.

But much as we loved them, we *weren't* The Shangri-Las. And Shadow was not the producer he once was. In fact, the only things I was aware of him producing all decade was a long-forgotten single by the early Mott The Hoople, and a band called Haystacks Balboa. And we weren't them, either.

There's no disputing that Shadow was a genius. But sometimes, you don't need genius, you need understanding as well. He was the most amazing producer, the most phenomenal talent. But if we were (or had ever been) the future of rock'n'roll, he was very much its past.

We were going into the studio to capture our signature sound, and Shadow completely wiped that out. We needed someone who would make us work, and Shadow didn't do that. And why would he? Nobody had told him any of that; he was just informed that David was the singer, and he was a star; Johnny was lead guitarist, and he was a star as well; and the rest of us were just the rest. So that's how he approached the sessions.

A lot of elements make up a band, and the members and their usual instruments are a lot of them. But what goes on around the edges is also important.

For example, Johnny and I always did backing vocals, and though we weren't what you'd call brilliant, or even very good, the sound we made was a key element within the New York Dolls. Shadow more or less banned us from the vocal booth and brought in some Brill Building backing singers instead. You really notice our absence (or their inclusion) during 'Stranded In The Jungle'.

Likewise, my piano playing wasn't exactly Elton John, but again it was a part of our sound – listen back to the first album, and you'll hear what I mean. Shadow didn't even let me sit at the instrument. He brought in another "real" musician, Stan from John Lennon's old sidekicks, Elephant's Memory. Every day in the studio, it felt as though another layer of the New York Dolls was being chipped away, smoothed over, buffed and beautified. I don't want to say the album was slicker, but it was ... slicker.

Shadow turned his attention to the songs. Most of what we brought in were leftovers from the first LP ... in fact, 'Chatterbox' was left over from the Actress days, and still Johnny had to fight his tits off to be able to sing it, because David was adamant that he was lead vocalist, and "What am I going to do if someone else is singing?" But Johnny was just as intractable, demanding that he play lead guitar on everything, even if he couldn't.

We did present a few new songs: 'Puss'n'Boots', which I'd written with David; 'Babylon', which was strictly a Johnny song; 'Mystery Girls', which I put together practically singlehandedly (but is still credited to Johnny and David alone); and what became the album's title track, 'Too Much, Too Soon'.

Or, at least, it would have been the title track if Shadow had allowed us to record it. Maybe he didn't like it; maybe he'd been told that David and Johnny wrote all the songs as well, and 'Too Much, Too Soon' was another of mine. But we never got around to taping it, and right towards the end, when I more or less insisted, he simply said we'd run out of time.

The only thing he gave me was to allow me to step up to the microphone to unleash my trademark "great God, shoogle-moogle, let me out of here" during our cover of The Jayhawks' 'Stranded In The Jungle'. (Although, to be truthful, I based our version on my old single of the same song by The Cadets.)

All that aside, I love *Too Much Too Soon*. It could have been better; we could have retained the sound that Todd Rundgren gave us. We could have worked without the session men. But it was what it was, the best album that we were capable of making at the time, and the best that

Shadow, beset on all sides by so many other opinions, could produce. The real problem with *Too Much Too Soon*, however, was that it wasn't a New York Dolls album. Or, rather, it was, but it was also the start of a David Johansen solo album.

They took away the piano, they took away the backing vocals. The guitars weren't as loud as they should have been (although the vocals were certainly upfront), and nothing stood up and punched you in the face. But I still love it.

The reviews were worse than last time; sales were lower than last time; and, even among our most devoted fans, the feeling was "Well, I like 'Human Bein'' well enough, but I like 'Jet Boy'' a whole lot more." You could play that same game with virtually every track on the album. Now, however, *Too Much Too Soon* is regarded as a classic New York Dolls recording, and that's how it should be.

We weren't ready to record. We should have been given more time to write new material and get it together. Instead, we were rushed back in and it shows. And, to be honest, the whole experience left me bereft, and the fate of 'Too Much, Too Soon' was simply the cherry on the dog shit cake. I'd been dying my whole life to work with a guy like Shadow, and he's saying, "See you later."

Again, there was no time to try and process anything. We came out of the studio and straight back out on tour, although I can't complain about the first show we had, another Howard Stein promotion, this time called the St Valentine's Day Massacre. Or, maybe Mascara would have been more appropriate?

Ably assisted by Bob Gruen (and Marty's young son, who played a newsboy), we shot a short piece of film with which to open the gig. A few days before the show, the five of us dressed up as Prohibition-era gangsters, leaped aboard a black Volkswagen beetle, and made our way down 14th Street, hanging off the sides of the car, waving our weaponry in the air, until we arrived at the Academy of Music.

Behind us, our take on the *Courageous Cat* theme imparted period menace (it was probably the best thing we recorded at A&R, one day when Shadow wasn't around), while captions warned the watching world of who was heading their way … Scarface and Freddy Boy and the rest of the crew, collectively known as the Lipstick Killers.

The film ended with us pushing through the doors of the venue – and, when it was screened on the night of the show, that was our cue to burst in through the back of the auditorium, swagger down the aisles, and then leap onto the stage. It was a brilliant opening, a terrific gig, and I even persuaded my parents to come down to see us. I have pictures of them backstage, my mom drinking Southern Comfort from the little plastic cup that closes the bottle.

Sable was there; Iggy, too. I remember handing him a pair of Rayban sunglasses; he snapped them in half, tossed one piece to the side, and then balanced the other on his nose. "This is how you wear these."

The St Valentine's Massacre lives on in my mind as one more truly glorious New York Dolls performance. Twenty-four hours later, we were in Bloomington, Indiana, with Lynyrd Skynyrd – one of several shows we played with them. I remember after one, in Springfield, Missouri, Ronnie Van Zant came up to me and said, "You know y'all don't know how to play," in that thick southern accent of his. He paused, then continued, "Yeah, but y'all boogie like hell." Later, I wrote a song about it.

I took it as a compliment, but such gestures were few and far between. Life started not to be fun. We had known all along that we'd be gigging, but even amid all the forebodings and warning signs, I don't think any of us realised just how low our stock had sunk.

Put it this way. Returning to towns we'd visited last year, if we played a theatre then, now it was a club. Our wages were now $200 a week, which was better, but everything else had gone down. Promotors weren't pushing as hard as they once had, and Mercury certainly didn't do anything with the album – and why should they? Even the biggest record labels in the world have to work to a budget, and you can imagine them sitting in the office, dividing up the promotional money.

Bachman Turner Overdrive were doing phenomenally well; they had a hit single, a monster album, they were the hottest thing Canada had produced in years. So they were at the top of the list. The Ohio Players, too. Paper Lace and Rod Stewart. Thin Lizzy were rising and Uriah Heep were massive. And the New York Dolls? "We didn't do shit with those guys. Or girls. Or whatever they are. Don't worry about it."

There was nothing we could do about it either. We could have sat down and written the most addictive songs in the universe. But when the industry decides that you're on the way down, and your management does not disagree, then you're sunk. Or, at least, sinking fast.

Round the country we went, growing more and more miserable with every passing day. The addictions were kicking in; Johnny and Jerry, forever searching out smack; Arthur and David were drinking.

Occasionally, though, we'd touch down in home territory, and it felt like a band again – in March, we played the Santa Monica Civic, completely sold out, supported by Michael Des Barres fronting Silverhead.

In fact, I bumped into Michael in the parking lot as I was heading in for the soundcheck; he stepped out of a Cadillac hearse, with his wife-to-be, Pamela Miller, on one arm, and in the other hand, a baby tiger on a chain leash and collar.

"Hey, can I pet your tiger?" I asked.

"No, not today," replied Michael. "He'll bite your head off."

We opened for Sly & The Family Stone in Rhode Island, and played a couple of nights at Max's, where we felt like homecoming heroes. Another show around that same time took us to the opening night of the Bottom Line, just up from where the Mercer once stood. Suzi Quatro was the actual headliner, but that was cool – 'Can The Can' had been a fabulous record, and we knew her audience wasn't too different to ours. And besides, this was our city.

We were given a small but comfortable dressing room, and clearly a lot of money had been spent on it – the walls were vast mirrors, floor to ceiling things ... perfect for checking your make-up before you took the stage. Unfortunately, we'd scarcely arrived when something pissed off Arthur ... namely, the fact he'd run out of booze.

Whatever he was holding in his hand – a now empty bottle, I think – he smashed it against the mirror. Which, of course, then shattered the mirror, and that was probably our fee for the evening taken care of.

Worse, however, was still to come.

The early to mid-seventies were a fraught time in New York, with both the Weather Underground and the Puerto Rican nationalist FALN detonating devices around the city (and elsewhere in the country). Bomb scares were almost routine, too, and when the Bottom Line received such a warning, the place was quickly evacuated.

The police arrived and the bomb squad too, and the venue was declared safe. We played our set; Suzi played hers; and we were all looking forward to reconvening for the second performance the following evening.

It didn't happen. Casting around for someone to blame for the hoax, the club seized on the notion that we'd made the call. That we knew we weren't doing so well, and were afraid of Suzi blowing us off stage. It was one of the most preposterous things I have ever heard, but it was enough for the Bottom Line to cancel our next show, and to ban us from the venue as well.

Thankfully, we had other places to play.

The biggest show we did in New York that month of April, 1974, was the Easter Parade at Club 82.

A bit of history. Club 82 had been around since the fifties, when it was opened as a lesbian bar by Anna Genovese, the wife of Mafia boss Vito. It took its name from its house number, 82 East 4th Street. The club itself was in the basement, and now it was being run by a pair of incredible lesbians – Butch, who I don't think I ever met, and Tommy, who was a tough, grey-haired Irish chain-smoker who reminded me of a really fierce Sunday School teacher.

We hung out there a lot during the early days of the Dolls, lounging around amidst the fake palm trees and tiki chic that was festooned everywhere, or looking at the photographs that hung on every wall, showing all manner of old-time Hollywood stars, Errol Flynn and the like, posing with the drag queens.

We'd never played there, though; nobody had. The only live entertainment they put on were drag shows. So when they invited us to do their Easter party we jumped at it. This is what the New York Dolls were made for!

David called each of us up. "Hey, it's Club 82, so let's do the drag thing. Let's all dress in drag."

Arthur and Jerry were fine with that. I was in love with the idea, and immediately decided what I would wear; a school girl's apron that I'd picked up at the flea market in Paris, a black smock with buttons all the way down, a pair of tights and high heels. Arthur, I knew, would be wearing the tutu because, let's face it, you cannot beat a tutu. Jerry found a light yellow prom dress, and painted huge rouge circles on his cheeks; and David was in Cyrinda's Marilyn Monroe dress, complete with convincing falsies.

Only Johnny resisted. In fact, he was resolute.

Have you ever seen the movie *Performance*? The scene where Mick Jagger and Anita Pallenberg are trying to persuade James Fox, the on-the-run gangster, to try a new look, a more feminine one? And he explodes with rage and maybe fear, too: "I'm not a woman! I'm a man! A man, I tell you."

Johnny was a lot like that. Even at the dawn of the New York Dolls, when people were genuinely uncertain whether we were boys or girls,

Johnny remained convinced that they weren't talking about him, and when we pointed out how many obviously gay guys were clustered around his side of the stage, that was nothing to do with him either. He couldn't help it if they were attracted to him, but the feeling was certainly not reciprocated.

Now all Johnny's old fears and prejudices came screaming into view. No way, he swore, was he going to dress up like a woman, and he was true to his word. He turned up topless, just bare chest and his long, long hair, and he spent the show playing more with his hair than his guitar.

You could still feel the tension between Johnny and David; the two of them wouldn't even sing together. But it worked; he looked terrific – we all did – and we started to formulate a plan.

Back in the early days, one of the things that made the New York Dolls so unique was we were constantly seeking out new places to play, venues that nobody had thought of in the past. It was as if we had come full circle; in a way, Club 82 was one of the places we started at, talking about the band if not actually being one. It might even have been where we first agreed to look off the beaten track for places to play.

Let's do it again. The promoter who put on the show, David Lee, was an old fan of ours, and he was willing to go along with us. In fact, that happened a few times, fans of ours becoming booking agents. It's a bit of a step down from having William Morris do it, but in a way it was more exciting.

We hit on the idea of a world tour – with the world confined to the five boroughs that constitute New York City: Manhattan, Queens, Brooklyn, the Bronx and Staten Island. We'd pull in a bunch of new groups to open for us – The Miamis at Club 82, The Ramones at the Coventry in Queens, The Stilettos, which was Elda and Deborah's group, at another. We weren't going to make a fortune, but at least it would be fun, and it was something new as well. And "new" is what we were craving.

And then it was back to the bowling alleys and night clubs, and the inescapable awareness that the last time we were in this city we were playing the big place up the road. The auditorium where tonight, someone else, someone new, was topping the bill. Once, we even played a state fair, the Minneapolis/Saint Paul-Falcon Heights State Fair, and that was weird, Johnny and I wandering around a huge field before the show, looking at the two-headed cow, and the Pet A Piglet exhibition. It was families, beer and motorbikes all the way, but there's still people out there today who come up and tell me, "Hey, I saw you guys at the state fair in 1974."

Too Much, Too Soon was released in May, and the next three months were mapped out for us. Scooping up Jerry's friend Buddy Bowser to add sax to the show, as he'd done on so many occasions before, we set out on our longest tour yet, a rollercoaster that was destined to drag us down to our lowest depths ever.

Nothing was predictable. Scanning the list of our upcoming engagements, we were delighted to see a couple of British dates pencilled in: a festival in Buxton with Humble Pie and The Faces, and something called the Rock Proms with 10cc and The Incredible String Band.

Unfortunately, that was the last we ever heard of the trip.

If gigs were feeling unreliable, life off stage was growing more turbulent too.

We were in Cleveland, playing the Allen Theater, and staying at the Holiday Inn. David and I were roommates, up on the seventh floor. Unless Cyrinda was along as well, that was usually how we paired up; David and me in one room, Johnny and Jerry in another, and Arthur on his own.

I was looking out of the window, down towards the landing where the swimming pool and the restaurant were located, and something was wrong with the picture. Broken furniture littered the place. Tables, chairs ... a television set. It was like The Who had just passed through, at the height of Keith Moon's lunacy.

I shrugged it off. Holiday Inns attracted all manner of strange people in those days.

We had a ten o'clock lobby call, so David and I finished our packing and made our way down, to find our road manager talking to the hotel manager and handing him a thick wad of cash. Of course I asked what was going on, but all I received as an answer was a nod to a figure sitting slumped in the corner, very quiet, very withdrawn.

Arthur.

"Well," he explained, "I had these two girls in my room and they were really nice, but then they said, 'You're boring, Arthur. We were with Deep Purple last week, and they destroyed their whole hotel room for us.'"

So what did Arthur do? He said, "Oh yeah, baby, well watch this." And he threw everything in the room out of the window. All $2,000 dollars worth of it.

Our opening act in Cleveland, and at a number of other shows too, was Kiss. Like us the year before, they were now regarded as the hot up-and-comers, hungry to tour and show off their moves – which, in fairness, had come on quite a way from the days when they were just a Dolls dress-up act. Management had even considered signing them at one point; maybe they still were. And it made sense to put us together, if only to pull a few more people in to see the show.

I wasn't a fan – they were superb musicians, but I like a little Rolling Stones in my music, and they just didn't have any. The concerts went well, though, and audiences seemed happy.

Of the four Kiss-ers, Paul Stanley was the member I seemed to spend the most time with, talking about life on the road as I had experienced it, to help him prepare for what he would soon be going through. And one of the first things I ever told him was, "You have to pay tribute to the king."

"What do you mean? Who's the king?"

"Who do you think? It's Alice!"

Alice was enormous at that time; even though the hits were winding down, and the band would soon be breaking up, Alice Cooper was hard-wired into every kid in America, to the point where any group that could be construed as "weird-looking", who had long hair and dressed outside the norm … "Hey! It's Alice Cooper." And they'd want your autograph.

"Never disappoint them," I told him. "Just smile and sign and go on your way."

A few days later, we were at Detroit airport, and I suddenly hear my name being called. I turn and there's Paul, hurtling towards me, completely out of breath. For a moment, I thought something awful had happened, but then he broke into a massive smile. "Sylvain! I just signed my first Alice Cooper autograph."

Trust David to go one better. We were on our way to California, sharing the plane with a high-school orchestra, a bunch of whom were flashing surreptitious glances in our direction. I was seated next to David and, sure enough, a little way into the flight, one of them plucked up the courage to approach us.

Now, I don't think I resemble Alice in the slightest, but I look a lot more like him than David does, so it was no surprise that the kid addressed me first: "Hey Alice, can I have your autograph? We love you man, the whole band is on the plane," so yeah, yeah, sure, I sign Alice Cooper.

Three more young musicians came up, then four more, five more, and all the while David was watching me with mounting incredulity and, perhaps, just a little envy. So finally, I asked one of the kids, "Say, don't you want Mick's autograph too? Mick Jagger?" And David went straight to work, signing every piece of paper he is handed. Wow. I thought I had something with the Alice Cooper thing, but add Mick to the equation and you've got absolute mayhem.

Chapter 23

THE POWER OF "WE"

We were spending so much time in Los Angeles that one visit simply blurred into another. We were there in March for the Santa Monica show; we were back in July to play the Roxy and shoot some scenes for Ralph Bakshi's new movie (they were deleted long before *Hey Good Looking* was released); and we were back again in October for the Hollywood Palladium.

We weren't complaining; at this point in our career, it was the only place outside New York where we felt even halfway at home. Although that didn't stop us getting kicked out.

Our Roxy run was slotted into a break in the long-running American debut of *The Rocky Horror Show*: four shows while Tim Curry, Meatloaf and co. spent a few days without their make-up on. Obviously, we were the perfect substitute.

Or not. Rocky was absent, but his equipment and set still decorated the venue and, on our very first night at the club, someone trashed it. Not all of it, but enough; and they never found out who was responsible. But the best guess was that it was either one of the New York Dolls, or one of their audience, and we were sent packing. The rest of the shows were cancelled.

What the fuck was happening to us?

The New York Dolls had always been a high-spirited mob, but we had always been light-hearted too. Yes, our parties got out of hand; yes, we could be loud and obnoxious, and make straight people run for their lives. But we had never been associated with violence, and we had never encouraged it either. Now it seemed to be following us everywhere we went, and even when it took a day off, the fates could not resist knocking us back in some other way.

The day after the ill-fated Roxy gig, we were due to record a spot for Don Kirshner's *Rock Concert* television show.

It was a big deal; like *Midnight Special* and the *Old Grey Whistle Test*, it was one of those programmes that most music lovers caught, regardless of whether they cared for whoever was on that week, while the producers were smart enough to ensure a mix so that even if one half of the audience tuned out, the other half would tune in. Once again, we had the opportunity to blast ourselves into living rooms all across America; and, once again, we blew it.

For some reason, Johnny's P-90 pick-up was screeching a lot of radio interference, which is noise that engineers really hate even if guitar players sometimes enjoy it, because it sounds so nasty-ass. We were happy to keep going, because we'd overcome far worse problems on stage in the past. But the engineers were stopping us every other song, disappearing with Johnny's guitar and then handing it back with another layer of shielding on it. By the time they'd finished, it was so covered in stuff that he couldn't even play it.

Take after take we tried, so there was no chance of getting anything even remotely approaching a groove underway. The audience was getting restless – most of them were there for the night's other attraction, Rufus, to begin with. And we were miserable.

The only performance that was worth its weight that day was 'Chatterbox', because Johnny wasn't yet that good at singing and playing guitar at the same time, so he left the latter to me. David was getting into it as well, leaping around going "yeah, yeah, yeah", and the five of us were all but melting in the heat.

I don't know what the audience made of it, either in the studio or on television later, but I know what Don Kirshner thought. "You can make your own choice if they're good or not," is how he introduced us, and when you hear the audience let out a mighty roar in response, just remember this: it was spliced in from Rufus's performance.

At the beginning of September, we returned to Canada for a couple of shows in Vancouver, which is where Johnny and Frenchie met up with some bikers who gave them a one ounce stash of methamphetamine.

Our next gig was in New York in four days' time, so they smuggled the stuff back into the country, divided it between them, and went their merry ways.

Johnny then did his entire half-ounce in one sitting.

Speed is not an easy drug at the best of times. It makes you edgy, nervous and fraught, but most of all, it can make you paranoid. Which, considering how paranoid Johnny was already feeling – particularly when there was no smack around – did not make for a good combination.

First, he went to see his sister Marianne in Queens, who called me in tears once he'd left. Apparently, Johnny walked in to find a couple of Con Edison workmen repairing an electrical fault. Convinced they were cops, he locked them in the basement, then took off in Marianne's Camaro. She hoped he might be heading my way.

A couple of hours passed, and then my door buzzer rang. Or, rather, somebody pushed it and then, deciding I wasn't answering quickly enough, kept pushing it, over and over until I finally opened up.

It was Johnny, eyes bugged, teeth grinding, and completely out of his mind. I let him in, sat him down and told him I'd make some tea.

"No! I need to hide. They're after me. They're coming after me."

The story unfurled. The cops were after him. The FBI and the CIA. They were all out searching for him and, to make matters worse, David Johansen was one of them. He was so gone … and I swear, something happened that day that never really came back. He got so fucking crazy that something snapped forever. Johnny had always been all about excess, but this was too much even for him.

He was staring out of the window and a taxi drove past. "Did you see that? Johansen was in the back of that car."

Another came by. "Look! Now he's driving."

Now he was on his feet, pacing back and forth, his bottom jaw working from side to side, stacking up books and cushions in piles, and every car that passed by the window, Johansen was in it, watching the apartment and reporting back to the cops.

He stepped to the door and went outside. Now he was kneeling down beside my bicycle, rummaging through my tool box, and pretending he was repairing something. Only he wasn't; he was smashing it up. He cut the brake cables, bent the spokes, the lot, and all the time he was ducking whenever another car passed, insisting he'd seen Johansen inside.

It took hours to even calm him sufficiently that I could call another friend over, to bring some downers to help him relax. Then, with him half asleep beside me, I took him back to his apartment on 24th and got him into bed. What a mess.

This sort of thing was happening more and more. That was extreme, but it wasn't unusual, and because I was the only one amongst us who was usually sober, I ended up as the one who played nursemaid to the boys.

They all had their moments. Arthur was beginning to suffer from the DTs. If you didn't hand him a six pack the moment the shakes started, he'd fall apart. David was drinking, and holding things together, but he could be a nasty drunk as well. Johnny was Johnny. Jerry was the only guy who seemed unaffected by his intake; he's the only person I ever met for whom heroin was the better drug.

We began having to cancel shows. Although we never had the best reputation for punctuality, that had rarely happened before. Now, however, it was occurring so often that management warned that we were beginning to get a reputation. When we played, and everyone was feeling fine, we were still the best band on earth – I remember an outdoor festival in Florida, with Leon Russell and Ike & Tina Turner, and riding the hotel elevator with all the Ikettes backing singers crammed in around me. Another time in the same state, there was us, Slade and 10cc, and I loved Slade. We lived up to all our praise at those shows.

But we did some gigs with the Blue Öyster Cult, and God bless them for sticking with us when our tails were between our legs. Arthur got really sick, so Peter Jordan had to sit in for him again, and although we did get a lot tighter, it didn't change what was happening to us.

Mercury dropped us. We'd had a three-album deal, but after the second LP failed, they'd had enough. We weren't writing new songs; we weren't putting new stuff together. There was absolutely no appetite for anything. The sicknesses were becoming more prevalent, the money wasn't there, the ticket sales weren't happening, our girlfriends were leaving us, all manner of things were going wrong, and management were crapping in their pants.

I know I disagreed with almost every decision they made for us, but at least they were making decisions, trying to come up with some way of transforming us into a money-making machine. And even now, they were still there; they were just spending less and less on the things we needed – travel, food, accommodation. It was as if they'd finally given up on trying to make us pay; now they just wanted us to work.

Things got so bad that Marty had to put his own home up as collateral, that beautiful mansion where we first went to meet him. The money just wasn't coming in.

We were going ever deeper into debt, because everything management gave us, from our weekly wage to the gas in the tank, all of it was a loan. We were expected to pay it back, whether through record royalties or ticket sales. And as neither of them were worth shit at that point, we just sank deeper and deeper. You have to eat and they're holding the plate.

But our world was changing in other ways, too, because it wasn't 1972 any more, it was 1974, and even in New York, there were so many more bands playing. Patti Smith, Television, The Ramones and Blondie, they were all stepping out of the garage and onto the stage, and when you mentioned the Dolls to the average club goer, you might as well have said Mitch Ryder.

It didn't matter that we were younger than a lot of these other, newer, outfits. We were the old, old men of the scene, and it was impossible not to despair a little. That beautiful thing with which we started out had gone forever. The blueprint we wrote with blood and glitter had been dumbed down, blanked out and spray-painted with everyday dullness.

Even the audience that we believed we had created in our own image was gone. No longer a part of the show, now they were just spectators.

But the New York Dolls were not dead yet. Not while I had something to say about it. We were the Dolls. We would always be the Dolls.

Still, the portents piled up, including one whose ramifications we would not understand for a few years more.

It was the Dolls who brought Nancy Spungen to New York.

We met her in Philadelphia, at whatever club we happened to be playing that night, but which was certainly smaller than the one we'd played the time before. Something happened – someone riled the locals, maybe, or looked at a bruiser's girlfriend wrong, but we had to peel out of there very quickly, with all these drunken heavies banging on the side of the van as we squealed out of the parking lot.

There were a few girls in the back of the van ... this is the night when Nancy later said she had sex with all of the New York Dolls with the exception of Arthur, who was in our other car. She may have been correct, as well.

We got to New York and she spent the rest of the night with whoever, and the next thing we heard, she'd found a ground-floor apartment on

23rd Street, between 9 and 10. A lot of nights, after going to Max's, I'd meander down there, and knock on her window. "Oh Sylvain," she'd say as she buzzed me in, "Come on in, you can fuck my girlfriend."

It's impossible to second-guess fate; nobody could ever have imagined the life that Nancy would go on to lead, or how short it would ultimately be. Even then, though, it was clear that she was a very troubled person, and she wasn't enjoying her life. She was miserable, and that's just how she was made.

We spent Christmas on the road, at an inn just outside Cleveland, playing a little dance hall that was more commonly used for weddings and things. It sounds grisly, but actually it was fun. The crowd was on our side, and David played Santa Claus, handing out Christmas presents to everyone. Then, from there, we went to Fort Lauderdale in Florida, to a club that a long-ago friend of mine now booked.

Back in the mid-sixties, there were three bands in New York – The Young Rascals, The Rich Kids, who our road manager Tony Machine used to drum for, and The Vagrants, who included a distant cousin of mine, named Roger Mansour. They were the ones who came out with 'Respect' before even Aretha got her hands on it.

The Vagrants broke up, life went on, and then one day Roger called me up, completely out of the blue, to offer us a gig at the Flying Machine. Which, believe it or not, really was a flying machine: a restaurant and night club built into the fuselage of an old air force B52 bomber!

It was the most phenomenal-looking place; plus, Florida is where New Yorkers go when they can't stand the winter cold any more, so some of the audience already knew us, and the rest really wanted to. It was a small club, but it was wall-to-wall screaming chicks, crazy kids and even some Floridian girls we'd met when we were in London. One of them, Debbie, later married Paul from The Clash; another, Lori, became the first Mrs Johnny Depp. We were high and they were gorgeous.

And it was another step down on the ladder from success. We spent New Year's Eve back in New York, left to our own devices for the first time since we started the band. We'd been booked to play the Nassau Coliseum alongside Chuck Berry and Little Richard. But the show was cancelled and I think that sums up 1974. It was cancelled.

Management had given up. Marty lost his house and, out of funds, was forced out; his erstwhile partners wanted to get out too. Their last hope lay with a new song that I'd come up with, 'Teenage News'.

Everybody who heard it agreed that it was a hit, a balls-out rocker in a Chuck Berry meets Eddie Cochran meets the Stones kind of way, with three separate hooks and a title I borrowed from a line in Gary US Bonds' 'I Dig This Station' – "It keeps us up to date on every day, the top tunes from the teenage news." Even the team who started *Punk* magazine, John Holmstrom and Legs McNeil, told me their original title for the magazine was going to be *Teenage News*.

We were sent off to record it. We were back at the Record Plant, where we recorded the first album, and Jack Douglas, our engineer on that occasion, was going to produce. He'd already heard the song; he came over to my apartment one evening, and I played him my little demo. "So this is the song everyone's talking about? God, I love it. You've still got the Brill Building in you."

But … the curse of the Dolls. I was there first, talking to Jack. Jerry was next; he set up his drums and we were just beginning to get the drum sound right when – let's say he got sick and had to go home. Arthur didn't show at all, and neither did Johnny. The only people in the room were Jack, David and I, and out in the hallway, John Lennon!

He was in the studio too, down the corridor in Studio B where he was recording his *Rock'n'Roll* album, and had popped outside for whatever reason. And now I was chatting to him; I mentioned I'd been in *Up Your Legs*, and now I'm in the New York Dolls. "Yeah, I know," he said, and he gave me one of those looks.

I changed the subject. "Hey, I've got a guitar that you're going to love." I took him into the studio, opened the case, and there she is, the 1959 hollow body White Falcon, with a little decal of a fifties pin-up girl with a black panther, and he just flipped. He couldn't help himself; he picked that baby up, started strumming, and, I swear, if he'd not been called back to the studio, he'd never have put her down.

We never did record 'Teenage News'. But hey, I met John Lennon again.

Back to the drawing board. Management were still adamant that we had a hit record on our hands. We just didn't seem to have a group that could record it. So how about this?

Back when Marty was at Buddha, the big boys on the block were a pair of producers named Jerry Kasenetz and Jeff Katz. They were responsible for a string of hits – 'Yummy Yummy Yummy', 'Goodie Goodie Gumdrops', 'Simon Says'. That whole bubblegum movement at the end of the sixties was their baby, and though it looked like they had a ton of different combos in their stable – The 1910 Fruitgum Company, Crazy Elephant, Ohio Express and so on – in truth, they didn't have any. It was just a bunch of session men playing the records, and then Kasenetz–Katz would decide what name to release it under.

They also picked up a few "famous" names – Freddie & The Dreamers was one; The Shadows of Knight, once one of *the* all-time greatest American garage bands, was another. Now they were looking to pick up the New York Dolls.

Once again, the rest of the group couldn't make it – they were all either sick or in rehab. But David and I agreed to meet with the pair, and so began one of the most surreal episodes in the entire life of the New York Dolls.

A driver came to pick us up, a long-haired kid in a groovy-looking love van with disco lights in the back. Out to Long Island, to a studio that looked like it had just been built, and there was so much glass it could have been a greenhouse. Inside, the biggest mixing desk I have ever seen seemed to reach all the way back to Manhattan.

We chatted for a while, and then one of them pressed a switch and the room was filled with music, a super-catchy, super-poppy song that yeah, you could easily imagine becoming a hit. Top 40 radio was crap at the best of times, and this thing would have felt right at home there.

"What do you think?" we were asked.

"Yeah, it's okay. What is it?"

"What you just heard is your next hit record. You don't have to perform it, you don't have to play it, you don't even have to sing it. It doesn't matter if Johnny shows up, or anybody else. All we want is the New York Dolls' name and we guarantee you a hit record."

Which is exactly how they operated in the sixties.

Well forget it. I looked at David, he looked at me, and basically we started talking about our clothes – "Hey man, where did you get that shirt? It looks really good." We were polite. "We'll consider your offer". We told them we'd let them know. Then we were driven back to New York, dropped at our apartments and the next day, on the phone together, I think we said the exact same words at the exact same time. "What the fuck was that?"

No way were we going to do it, but that shows you how desperate management were, and it also shows you how weak the band was, the fact that it was David and I who were making the decisions, and the others didn't even know what was happening. Something else that I wasn't at all comfortable with.

And that was it for management. The last we heard from them. Marty was already gone; he couldn't put up any more collateral to pay for our salaries and expenses so he was basically kicked out – and he was the one who signed us in the first place! The last we heard from his partners was an offer to play a festival in Japan in July, and I don't think we even got back to them about it.

I was so disappointed about what happened to Marty, and the whole Kasenetz–Katz business, that I wasn't going to do anything for them – although, ironically, we did play the Japanese festival, after the organisers got in touch with Bob Gruen, to arrange for him to photograph the event, and happened to ask if he knew where we were. But, although we used the name, it wasn't the New York Dolls; Johnny was gone, Jerry and Arthur, too.

And therein hangs my final story.

Chapter 24

THE SEX PISTOLS, THEY'RE YOUR BAND

It was a beautiful summer day around the middle of February, 1975. I was walking past the Chelsea Hotel when a familiar voice suddenly hailed me. "Oi! Sylvain!"

It was Malcolm! He was in town to meet wholesalers and distributors, introducing Vivienne's latest lines to America. They'd just changed the name of the store from Let It Rock to Sex, and he was having a little trouble with some of his would-be customers not being keen on the name of the line, Sex Original, emblazoned on all the labels. In the end, he started unpicking them all, because that's the only way they would stock his clothes.

He was full of news and excitement, though. At least until he asked me what the New York Dolls were up to, at which point he turned quiet and thoughtful.

Malcolm loved the Dolls. From the moment I met him in 1971, and every time we saw him thereafter, all he could talk about was how much he adored the group; how refreshing we were compared to the rest; how the New York Dolls could change the world. The other groups who came along in our wake … he liked a few of them, dismissed a few more, but not one, he insisted, would have existed without the New York Dolls to show them the way. "If only you could have stayed in London," he'd say. Or, "If only you had better management."

"Like who?" I asked. And he smiled.

"Let's get together and talk about it."

We started meeting up every day. A friend of his ran a second-hand store right on the corner of 8 and 22nd, a couple of blocks from Malcolm's short-lease studio apartment on 20th. We'd meet at the store, then cross over the road to a coffee house. And we'd start making plans.

There was a loft down the road on 23rd that he knew of, that had just become available. Its last occupants were the funk group Mandrill, who had fixed it up as a rehearsal space and all-purpose hang-out. "It sounds perfect for you lot. Let's go take a look."

I followed him. When Malcolm got a bee in his bonnet, he was like a force of nature, completely unstoppable, simply flattening you with the weight of his enthusiasm. But he was right, the loft was perfect. It was on the third or fourth floor, above an off-track betting shop on a street that was otherwise occupied by piano showrooms. The rent was reasonable. "We'll take it," he said, and he rented it on the spot.

The place was huge; fourteen-foot-high ceilings, and vast arched windows, caked with decades of filth – or, at least, they were until Malcolm got it into his head to clean them up, balancing on the tiny ledge that hung out over a four-storey drop, a squeegee and a rag in each hand, while Frenchie and I clung onto his legs because one good wind would have swept him off his perch.

So now we had a loft, just like we did in 1972. Frenchie moved in as a kind of caretaker, and we got all of our equipment out of storage and prepared to move it in. And this is where Hilly Kristal comes into the story because ... although I've already mentioned that there was no CBGB when the New York Dolls were around, there *was* a truck rental place right across the road from where the club would be, and it was owned by Hilly. All the New York bands used to rent from him, too, not only because he was cheap, but also because he didn't care if you had a funky licence. He'd rent to anybody.

The loft was convenient for everybody. I still had the place on Charles Street, David lived just a short walk away on 17th and 9; Johnny and Arthur weren't far away. The only one I'm not certain about was Jerry; I never quite figured out where Jerry lived.

Malcolm's enthusiasm swept through the New York Dolls like a plague. You have to remember, it was only a few weeks earlier that I couldn't even get three-fifths of the line-up to the Record Plant to record the best song I'd ever written. Now, you could scarcely keep us apart. Sometimes I'd arrive at the loft at whatever time we said we'd meet, and they'd already be there, already playing, and looking over at me as if to say, "What kept you, man? We've been here for hours."

Songs and new arrangements were pouring out of us. 'Red Patent Leather' just leaped into the world, fully formed before it was even completely written. 'Teenage News' was growing even tighter, and it had already been seamless to begin with. 'Downtown' was coming back and it was on fire. Johnny came up with one of the greatest songs he ever wrote, 'Pirate Love'.

I introduced 'Dizzy Miss Lizzy' and Eddie Cochran's 'Something Else', and we made them our own; and 'Daddy Rolling Stone', which I wanted us to play like The Who used to, back on their very first album. But Johnny could never quite get the riff together, so he changed it and it became even better. One of my favourite records of all time is the version of 'Daddy Rolling Stone' which he included on *So Alone*, with Steve Marriott and Phil Lynott trading verses with him. That came directly out of the New York Dolls' version.

I was singing lead on a song or two, and playing keyboards too, a lovely Fender Rhodes 88. You should have heard our version of 'Ain't Got No Home', that terrific old Frogman Henry blues; or the original vision of 'Girls Girls Girls', which would wind up on David's first solo album. Everything we touched turned to gold; half a new album had already come together, and we'd worked up a killer set list as well. We even threw in a few of our oldies!

We had some fantastic jams in that loft. Just like Christie Street, it became a magnet for other musicians who would drop by to hear us, and then pick up an instrument. We were spending time, too, with a band called The Demons – we used to let them rehearse at the loft when we weren't around (and Frenchie wasn't asleep), and their guitarist, Walter Lure, really hit it off with Johnny, a nascent partnership that would have its own consequences a few months later.

All manner of schemes were dreamed up in that loft; all kinds of crazy ideas and wacky notions that we could sit up all night discussing, and it didn't matter that a lot of them would be forgotten by morning. We were communicating again, we were brothers. We were alive.

Malcolm was in on most of these conversations, but for the most part, he kept quiet. He might add a thought or two on occasion, but he was happy just to see the band become a band again, and it was only later that I realised that *that* was perhaps his most impressive talent.

So much has been written over the years about what a Svengali Malcolm was; how he could shift and twist situations to meet his own requirements; how he could have led the Devil astray, if he thought it would serve his purposes. And maybe that's true.

The Malcolm we knew, though, never asked us for anything, and never suggested, even quietly, that *this* might be a good thing to do, and *that* would be even better. Every decision that we took came out of the group; if not all of us, then one of us, and the rest would agree.

Malcolm saw his role as the one who would then make things happen. He loved the New York Dolls, but, more importantly than that, he loved what we were already saying. He didn't need to add ideas of his own; what we were coming up with was already perfect. All he did was give us comfort, after we'd been abandoned by everyone, and I wish we'd had him at the beginning.

He gave us new reason to hope, and maybe it *was* a practice run for him, like people would write later on. But even if it was, so what? He never had a contract with us or any kind of written deal. It was just him saying, "Hey, I'm going to help you," and us replying, "Thanks very much."

I don't think he even took a commission. We were hardly making any money anyway, but he didn't take a penny. He spent money, though, hiring a lawyer to make sure the old management couldn't touch us, getting us out of the old contracts because they were so screwed up, and buying us everything we needed.

He didn't even originate what history describes as our "Communist" phase.

In fact, that whole business started with a simple request. We were sitting around the loft one night after rehearsal, and somebody asked Malcolm, "Hey, do you think Vivienne would make me a pair of red shoes."

"Sure," Malcolm replied, and then someone else spoke up. "Hey man, I want red shoes too"; then someone else, and all of a sudden, we were all getting red shoes. Then Arthur asked, "Do you think she could make me a red shirt?" and Johnny, "Me, too." Now we're all getting red shirts. Then red pants and red hats, and David's getting a complete red gaberdine suit. We already have the song 'Red Patent Leather', which David and I wrote, and, very loosely, there was a theme developing around that.

Malcolm fired off a telegram letting Vivienne know what we all wanted, which was basically a wardrobe full of bright red and shiny stuff, and then David turned to Malcolm and said, "Hey why don't we just hang up the red flag?"

It was one of those moments when ... Malcolm and David were never especially close; it was rare for them to really connect. But, at that moment, they did. I could see it happening; they were both silent, just looking at one another, and you knew they were both having the exact same idea at precisely the same time.

The next thing, Malcolm turned up at David and Cyrinda's apartment with all the material, and Cyrinda started sewing the flag, sitting on their bed with the hammer and sickle. There was no political agenda at work, and no cultural one either. Like Johnny with the swastika at the Waldorf Astoria, we were playing with imagery, not politics, and while we knew there was potential for people to misunderstand, we (perhaps naively) believed that art would conquer all. Because that's what it was. Art has always been closer to magic than logic, and this was more magical than most. Only, instead of planting it in a museum, we were going to take it on tour.

Or maybe we just didn't give a fuck what people thought. Again.

We had even written the song that would announce our return – 'The Kids Are Back', a triumphant rocker whose chord progression was so good that Johnny would later add it to the song he wrote with DeeDee Ramone, 'Chinese Rocks'. It turned an okay number into a classic.

The day the clothes arrived from England was like Christmas, two huge boxes, with every garment conscientiously labelled with its intended recipient's name. She needn't have bothered. Sweaters, bow ties, jeans, shirts, shoes, jackets, and everything in red. We piled in and pulled out whatever we could, then traded back and forth until we all had what we wanted.

Some film-makers got in touch. They were looking to test drive a new invention, a hand-held 3D camera, and they wanted us along for the ride. We had already recorded 'Teenage News' by now – not much more than a very competent demo, but we were happy with it, and the idea of being able to present it to record companies with an accompanying 3D movie was irresistible.

We filmed in an old television studio in Astoria, Queens. It was the creepiest place, dark and desolate, as though it hadn't been used in years; walking in, all you could see was one stage light in the middle of nothing.

There were a couple of fake brick walls that we'd be using as a backdrop; David got to work, painting "Heavy Mental Kids" on one of them. Somebody brought in some garbage cans, and we arranged ourselves around them, some of us perched on top of them and Jerry using a couple as drums. The tape started rolling and we lip-synched 'Teenage News' – and we never heard from the film-makers again.

Years later, during the eighties, someone in Canada got in touch with me and said he knew the mother of the guy who made it. Nothing ever came of it, but somewhere out there, there's a 3D film of the New York Dolls playing 'Teenage News', just like somewhere else out there, there's the film of our Bataclan riot.

We hadn't played many live shows that year: a couple with The Dictators in Queens back in January 1975; a few nights at My Father's Place, out on Long Island (I wondered whether Kasenetz–Katz were there, to see if we'd play their song?); and then a week-long residency at the Little Hippodrome at the end of February, where we seriously road-tested the new material and outfits. It sounded perfect, it looked magnificent.

To coincide with the shows, Malcolm unleashed the manifesto that would let the world know we were back, a masterpiece of tongue-in-cheek humour that fit perfectly into our mood.

"What are the politics of boredom?" demanded the headline, before explaining how the Dolls had "completed the first Red 3D rock'n'roll movie ..." and now "assumed the role of the People's Information Collective, in association with the Red Guard". It was signed by the New York Dolls, and "produced by Sex Originals of London".

The show did not go down well; not in New York and not beyond either, as we set out on the short ... very short ... tour that Malcolm and Roger Mansour had strung together. Essentially, we just skipped down the east coast in our army-coloured Fury 3 station wagon: three shows in South Carolina, and then a handful of dates in Florida, and everywhere our arrival was greeted with confusion.

Asking the musicians about our stance was not going to enlighten anybody either. Malcolm and David knew about Communism – David had been going through a Maoist phase even before Malcolm arrived.

But Arthur, Jerry and Johnny didn't care; they probably thought it was all about clothes, and I saw it strictly from the visual angle, which I still say was fucking fantastic.

Audiences were equally divided. Either we were the heroes of the revolution … or we were a bunch of Commie cocksuckers who should be driven out of town with pitchforks and shovels. Which might have been an improvement on what they wanted to do to us before, back when they thought we were just a bunch of faggots, but it still didn't sound very comfortable.

What was important, however, was how we felt, and there were no complaints at all. From our point of view, as musicians and performers, the shows were going very well. We were so tight, probably as good as we had ever been in the past. We were reading one another instead of just following somebody's lead, and the fans who liked what we were doing were really latching onto 'Teenage News' and 'Pirate Love', so that was just like the old days as well, when we were having hits before they'd even been recorded.

The only cloud was that Arthur didn't make it to Florida. He was still drinking heavily, and had even gone into rehab for a short while after the 3D shoot. I remember Jerry, David, Malcolm and me going to visit him at the hospital in Yonkers. He came out before we went on tour, but we had barely arrived in South Carolina when it was clear that the poor guy just couldn't go on. Malcolm drove him to the airport, and we called in Peter Jordan for the next few gigs.

That aside, I'm making this all sound very idyllic and, strictly from a musician's point of view, it was. In the "real" world, however, things were growing fractious once more.

A lot of the difficulties were down to money – basically, there wasn't any. Anything we earned went on food and transport and whatever; we weren't socking it away in the bank, that's for sure.

Johnny and Jerry were sick and getting sicker; David was growing distant again, maybe thinking of the golden horizons that people said awaited him once he stopped being a Doll; and I was just trying to keep the group together. I remembered the party we attended in Paris, and Vivienne turning to me to ask, "Are you always this happy?" "Yes," I replied, because I was. But sometimes, it was hard to keep it up.

Home throughout our time in Florida was at Jerry Nolan's mother Charlotte's house. She'd remarried and they had a place just outside Tampa which she operated as a kind of motel, only instead of having cabins or rooms, she had half a dozen trailers which she divided up between us. Jerry, of course, stayed in the house and we'd meet in there every evening while Charlotte cooked dinner for us all, these big bowls of sweetcorn and mashed potato and gravy, good southern cooking.

There were a few other people staying there, but the only one we really saw was this guy who used to sit outside his trailer, cleaning his gun. He'd take it apart, put it back together again, take it apart again ... what a sight that was. Jerry's stepbrothers were there as well, and they would come in during dinner and demand, "Y'all faggots? I know you're from New York City, but are y'all faggots?"

Poor Malcolm would be sitting there, choking on his food. He'd never been to the south before, never met real rednecks. It might look good in the movies, but when you're actually living it, it can be scary.

The mood continued deteriorating. I talked to Malcolm about it a couple of times. We were sharing one of the trailers, so we had time for those discussions that needed to be had, and even he was losing some of his early optimism.

Back when this whole adventure got started, Malcolm sat us all down at his friend's shop for a "clear the air" session. Everything, he said, should be out on the table – every petty dispute, every simmering resentment, every problem we had with one another.

It was difficult, but we did it. That was how desperate we all were to keep the New York Dolls alive.

Somebody brought up Johnny's and Jerry's drug use. They promised to try to clean up and, for a short time, I think they did. Arthur promised to scale back on his drinking and, of course, that didn't work out, but again, he gave it a go. David was asked to stop behaving as though he was the boss, and he agreed, on condition that the others stopped behaving in a way that left him with no alternative – because, and he was right on this score, somebody needed to make decisions, and if the others didn't want to, then he would.

All of this was ironed out and, for a while, it held. But old habits died hard, and all the old problems were surfacing again.

Arthur returned, and that lightened the mood a little. We were always stronger when we were five. But one night as we were sitting around talking after dinner, Johnny and David started arguing about something.

No surprise there; they'd been doing it for years. But this time, the argument didn't stop. Voices raised, tempers frayed, and suddenly David came out with it. "I'm sick and tired of this. You're all replaceable."

I almost choked on my food, but Johnny and Jerry just looked at one another, leaped out of their seats, and slammed out of the room.

I followed them outside. They were already out of sight, in the trailer packing their stuff. But Malcolm and I drove Johnny and Jerry to the airport the following day, and, as we dropped them off and they were walking away, it hit me what was happening. My throat constricted, my eyes were watering. I looked at their retreating backs and suddenly called out, "Hey, Jerry, Johnny, what about the New York Dolls?"

They both turned around. Johnny was silent. He was hurting, too. But Jerry looked me in the eye.

"Fuck the New York Dolls." And they disappeared into the airport. It was the end for us ... but it was the beginning for everybody else.

It was so fucked up, and it was all Johnny and David. They just didn't want to play together any longer, and it really didn't matter what the argument was about. David could have said anything, Johnny could have answered anything ... "I'm sick of your red shoes," or "I hate that I can't get any dope," or "Malcolm is a clown." Anything. Just one little push, that's all it needed, and that's what happened.

More than anything, I wished Frenchie had been with us. We'd left him behind in New York because we couldn't afford to bring him, but now I realised what a mistake that was. Because he would have quenched the fire, just as he had on many occasions in the past. He'd have given David one of his Frenchie looks, and have said, "Come on, Rocky ..." He always called David that. "Come on Rocky, take it back." And David would have.

But not tonight.

The next I hear about Johnny and Jerry, they're back in New York, back at the loft, rehearsing a new project with Richard Hell, who had just departed from Television. The funny thing about this new band, though, was where they got their name from.

Back when we were in Florida, driving around in the station wagon, I was playing with the radio like I always did. There's *always* an AM station that's playing the oldies, and finally I found it, just as 'Heartbreak Hotel' came on.

Jerry and Johnny were sitting behind me, and I turned around to them and said, "Man, wouldn't that be a great name for a band? The Heartbreakers!" And what happened? They looked at one another like lovers do, and when they went back to New York, they took that name with them.

Some time later, I was visiting Frenchie and I happened to run into Johnny. "Hey man, you took my name … and that's the second time you've done that." And he replied, "Don't worry, I've got a great name for you." He then gave me The Criminals, which became my own next outfit.

All of that, though, was away in the future. Right now, it was me who was heartbroken. All that night, the only thoughts going through my mind were was this *really* it? Were those *really* the last words?

I traced our story in my mind. I thought about Billy, that first meeting in the gym and the friendship that developed when Alphonso tried to make us fight. The years we had spent playing, learning, honing our skills. Meeting Johnny, and those early guitar lessons. Finding Arthur at Nobody's and David in his apartment. Rusty Beany's, the Mercer and Max's.

I remembered those days when we truly believed that the Dolls were going to conquer the world; the thrill of those first gigs; the excitement in England. Recording the albums. Touring the country. I even thought about our roadies, Frenchie and Peter, of course, but also Max Black and Desmond Sullivan – the one a beautiful cat with glasses, who never removed his motorcycle jacket, and worked my and Arthur's side of the stage; the other responsible solely for Johnny's side, which gave him more work to do than anybody else, but who kept us amused with his tales of touring around with Tiny Tim.

The hopes, the dreams, the triumphs. And all of it leading – to this? I couldn't believe it.

Back inside the house, David, Arthur and Malcolm were still sitting quietly, but there was business to attend to. The Dolls still had one or two more gigs scheduled before we could go back to New York, and we couldn't afford not to play them. So we hooked up with a local guitarist whom Arthur was hanging out with, named Steve Duren, and a drummer he knew whose name I cannot remember.

We kept Johnny's departure a secret; we knew how disappointed the audience would be if we appeared without him, so, before we went on, I teased up Steve's hair into a rough facsimile of Johnny's trademark mess, and instructed him never to look anyone in the eye.

Poor kid. I think he spent most of the show with his back to the crowd, although the experience clearly didn't do him any harm. The next time I saw him, he was Blackie Lawless of WASP.

Chapter 25

TAKE NO PRISONERS

The gigs at an end, David and Peter flew back to New York, and Arthur went off with Steve. But I decided that Malcolm really needed to see New Orleans. As I told him, it was only just up the road, and if you look at the map, it is. No need to mention that you had to drive through Alabama, Mississippi and a serious chunk of Louisiana first, or that it's 700 miles away, at a time when the speed limit had been reduced to 55 mph because of the oil crisis.

Or even that I didn't have a valid driving licence.

Actually, that turned out to be the least of our worries because, out one evening, I ran into a couple of girls who were both willing and able to take the trip with us, and they both were legal drivers.

We paid off the roadie we'd picked up for the shows. Malcolm left Arthur some money, and then we packed up our stuff, or as much as we could carry, and I've regretted this ever since. I had my favourite amp in the whole world down there, a cream-coloured Fender Tremolux which sounded so cool with the white Gibson I was playing, and I left it with Arthur, telling him to return it the next time I saw him. Instead he gave it to the future Blackie Lawless, and that broke my heart almost as much as the New York Dolls had.

We got into New Orleans a couple of days later. The girls already had somewhere to stay, so Malcolm and I booked into a place I'd found the first time I was there with the Dolls, this lovely old hotel with the wrought iron balcony wrapped all around, and cast in the shape of corn stalks … so, the Corn Stalk Hotel.

Malcolm was a friend, but he was also a fan; every chance he got, he'd be asking questions about the Dolls, or demanding stories about us. In New Orleans, I could tell him tales and show him where they happened, the last time the New York Dolls took New Orleans, back in July 1974.

I told him about the elevator full of tourists that I happened to walk into, who took one look at the tassel pants I was wearing (yet another trade with Johnny) and immediately asked if I was "a performer".

I remembered Johnny rushing into my room to announce that Frogman Henry was playing around the corner, fifteen minutes on, five minutes off, from early evening until late into the night. I was there for every set he played, *and* I got his autograph on a napkin.

We laughed at the picture I painted of Arthur, so excited by "the girl on the swing" – a pair of bare legs that swung back and forth through the window of one of the strip clubs. I showed him the T-shirts with tits painted on them … in fact, I bought one for Malcolm while we were there, and soon enough Vivienne was selling the same kind of thing.

And I told him how we got so damned drunk, more than I had ever been in my entire life.

All of that, and we didn't even play a show! The venue burned down a few nights before we got there, but our previous show, in Baton Rouge, was so close at hand, and now we had a few free days. It's party time.

Now, as then, I thought of New Orleans as a kind of vacation. I'd not had a genuine break in a year, since my friend Janet Planet and I took a few days in Jamaica, in the hills above Negril, after we finished recording *Too Much, Too Soon*. There, we fell in with the cast of the movie *O Lucky Man!*, devoured ganja cake and skinny-dipped on the beach, and were chased away by an old Jamaican lady, with hardly any teeth, but a very big broom: "How dare you do this in front of my home?"

Malcolm, however, never rested. One night, I returned to our hotel room to discover he had brought home … I don't want to call her a midget, but she was a very short young lady. Very very short. It wasn't even a sexual thing, although I do remember thinking, if anything should kick off, I'm out of there.

He was fascinated by what people used to call "freaks", and all he did was sit there asking questions about how she coped with everyday life;

how she did this, that and the other thing. He was genuinely interested in how she lived. And, of course, this carried on into the Sex Pistols, too, and the entourage he built up around them. He was brilliant, and he wanted to know everything. But some of the things he wanted to know were definitely weird.

Other times, I'd wake up to find him already on the telephone, calling up record shops to find out what their hours were, and then telling me to get dressed up a little, because we were going out to visit them.

Maybe you don't hear about it so much any more, but back in the days before the music industry became a centralised monolith, New Orleans was one of the regional capitals of American music, with a sound and a flavour that was completely unique, and countless local labels pumping out some of the most important records ever made.

That universe was still alive when we were there, and Malcolm must have called up every name he knew – arranging meetings, setting up dinners, and all of them so that *they* could meet *me*. Maybe the Dolls are finished, he'd say. But Sylvain Sylvain is just getting started.

He even set us up with Allen Toussaint, one of the most distinctive producers who ever lived, at the studio where he'd made so much magic. I really dressed up for that one, with my red patent leather and my make-up bag of course, and Malcolm couldn't believe it. "You look like you're going to do a show," he said, and I just looked at him ... . every day! And besides, he'd got all those wild suits that he always wore, so what was he even on about?

We got into the cab, met up with Toussaint, and suddenly Malcolm was pitching me as the next big thing to be launched out of England. We were going to form a new group, Malcolm would be our manager, and we were going to be bigger than Marc Bolan, because I was already a million times cooler.

Poor Toussaint! I don't think he knew what to make of it all. But he took us on a tour of the studio; he tinkled on the piano, some gorgeous bluesy stuff – what an experience! He was such a nice guy, what a gentleman.

Meanwhile, my mind was working overtime. England? Yes, we'd talked about it a little. There were some kids who hung out at Sex, just teenagers like we were when the Dolls first started, but they needed a guiding hand. I was to provide that hand. Between my name as a Doll and my years of experience, and their rough-hewn charm and love of rock'n'roll, Malcolm was convinced we could put something together that would blow the music scene apart.

It all sounded very interesting. Tell me more.

It was time to leave New Orleans. The girls had already left … years later, I ran into one of them and she swore that we'd just dumped them there, but it really wasn't like that. Besides, I'm French! I don't dump girls!

The only thing I needed to do was become a legal driver. I arranged to take my driving test in New Orleans. Malcolm, of course, appointed himself to test me with the book before I went in, and I have to say, being coached by an Englishman who doesn't know how to drive (and would be on the wrong side of the road even if he did), standing on the sidewalk outside the motor vehicle department, is a total thrill. It was a blazing hot day, and Malcolm was standing there with the book, in whatever garish suit he'd donned for the occasion, a demented ginger schoolmaster with the vocabulary of a street hoodlum.

"All right, you come to a stop sign, what do you fucking do?"

"You fucking stop," I replied.

Thank goodness the actual instructor was somewhat more polite.

I passed. The guy said I was the smartest Caucasian he'd seen in weeks, and for the first time in my life, I was officially permitted to drive. I collected my temporary permit, which was good for thirty days (they'd mail the full licence at the end of that period), and now we were driving all over the place.

Back to all the record shops we visited, loading the car up with 45s – things like 'Check Mr Popeye' by Eddie Bo; 'Handa Wanda', which I would later play with The Stilettos, with Johnny and Jerry at Buddy Bowser's loft; old Little Richard and Frogman Henry, Professor Longhair, Jerry Dorsey, all the dudes. Then we packed up the rest of our stuff, paid off our hotel bill and headed north – New Orleans to Nashville and on to New York. Passing along the way through Mississippi and Alabama.

That was an experience in itself. Particularly the time we had to turn off the highway and find a gas station.

Now remember, this is 1975, the Deep South. It's still very rural. The fast food chains and Walmart stores haven't yet started moving in, and even though a major highway was just a few hundred yards away, the road we were on was little better than a dirt track.

We pulled into the filling station, which was barely more than a dirty hut and couple of pumps, and suddenly we were surrounded by maybe half a dozen African-Americans. One started cleaning the windows, another was looking under the hood, another was checking the tyres; they were scurrying around doing this and that, and then this white guy came out in his green gas attendant outfit, with his name written on it.

He filled the tank and Malcolm handed him a traveller's cheque, which is how you did things in those days.

Except here. "What do you mean, traveller's cheque? This is cash only." Then he went back inside and picked up a big-ass gun.

I had never seen Malcolm move that quickly. Nor me, for that matter. We were digging behind the seats, reaching around on the floor, scrambling through our pockets, emptying our luggage, searching for change wherever it might have fallen, and finally we scraped together however much it was. I thrust it out of the window to the guy and we screeched out of there as fast as we could.

Our other problem was a little more familiar, at least to me. In the same way as Billy's stomach had problems adapting to the kind of food that was served up on English motorways, when we visited the UK in 1972, so Malcolm's was having much the same trouble with American highway cooking.

For more than half the journey, he was stretched out in the back seat, clutching his stomach and groaning in pain. "Oh you've got to stop, mate ..." He really was hurting. "Oh blimey, I shouldn't have eaten that steak, I don't know why I did." If we weren't pulling off the highway to pick him up medicine, we were pulling into every rest stop for him to use the bathroom. There were times when I didn't think we'd ever get to New York.

Finally, however, we did, and during respites from his intestinal sufferings, we mapped out a course of action. First and foremost, he needed to sell the last of his merchandise, because that was the reason he'd come to New York in the first place. But he also wanted to get me fixed up as well. The notion of the London-based project was growing firmer in his mind every day, only now it had expanded.

I told him about a girl I knew who, as far as I was concerned, was going to become one of the biggest superstars ever, and how I really wanted to put a band together with her.

"Fine, she can come to England, too. What's her name?"

"Deborah Harry."

"Terrific. Let's meet her."

Malcolm set up the meeting. I think he lured her by giving her clothes, and a few days later we were gathered round a table at McSorley's Ale House on East 7th Street, one of those old-time bars that didn't even allow women to cross the threshold until sometime in the late sixties. Sawdust on the floor, and all they served was beer, and plates of cheddar cheese and onion.

We ordered and Malcolm launched into his pitch. "We're going to England, I'm bringing Syl, my wife does this and I can do that, and he wants you to come with him."

We could see her thinking it over, and maybe she was torn. But finally, she turned us down. "I'm sorry. But I don't think I could ever leave Chris Stein." Which I had also suspected might happen, but it was worth a try. Besides, all of my other instincts were spot on. Out of the whole movement that the Dolls opened the door for, in New York and every place else, Deborah indeed became the biggest star.

Meanwhile, we still had to get rid of the clothes. I took Malcolm to this place on 8th Street where Billy and I used to sell stuff, and he offloaded a bunch. He went down to Christopher Street and got rid of some more. Deborah bought a few more things, and he sold more to Rick and Liz Derringer when we stopped by their brownstone on 13th Street.

That was interesting too, because staying with them at the time was a model who'd come up from Texas, named Jerry Hall. This was before she met Bryan Ferry, Mick Jagger and the rest. She was really at the start of her supermodel career, and she fell head over heels in love with this sleeveless top that Vivienne had made, a really cool red latex S&M thing with a black zipper that ran across the chest area.

She wanted to try it on, so she disappeared upstairs for a few moments, then returned to see what we thought. She looked ... well, you can imagine. Even Malcolm was going "Blimey, mate", while Jerry was giving us a twirl and saying,"Oh, isn't this nice!"

"Yeah, it looks so good, it's beautiful," said someone, and then Jerry answered, "Yeah, but this is the way to wear it" – and she unzipped it. My heart skipped a couple of beats, and Malcolm's jaw just dropped. "Oh, my gawd!" Even the girls were stunned.

One afternoon, I was dropping Malcolm off somewhere and this guy I knew who lived across the street, Derwood, opened his window and shouted across, "Hey, I hear you guys broke up."

I shouted back "yeah", not sounding too happy, but all I got in return was "fucking assholes", and he slammed the window shut. And I knew we were going to get hell from people for giving up so quickly.

But it was a good time. We were still deciding exactly what we were going to do, the actual logistics of our plans for London, and meanwhile the whole New York punk movement had taken off. Johnny, Jerry and Richard Hell had The Heartbreakers up and running, and Malcolm was obsessed with Richard.

In fact, he was absorbing everything, hanging out at all the clubs, watching all these new acts learn to walk, and he wanted to transplant the entire scene to the UK. Plus, he was hanging out on the West Side as well, taking in the leather bars and the gay scene, and everything was soaking into him: not just the music, but the fashions as well, and that's what he introduced to Vivienne once he arrived back in London – not just the tits top from New Orleans, but Richard Hell's torn T-shirts, the heavy-duty sex clothes, the safety pins, everything.

It was time for him to leave. We agreed that I'd give him my Fender Rhodes piano and my white Les Paul Custom, and he'd take them over with him. Then, once he was settled again, he'd send me a plane ticket; I'd fly over and he'd hook me up with the band. My future, he said, was his future. And then he flew home.

What happened next?

First, I received an airmail letter from him at my parents' house, a seven-page missive, outlining everything, all that Malcolm and I had talked about. How I would be flown over to London; how he had my group together; how they'd found a singer whom they named Johnny Rotten – "He can't sing, but he's definitely better than Johansen." He even sent pictures, little photo-booth black and whites of my four future bandmates. Rotten was wearing a beret and looked strangely French. I liked that.

I lost track of that letter for a long time. I read it, and then filed it away. It would be another sixteen years before I saw it again, when I was cleaning out the house following my mother's death in 1991, still tucked away in the drawer where I'd left it in 1975. It's now in the Rock and Roll Hall of Fame, the first thing you see when you enter their punk rock exhibit.

There was a phone call from Vivienne's. I chatted to the boys – Paul Cook, Steve Jones, Glen Matlock and, very briefly, Johnny Rotten, then

Malcolm reiterated his pledge. "You've got to come over, we'll send you a ticket, we'll get some songs together, it's going to be fantastic."

I'm still waiting for the plane ticket, but I know Malcolm will come through with it one day.

Meanwhile, I was living across the street from David; we were talking, we were wondering. We did the Japanese tour with Peter Jordan, Tony Machine and Chris Robison, and every day I'd check the mail to see if the ticket had arrived yet. It never did. But we were getting gigs as the Dolls, and David's solo career was beginning to take shape, so I worked with him on that.

My own band, The Criminals, came together, and after that, The Teardrops. Arthur reunited with Big George and launched the Corpse Grinders; and Johnny and Jerry replaced Richard Hell with our old friend Walter Lure and went to England to tour with the Sex Pistols. Later, I heard that Steve Jones was playing my old Les Paul Custom, but the Fender Rhodes piano had been sold to pay for the Pistols' rehearsal space on Denmark Street.

The New York Dolls had never been spread so far apart, but we never really separated either. None of us knew when the phone would ring and a familiar voice would come on the line, to ask if you wanted to get together, see what happened, try something out.

That went on for years, all the way up until death got in the way of life. Johnny was the first to go, in 1991, just thirty-eight years old. Jerry followed, barely nine months later, aged forty-five. And then Arthur, only fifty-five, less than a month after he joined David and me to reform the New York Dolls for the 2004 Meltdown festival curated by Morrissey.

Just like Billy, and so many others in this story … my mom and dad, Valerie Sutain, Cyrinda Foxe, David Bowie, Marty Thau, Leee Black Childers, Sable Starr, and far too many others … I think of them all almost every day, both the good times and the bad, both the laughter and the tears.

In rock'n'roll years, I am now about 300 years old. But, even if I live for 300 more, I doubt I'll ever have such times again.

EPILOGUE

The New York Dolls played their first live concert, without me, on December 24, 1971 at the Endicott Hotel in New York City, and their last – without Billy, Johnny or Jerry – in April 1975 in Florida. David and I then kept the name, at least, alive for another eighteen months, until we played our final show as the Dolls alone, on December 30, 1976.

It wasn't a bad lifespan – five years is more than many acts survive. Even The Beatles only had eight years at the top, and the Sex Pistols – the group I came so close to joining – barely made it to three, and might not even have lasted that long if I had gone to England.

The world they inherited, after all, was very different to that in which I was born, and that's ironic because it was also a world that I'd helped create.

In the annals of British punk rock, when it was still a newborn monster, snarling and cursing its way into being, there were just three groups that everybody seemed to agree were "responsible" for its arrival.

There was The Stooges, crashing nihilistic three-chord garage rock around their frontman's penchant for onstage self-destruction; there was The Velvet Underground, pumping discordance and drug drama out of Warhol's most distended art-mare …

… and there was the New York Dolls, shattering the somnambulist reveries of the *Old Grey Whistle Test* with a blur of colour, noise and gesture. Like the paper said back when newsprint was still new to us, "subterranean flash and sleazoid rock", oozing out of the TV screens to polarise a nation of rock'n'roll addicts.

You can throw other names into the brew as well – MC5, Pink Fairies, Bowie and T. Rex, but the apple never falls far from the tree. Read my story; if we didn't know all of those people, we at least loved them to death. 'No Fun', 'Waiting For The Man', 'Kick Out The Jams'; by the time the Dolls ended, I'd loved those songs for so long they felt like brothers and sisters to me. I wore clothes that were handed down from Bowie, and what was the first rule of songwriting throughout the life of the Dolls? "Let's T. Rex the shit out of this thing."

Of course the New York Dolls were beloved by the punks. There was nothing there *not* to love.

What the history books like to term our "rehabilitation" began quickly. Our transformation from the no-hope zeroes who fell apart in Florida (but started crumbling long before that) to the all-conquering heroes whose every song was an integral strand in punk's DNA barely took six months.

When David and I played the final Dolls show at the end of 1976, our two albums together had been out of sight for at least a year. I don't think they were ever deleted altogether, but they might as well have been. They were invisible.

It was public demand that brought them back, an army of kids who heard our name from the mouths of their newfound idols and wanted to know more. In spring 1977, less than six months after that final concert, *New York Dolls* and *Too Much Too Soon* were reissued in the UK as a double album.

I wasn't, I must admit, impressed by it. I looked at the cover, our five faces cut out against a black background, and all I could see was the sleeve from the first Kiss LP. Go check it out; I don't know who our designer was for that one, but they clearly had a very different idea about the New York Dolls to the kids who lined up to buy the record.

It didn't matter. It sold, and it kept on selling, even after one, two, three … I don't know how many more … other New York Dolls albums appeared to join it on the shelves. Over the last forty years, I've had fans come up and tell me they own over a hundred New York Dolls albums, and I'm astonished every time because that's more songs than we even knew how to play! Out-takes, demos, concert recordings; if we switched on a tape recorder, it appears that somebody else took the tape and released it. Then re-released it with a different cover, a different track listing, a different mix. And that includes Arthur!

It's an incredible output and it doesn't show any sign of slowing down. Even as I was writing this book, word reached me that our two LPs are about to be re-released again, this time as part of a four-CD box set; and barely three weeks after I finished it, I was off to New York City to play a New York Dolls tribute at the Bowery Ballroom, organised by Elda Gentile's sister Diane and featuring Alejandro Escoveda, Walter Lure, Kenny Aaronson, Steve Conti and more.

There is more. David and I (plus Arthur, for far too brief a period) led a reborn New York Dolls through seven years earlier this century, and released three new albums in the process. And I never tired, every night we played, of hearing another fan tell us how much we meant to them – at the time if they were old enough, or growing up since then if they weren't.

And why do we mean so much to so many people?

Because the New York Dolls' music was, and is, timeless. The New York Dolls are timeless. I don't say this out of arrogance, boastfulness or ego, either. It's the truth. It doesn't matter when you first heard us, or where or why. Whether you came to us through Johnny's solo albums, or via Buster Poindexter; whether you first heard our music being covered by Sonic Youth or Guns N' Roses, Slaughter & The Dogs or Morrissey. The fact is, you heard us, and something spoke to you when you did.

Something deep inside, a voice that told you to look at your life and the world around you; to look at your friends and your job and your family …

… and then T. Rex the shit out of them.

Because what I realise now is that Daffy Duck got it wrong.

It's a great show and you *can* do it forever. The New York Dolls are living proof of that.

NOT THE END … NEVER-ENDING

POST OFFICE
EXPRESS
DELIVERY
Air Mail
C/O MRS MIZRAHI
SYLVAIN MIZRAHI
14-10 59th AVE
APT 6B
REGO PARK
N.Y.C. N.Y. 11373 U.S.A.
MRS MIZRAHI
URGENT
PLEASE GIVE TO
SYLVAIN AS
QUICKLY AS POSSIBLE
HIS FRIEND
MALCOLM.

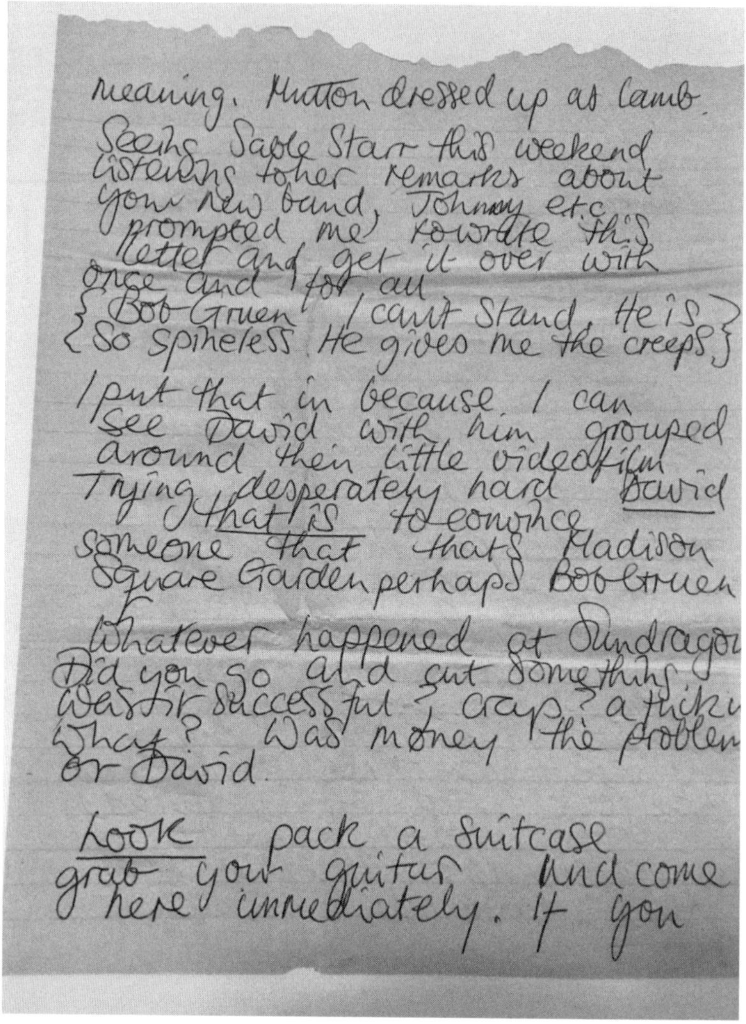

meaning. Mutton dressed up as lamb.
Seeing Sable Starr this weekend
listening to her remarks about
your new band, Johnny etc
prompted me to write this
letter and get it over with
once and for all
{Bob Gruen I can't stand, He is}
{So spineless He gives me the creeps}

I put that in because I can
see David with him grouped
around their little videofilm
Trying desperately hard David
that is to convince
someone that thats Madison
Square Garden perhaps Bob Gruen

Whatever happened at Sundragon
Did you go and cut something
Was it successful, crap? a flicki
What? Was money the problem
or David.

LOOK pack a suitcase
grab your guitar and come
here immediately. If you

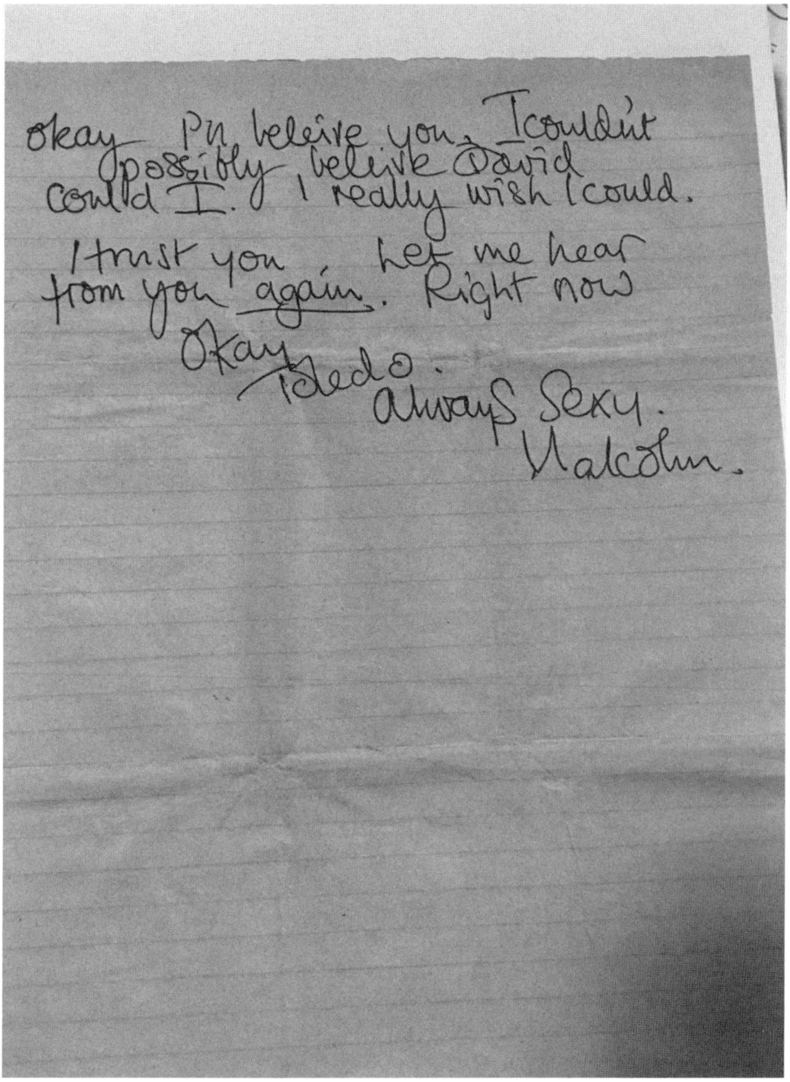

Okay I'll beleive you, I couldn't possibly believe David could I. I really wish I could.

I trust you. Let me hear from you again. Right now

Okay Toledo.

always Sexy.

Malcolm.

JOHN
ROTTEN
SINGER.

STEVE
GLEN
BASS

Acknowledgements

This book is dedicated to Wanda O'Kelley and the Dolls that are no longer with us: Billy Doll Murcia, Johnny Thunders, Jerry Nolan, Arthur Killer Kane Jr, and Sable Starr and Cyrinda Foxe (Kathleen Victoria Hetzekian).

Special thanks go to: David & Mara Johansen, Paul Fakler, Bob Gruen, (Janet Planet) Juanita Ballard-Samz, Valerie Sutain, David & Cyrinda Foxe (Kathleen Victoria Hetzekian) and their duplex penthouse apartment, David Bowie, Marty Thau, Malcolm McLaren, Vivian Let It Rock Westwood, Chris Stein, Clem Burke, Deborah Harry, New York City, the island of Manhattan, London (England), Hollywood (California), Paris (France), Cairo (Egypt), Detroit (Michigan), Toronto/Vancouver & Montreal (Canada), Spain 1973 for banning The New York Dolls for their sexuality, The GTOs and Pamela & Michael Des Barres, Chelsea Hotel and Stanley Bard, Candy Darling, Jackie Curtis, Max's Kansas City and Mickey & Yvonne Ruskin, Danny Fields, Joe Dallesandro Closepens, Rodrigo Salomon, The Different Drummer, Rosie Rexach, Christian Hoffman, Lance Loud, Christian Rodriguez (Frenchy), Shoo-be-doo, Esther Katz, Quintano's School (for Young Professionals), SS United States Line, 1965 Chevrolet Impala, Roller-skates, Stretchlamey, Desmond Sullivan, Peter Jordan, Max Blatt, Nite Bob, Heidi Murcia, Hoffman Murcia, Alfonso Murcia, Alfonso Murcia Junior, Mercedes Murcia, Walter Lure, Phyllis Stein, Lynette Kral, Mireille Protonotarios, Mizrahi, John Speedy Carlucci, Marky Iannello, Andy Cole, Billy Rene,

Uncle Victor Hamell, Philippe Marcade, BP Fallon, Corel Shields, Sable Starr, Jean-Pierre Kalfon and Caffe Reggio.

New York City book locations include: The Different Drummer (792 Lexington Ave), New York Doll Hospital (787 Lexington Ave), Dolls loft (119 Chrystie St), Sylvain & Janet (9 Charles St), David & Cyrinda Foxe (65 E 11th St), Mercer Arts Center, Hotel Diplomat, Chelsea Hotel, Rusty Beanie Bicycle Shop (108 W 81st St), Johnny, Billy, Sylvain & a monkey (238 E 14th St, Apt 4FW), Max's Kansas City (213 Park Ave South), Elda Stiletto Gentile (190 First Ave) and Johnny's first apartment (182 Ave A).

Dave Thompson would like to thank our agent Lee Sobel for bringing everything together; Amy Hanson, for keeping it on course, Jo-Ann Greene, Oliver, Trevor and the fish... and, of course, Sylvain. Thanks, Jackson, it's been great.

"It's torture, yet compulsive." – *Kerrang!*

TOO MUCH, TOO SOON
THE MAKEUP AND BREAKUP OF THE NEW YORK DOLLS
by Nina Antonia

Too Much, Too Soon is the definitive story of the most outrageous glam rock band of them all: the New York Dolls.

The Dolls, peddling transgender posturing and incendiary rock 'n' roll, were dumped by the record business after making just two albums. But their influence lived on when Malcolm McLaren injected the last of the Dolls' lifeblood into the Sex Pistols and changed pop forever. From punk to grunge, practically every new sensation in the contemporary rock scene has been a delayed reaction to the New York Dolls. *Too Much, Too Soon* celebrates all the glorious sleaze and excess of the Dolls' brief auto-destruct career through interviews with the survivors, including band members, managers, roadies, groupies and hangers-on.

No one could hold a candle to the Dolls, so they set themselves alight.

In this new edition, music journalist and author Nina Antonia takes the story up to the Doll's reformation for Morrissey's Meltdown in 2004 and the tragic death of Arthur Kane shortly afterwards. Illustrated and including a comprehensive discography.

Available from all good book shops & www.omnibuspress.com

ISBN: 978.1.84449.984.7
Order No: OP51040